A BROOKLYN DODGERS READER

This book is lovingly dedicated
to my wife, Mildred,
my daughter, Christine, my son, Andrew,
and my granddaughter, Alexandra —
my first inning, my last inning
my whole ball game

And in memory
of my father, Paul Andrew Mele,
who showed his son everything a father should —
Love, Honor, Strength of Character
and Baseball

A BROOKLYN DODGERS READER

Edited by Andrew Paul Mele

Foreword by CARL ERSKINE

McFarland & Company, Inc., Publishers
Jefferson, North Carolina, and London

LIBRARY OF CONGRESS CATALOGUING-IN-PUBLICATION DATA

A Brooklyn Dodgers reader / edited by Andrew Paul Mele ;
    foreword by Carl Erskine.
        p.   cm.
    Includes index.

    ISBN 0-7864-1913-X (softcover : 50# alkaline paper) ∞

    1. Brooklyn Dodgers (Baseball team) — Miscellanea.
    2. Brooklyn Dodgers (Baseball team) — Fiction.   I. Mele,
    Andrew Paul, 1938–
    GV875.B7B77   2005
    796.357'64'0974723 — dc22   2004025787

British Library cataloguing data are available

Cover photographs ©2004 PhotoSpin

Manufactured in the United States of America

*McFarland & Company, Inc., Publishers
    Box 611, Jefferson, North Carolina 28640
    www.mcfarlandpub.com*

CONTENTS

III. Middle Innings

"Loyalty to the Dodgers
is perhaps the strongest emotion
man can experience"

—*Life* magazine,
October 13, 1941

PREFACE

In April 1947, when Jackie Robinson played his first major league baseball game, I was eight years old.

In September 1957, when the Dodgers played their last game in Brooklyn, I was going on nineteen.

The years between were filled with fun, excitement, disappointment, elation, and devotion to the Brooklyn Dodgers.

Forty-six years later, after hungrily reading and rereading articles, novels and nonfiction books about the team of my youth, I collected what struck me as the strongest and most lasting writing I'd come across.

Baseball has always been a passion with me, and never more so than when I'm playing. More than watching, reading, or discussing it. To feel the sun on the back of my neck, to lope across fresh cut grass (real grass, of course) and eye a lazy fly ball into the glove, supersedes all other venues for the outpouring of that passion. It is challenged only when I'm working out with a group of friends (we call ourselves "The Old Boys of Summer") because it is countered by their passions for the game, equally extreme.

The devotion to the Brooklyn Dodgers came with a love for the game and a father who loved the game and the team. These conspired to produce in a young boy a lasting emotion that he continued to nurture long after the ballclub had ceased to exist.

Growing up in Brooklyn, we got to go to Ebbets Field a lot. The Dodgers provided free bleacher seats through a program called the Knot Hole Club. When I played sandlot baseball, on two occasions a teammate of mine appeared on Happy Felton's pre-game show, the *Knot Hole Gang*. They came back with brand new equipment and stories about meeting the players.

The Dodgers also bonded with the populace of Brooklyn by heavily scouting the local parks, particularly the Parade Grounds in the Prospect section of the borough — a mecca for young talent. I can still see Al Campanis and Steve Lembo behind first base, keeping alive the dreams of kids like myself.

And there was that Tuesday in October when we celebrated on the streets of Brooklyn, little knowing that it would be a solitary festivity frozen in time. That was almost 50 years ago. When that fact dawned upon me recently, it seemed a good time to reread and rethink this wonderful ballclub. What better way to do so than in the words of the best writers ever to have written on the subject?

In the 1930s the New York Yankees were managed by Joe McCarthy. After winning four consecutive World Titles (1936–1939) he was being called not just a great manager, but a genius. When confronted with this, "Marse" Joe reflected a moment, then agreed. "I am a genius," he said. "Every day I do something brilliant. I take my pencil and I write Henrich, Keller, DiMaggio, Dickey, Gordon."

The first part of my job was easy. I did what McCarthy did. I made out a lineup. I wrote Kahn, Smith, Young, Honig, Heinz, Holmes. I then decided to list the contributors chronologically so that the completed work would read like a history of the ballclub. As a guideline I listed all of the significant events in Brooklyn Dodger history and tried to touch on all of them. It was not difficult choosing the items to include. The hard part was determining what to leave out.

Then came the real difficulties. Each item to be included required permission from the author or the publisher before it could be reprinted. Sometimes, tracking down permission required the investigative acumen of Hercule Poirot and the persistence of a bloodhound. In some cases the process was time consuming and needed second and third follow-ups. Frustrating, at best. But in other cases it was smooth, efficient, and rewarding. Some of the people I contacted offered advice and assistance beyond what was required of them, and to those individuals I am profoundly grateful.

I knew that there were Brooklyn Dodger fans all over the country, but I had supposed that they were for the most part transplanted Brooklynites. But when I spoke with authors Ron Oakley of Lexington, North Carolina, and Tot Holmes of Gothenburg, Nebraska, I learned that these natives of their states had been Brooklyn Dodger fans for many, years.

The Dodgers of Brooklyn were one of the most popular and beloved baseball teams in the history of the game. Immortalized as the Boys of Summer by Roger Kahn, they came into being in the late 19th century and by 1920 had won five pennants. They contended once or twice during the twenties but never could win it all. In the thirties they were known as the *Daffiness Boys;* 'nough said!

They had their share of heroes. Some were great ballplayers like Vance, Wheat and Nap Rucker. Some were colorful—Bordagaray, Mungo, Uncle Robbie and Casey Stengel. Some were a combination of both, like the irrepressible Babe Herman.

In 1938 Larry MacPhail came to Brooklyn and brought night baseball, radio broadcasts, Red Barber, Leo Durocher and a winning ballclub. In 1941 the Dodgers won a pennant and began a new tradition: losing to the Yankees in the World Series. They were colorful, innovative, and exciting, and their Flatbush home, Ebbets Field, was a house of worship for the faithful.

The real legacy of the Brooklyn Dodgers, however, was built over the last decade of their existence. Between 1947 and 1957 they won six pennants, lost twice in the last inning of the last game and won the only world's championship Brooklyn would ever see. This was undeniably a great ballclub, but the cornerstone of this legacy was Branch Rickey's "great experiment": the emergence of Jackie Robinson as the first African American to play in the major leagues in the 20th century. With ability and courage unparalleled, he destroyed the Jim Crow barriers in baseball.

Following the 1957 season, Dodger president Walter O'Malley whisked the financially successful franchise away from the fans to whom they were so much a part of life, leaving a void that has never been filled.

But Brooklynites who remember trolley cars, Coney Island, and egg creams also remember the Brooklyn Dodgers, in images as vivid as they were when young men in white flannel knickers glided over emerald seas and the Dodgers were as much a part of Brooklyn as the Bridge.

I wish to thank three friends, Mark Levine, Tony Sogluizzo, and Tom Miskel, for their guidance, encouragement, and advice.

My appreciation to the librarians at the Brooklyn Public Library Brooklyn Room for their able assistance.

Carl Erskine kindly consented to write the foreword, and for this I am grateful. Speaking with this Dodger hero was a highlight of this whole experience.

The only regret I have is that my Dad is not here; he would have enjoyed it. Until he passed away in September of 2000, we talked Brooklyn Dodger baseball. We still reminisced about that October 1953 afternoon when we sat in the bleachers at Ebbets Field and watched "Oisk" dazzle the Yankees with his overhand breaking ball. When we last spoke of it, my dad said, "Remember how that ball was breaking down?"

I remember.
To Brooklyn and its beloved Bums.
Thanks for the memories!

Andy Mele
Staten Island, New York
Formerly of 35th Street, Brooklyn

FOREWORD

Carl Erskine

When I grew up in Anderson, Indiana, I was Carl Erskine. The first day I arrived in Brooklyn, I became "Cal Oiskine," and for the next ten years it was, "Hey, Oisk, whadayasay," and "Hey, Oisk, strike da bum out." And I loved every minute of it. Playing for that glorious team, in that glorious place, in that glorious era was all that I could have hoped for in baseball.

An added dimension to those years was my nine seasons as a part of the historical social event that was Jackie Robinson's career. Branch Rickey could not have chosen a more ideal location for this "great experiment" than Brooklyn.

We were a young family living summers in the Bay Ridge section of the borough among the people who were both our fans and our neighbors. We grew to be a part of the community and were made to feel that we belonged.

The Brooklyn Dodgers were a special team with a special place in history that transcended baseball. In this volume you will read about the things that made them special and in the words of some of the greatest and most prolific baseball writers of the past seventy years.

Welcome to Brooklyn.

Carl Erskine #17
Pitcher, Brooklyn Dodgers
1948–1957

I. Warm-Ups

I keep a clear eye and hit 'em where they ain't

— Wee Willie Keeler, outfielder,
Brooklyn Superbas 1898–1902

Baseball was played in Brooklyn years before the Trolley Dodgers joined the American Association and, in 1890, the National League. The game grew up in New York City during the middle decades of the nineteenth century, when clubs such as the Atlantics and Excelsiors dominated — and exported — an amateur game that would sweep through the Northeast and Midwest and capture the attention of the national sporting public.

IN THE BEGINNING

James L. Terry

Contrary to popular myth, organized baseball was born not in the sylvan landscape of Cooperstown, New York, but in the burgeoning urban environment of New York City and Brooklyn. Various games of ball, such as old cat, stoop ball, rounders, and town ball, had been played throughout the country from the time of the nation's early settlement. But the game we know today as baseball was shaped by the forces of modernization that impinged most directly on the rapidly changing urban enviroment.

Brooklyn at Mid-Century

In the early nineteenth century, Brooklyn, which occupied a small corner of Kings County along the East River, was a sleepy bedroom community of wealthy merchants who had amassed their fortunes across the river in Gotham. Most of Kings County was farmland where the largely Dutch landowners continued to own slaves as late as 1827. But, with the opening of the Erie Canal in 1825, New York City and Brooklyn soon developed into the industrial and commercial center of the country. Brooklyn's population and economic growth were phenomenal. Between 1810 and 1840, wealth increased 2,000 percent and population 1,000 percent. From 1835 — when Brooklyn received its city charter — to 1855 the population grew from 24,592 to 205,250, making Brooklyn the third largest city in the nation....

At mid-century, technological developments and ideological changes would facilitate the rapid development of baseball in the New York area. Revolutions in communications and transportation promoted the growth of the game. The sporting press, centered in New York, which had largely covered horse racing and cricket, devoted increasing coverage in the late 1850s to baseball. Weeklies, such as *Spirit of*

From *Long Before the Dodgers: Baseball in Brooklyn, 1855–1884,* ©2002 by James L. Terry, by permission of McFarland & Company, Inc., Publishers, Box 611, Jefferson NC 28640. *www.mcfarlandpub.com.*

the Times, Porter's Spirit of the Times, Wilkes' Spirit of the Times, and especially the *New York Clipper,* became promoters of the sport, introducing it to a nation-wide audience. In Brooklyn, the *Daily Eagle,* the *Daily Times,* and the *Daily Union* increasingly provided coverage of baseball matches of local clubs. The development of the telegraph allowed reports of games in the New York area to be sent to newspapers, at first in the Northeast, and eventually throughout the country. When the Brooklyn Excelsiors made their first road trip to upstate New York in 1860, their reputation had preceded them.

The building of intercity and intracity railroads facilitated the expansion of commerce and was also means for baseball clubs and fans to travel to matches across town and between cities. In 1854, the Brooklyn City Railroad purchased the local omnibus (horse drawn stage) companies and began replacing them with horse drawn railroad lines. By the 1860s, horse drawn lines crisscrossed the city, providing easy and cheap access to baseball grounds in Williamsburg, Bedford, and South Brooklyn....

The Culture of the Early Game

Although historians credit the New York Knickerbockers, established by Alexander Cartwright in 1845, as the first organized baseball club, documentation of the existence of baseball clubs in New York City dates back to the 1820s. A recently discovered communiqué in the April 23, 1823, issue of the *National* Advocate describes a baseball club that played on Saturday afternoons in New York City. "A Spectator" wrote to the newspaper:

> I was last Saturday much pleased in witnessing a company of active young men playing the manly and athletic game of "base ball" at the retreat in Broadway (Jones') [Broadway, between Washington Place and 8th Street]. I am informed they are an organized association, and that a very interesting game will be played on Saturday next at the above place, to commence at half past 3 o'clock, P.M. Any person fond of witnessing this game may avail himself of seeing it played with consummate skill and wonderful dexterity. It is surprising, and to be regretted that the young men of our city do not engage more in this manual sport; it is innocent amusement, and healthy exercise, attended with but little expense, and has no demoralizing tendency.

...Prominent Brooklyn clubs, like the Atlantics and the Excelsiors, might have a hundred members or more, most of whom were spectators and not players. In the press they were referred to, for example, as the Atlantic Base Ball Club or simply the Atlantics. This nomenclature continues today as even major league franchises are still referred to as clubs. Teams might also pick up additional monikers. For example, the Atlantic Club was at times in the press referred to as "the Bedford Boys" in reference to the locale of their home grounds.

Typically a club would form, officers would be elected, the location of a home ground would be established, and written invitations would be sent to other clubs proposing a series of matches. As the following item in the *Daily Eagle* illustrates, clubs would send announcements of their club's formation to the local newspapers and sports weeklies in order to make themselves known to the "base ball fraternity."

A Challenge — The undersigned is authorized, by a nine selected from the firm of Stratten & Chappel, Plumbers, 103 Orange Street, to issue a challenge to play a friendly game of Base Ball, with a nine selected from any shop in the city of Brooklyn. By addressing a note to me at the above address, a match can be arranged. W. J. Rocae. Who will take it up?

The First Brooklyn Baseball Clubs

By 1855, New York and Brooklyn each had four prominent baseball clubs. In New York, the Knickerbockers, Eagles and Empires played at Elysian Fields while the Gothams' home ground was in Harlem. Brooklyn boasted the Excelsiors of South Brooklyn, the Putnams of Williamsburgh, the Eckfords of Greenpoint/Williamsburgh, and the Atlantics of Bedford.

Following the example of the Knickerbockers, John H. Suydam and some of his friends of the Jolly Bachelor's Club founded the Excelsiors of Brooklyn in December 1854. Among its members were representatives of some of the oldest and wealthiest families in Brooklyn. Club official and Brooklyn coroner Dr. Joseph Jones would be an influenctial voice in the amateur baseball association throughout the 1860s. When the Excelsiors left the arena of competitive play, he would fight a losing battle against professionalism. Two club members — Henry B. Polhemus and Joe Leggett — would be noted for not only their outstanding playing ability, but also for teaching the game of baseball to their business associates in the city of Baltimore.

The Brooklyn Excelsiors played in South Brooklyn, initially on grounds at 3rd Street and 5th Avenue, the site of a major battle in the Revolutionary War, and currently the location of Byrne Park. They later moved to grounds near Carroll Park and by 1859 began playing at grounds "at the foot of Court Street," the present location of Red Hook Park. On the eve of the Civil War the Excelsiors had built one of the strongest baseball teams in the country. But, following the death of their star player, Jim Creighton, in 1862, the club would never be as competitive again. Although club members would continue to play for the pleasure of the game, they would spend more time socializing in their club headquarters in the row house that still stands at 133 Clinton Street.

The Putnam Club of Williamsburgh, organized in May 1855, played on grounds at Wheat Hill at the corner of Hooper Street and Lee Avenue. According to William Rankin's 1909 history of baseball, the members of the Putnams included "some of the leading men in the vicinity of New York in the commercial and social world." The team's pitcher, Thomas Dakin, would be elected the first president of the National Association of Base Ball Players in 1858 and would later become brigadier general in the Brooklyn militia's Fifth Brigade. Because so many members volunteered for military service during the Civil War the club was forced to disband....

The first recorded Atlantic game was with the Harmony of Brooklyn on October 21, 1855. The Atlantics won the match, 24–22, and won the November 5 return match, 27–10. The following year, the Atlantics would merge with the short-lived Harmony and add five players to their roster who would make the club virtually unbeatable: Charlie Price, Dickey Pearce, Polkert Boerum, and Matty and Pete O'Brien.

In the next few years, baseball's growing popularity gave rise to the formation of more clubs in Brooklyn. The Continental Club, established in October 1855, shared grounds at Wheat Hill in Williamsburgh with the Eckfords. Although they played competively only for a couple of years, the club sponsored the Silver Ball Championship trophy awarded to the championship teams in the early 1860s.

The Pastime Club, which played on the grounds of the Long Island Cricket Club in Bedford, like the Putnams, was comprised of prominent citizens of Brooklyn. Among its members was a prominent Flatbush realtor, the county register, the commissioner of jurors, a prominent sculpter, and the superintendent of the Coney Island Railroad. Like the Putnams, the Pastimes would leave the playing field during the Civil War.

Two other clubs, the Enterprise and the Exercise, are notable for developing players who would become star players for the Atlantics. Organized in June 1856 in Bedford, during the 1860 and 1861 seasons, the Enterprise roster would feature John Chapman, Joe Start, and Fred Crane. The Exercise Club, which played on grounds in South Brooklyn at Third Avenue and Tenth Street, featured both John Galvin and Joe Sprague in the 1861 lineup.

Although initially formed as a "junior club" in October 1856, the Star Club of South Brooklyn would advance to the senior circuit in the 1860s. The Stars, who shared grounds with the Excelsiors, were the dominant junior club in their early years and developed such talented players as George Flanly and star pitcher Jim Creighton. In the late 1860s, the Stars would continue to field a competitive amateur club led by the team's second outstanding pitcher and future Hall of Famer, Candy Cummings....

In 1856, baseball was being played throughout the New York metropolitan area. *Porter's Spirit of the Times* observed that "Matches are being made all around us, and games are being played on every available plot within a ten mile radius of the city." The proliferation of teams and the growing interest in the game led the Knickerbockers to call a meeting of club representatives in Manhattan in 1857 to form the National Association of Base Ball Players (NABBP). The following year, representatives met to elect officers and draft a constitution. After initially adopting the Knickerbocker rules, the most significant function of this and subsequent annual winter conventions was to approve rule changes....

A regulation ball was to weigh between 5¾ ounces and 6 ounces and measure between 9¾ and 10 inches in circumference. It was to be made of India rubber and yarn, covered with leather. The bat was to be made of wood and not to exceed 2½ inches in diameter. There was no limitation on length. The bases, to be made of canvas, were to be arranged 90 feet apart. The pitcher's plate, to be made of iron, was set at 45 feet from home base.

At the 1858 convention, the outcome of games was changed from the 21-run rule to the completion of nine innings. The following year, a rule was instituted allowing the umpire to call strikes if the striker refused to swing at good pitches. A rule allowing the umpire to call balls was not instituted until the 1864 season. Until 1865, when the "fly rule" was put into effect, outs could be made by catching a hit ball on one bound....

Baseball and the Fourth Estate

No single individual did more to promote and influence the game than Brooklyn's sportswriter Henry Chadwick. Born in England in 1824, Chadwick moved with his family to Brooklyn when he was 13. An avid cricket enthusiast, he played the game as a youth and in 1856 began reporting on cricket matches for the *New York Times* and the *Brooklyn Daily Eagle.* But, after watching baseball matches in the mid–1850s, his passion turned to the new sport. He quickly became an expert on the game, and at one time or another reported on games for nearly every major New York metropolitan area newspaper: the *Times,* the *Sun,* the *Herald,* the *Mercury,* the *World,* the *Daily Eagle* and the *Daily Union.*

Chadwick was more than a mere reporter; through his writing he was a promoter and moralist who shaped readers' perceptions of baseball. Joining the staff of the *New York Clipper* in 1856, Chadwick's views of the game would be read by a national audience until the turn of the century. In addition to writing, Chadwick helped to organize the National Association of Base Ball Players (NABBP) and its successor, the National Association of Professional Base Ball Players. He also served on the rules committee of the NABBP, helping to shape the contours of the game. For better or worse, Chadwick must be thanked for his passion for numbers. He developed the first scoring system for games and the box score that would be a regular feature of newspaper reports of games. He also inaugurated the elaborate compilation of statistics that to this day is a prominent feature of baseball.

From his arrival at the age of 13, Brooklyn would forever be Chadwick's home. After his death in 1908, his body was interred at Greenwood Cemetery, not far from the grave of baseball's first star player, JimCreighton. Albert Spaulding, his friend and associate, encouraged the National Baseball League to finance an impressive monument over his grave, a tribute to Chadwick, but also a tribute to the game that he helped to establish. In 1938, Chadwick was elected as a charter member of Baseball's Hall of Fame, the only writer elected before a sportswriters division was established.

The New York–Brooklyn Rivalry

Just as the baseball epidemic hit the metropolitan area, baseball promoters in 1858 struck on an idea that would capture the attention of New York area baseball fans to the present day, a series of matches between New York and Brooklyn. All-Star squads, "picked nines" of the best players representing clubs from the two cities, would square off in a best of three series. The intercity rivalry, later to become the "subway series," was born....

The first match was scheduled for July 13. Under a threatening sky, 2,000 fans made their way by horse-drawn vehicles or by the Flushing Railroad line. But, by game time a heavy storm forced the match's postponement. The disappointed fans would have to wait another week.

On July 20, under more favorable skies, an even larger crowd gathered at the ball grounds. Spectators arriving by train had to pass through a group of petty entrepreneurs hoping to capitalize on the event. Tables lined the route from the station to the ball grounds with card sharks and carnival games of chance such as "try your strength," "guess your weight" and "ring-toss."

...Brooklyn took a 3–0 lead after the first inning, stretching it to a 7–3 margin after three. In the fourth inning, the New Yorkers struck for four runs to tie the game. In the following inning, New York took the lead and held it through the remainder of the game.

The second match of the season was played on August 17 before an even larger crowd, estimated at 5,000. Brooklyn juggled its lineup, replacing Holder and Burr with Oliver and Pearce from the Atlantics. Pigeon, who played shortstop in the first match, pitched in the second. The changes apparently made a difference in the outcome, as Brooklyn convincingly beat New York 29–8 to tie the series.

In early September, New York won the "rubber" match of the intercity series by a score of 29–18. For the time being, New York could claim bragging rights to having the best baseball players in the metropolitan area, if not the entire country. But, in a short time the entire baseball fraternity would recognize Brooklyn as the championship city of baseball.

The first all-professional baseball club was the Cincinnati Red Stockings, formed in April 1869. Traveling the country over the next year, they compiled an astounding record of 92 games without a loss (one tie with the Troy, New York, Haymakers). Then on June 14, 1870, they suffered their first defeat, at the Capitoline grounds in Brooklyn where the Atlantics beat them 8–7 in eleven innings. The Brooklyn Daily Eagle *covered the game. Note the terminology then in effect in describing the events of the game.*

THE ATLANTICS TRIUMPHANT

Brooklyn Daily Eagle

A Glorious Victory for Brooklyn

The Local Nine Beat the "Picked Nine" from the West

Gallant, Though Unsuccessful Struggle of the Red Stockings

Fair Field and No Favor

Intense Excitement

The most remarkable game, in more respects than one, was played upon the Capitoline ground yesterday between the celebrated old Atlantics and the celebrated young Red Stockings. Notwithstanding the energetic protests of the Atlantics, they were compelled to charge fifty cents admission to the ground, and yet from nine to ten thousand people congregated there, and in the hot sun, watched with intense interest the progress of the game. The general impression previous to the game was that the Atlantics would lose the game; none but the nine knew, however, how hard they were going to play. The Red Stockings were bound to defeat their strongest foes, and played throughout with the same determination. The result therefore was, that the most stubborn game ever played, was finished yesterday upon the Capitoline ground.

The Game

As early as one o'clock, the crowd began to gather upon the Capitoline, and by two o'clock although an hour previous to the game, the seats were all occupied. The

"Brooklyn Atlantics v. Cincinnati Red Stockings," originally published in the *Brooklyn Daily Eagle*, June 15, 1870.

crowd that came in afterwards were compelled to stand upon the banks and around the field as best they might. That portion of the ground devoted to carriages was covered with vehicles, in which were standing and sitting interested spectators. It was after three o'clock before the game was commenced, and the satisfaction of the Atlantic adherents was very great when it was found they went first to the bat. Save an overthrow by McDonald, in the very first innings, the game of the Atlantics was almost without a blemish. Save two mistakes by the Red Stockings, their game was without an error. The excitement began in the second innings, when both clubs were "whitewashed," and kept increasing until the sixth innings, when the Atlantics showed one run ahead. The hopes, however, of the Atlantic adherents went down, when in the seventh, the "Reds" went ahead, and were raised when in the eighth, where the Atlantics made one run, thus tying the game. The ninth resulted in a whitewash, and the excitement fairly boiled over, nor was allayed when another "whitewash" was given to each side. The eleventh innings was commenced amid breathless silence. A collision between Hall and McDonald seemed to throw the game into the hands of the "Reds," for they made two runs, but the accident only served to nerve the boys to superhuman exertions.

THE GAME WAS WON by the fine batting of every one who went to bat. Smith hit a corker out of reach upon the ground. Start sent a horrible one into the crowd, giving Smith his run. Chapman was put out, and Start still remained on third base. "Fergy" then took the bat, and with commendable nerve batted left hand, to get the ball out of George Wright's hands, took his base and sent Start home. Zettlein, the magnificent pitcher, sent a "terrific" past Gould, sent Fergy and took his second. Little Halley was then the man on whom the hopes of the Atlantics rested. He was equal to the occasion, and although he batted Zettlein out, Ferguson went bounding over the home place, amid the most deafening cheers and the utmost excitement. There was a stern retribution in Ferguson being allowed to make the winning run, inasmuch as he has been of late so much abused and advised to take pattern by Harry Wright, if he wanted his nine to win.

THE EXCITEMENT had now reached fever heat. Hats, coats, sticks and crutches even, darkened the air, thrown up by enthusiastic attendants on the ball field. The crowd broke from their confines, and rushed upon the Atlantic players, most of whom they elevated upon their shoulders and carried to the clubhouse. As the face or uniform of an Atlantic was discovered struggling through the crowd, he was immensely cheered, and as they drew near to the house, the ladies occupying the windows waved their handkerchiefs, and sent up their shrill voices in behalf of the "Brooklyn" boys. One enthusiastic individual mounted a shed and began ringing a large bell he found there, much to the delight of the crowd. The following is the score:

	1	2	3	4	5	6	7	8	9	10	11
Red Stockings	2	0	1	0	0	0	2	0	0	0	2
Atlantics	0	0	0	2	0	2	0	1	0	0	3

	Batting Score						Fielding Score				
	O	R	1B	TB	E	L	B	F	LD	T	A	E
G. Wright, ss	2	2	2	2	2	2	1	1	0	2	3	0
Gould, 1st b	6	0	0	0	0	0	3	1	0	9	0	3
Waterman, 3rd b	4	0	1	1	0	1	1	2	0	3	4	1
Allison, c	2	1	2	2	1	2	0	2	3	5	0	0
H. Wright, c.f.	4	0	1	1	0	1	0	2	0	2	0	0
Leonard, l.f.	5	0	0	0	0	0	0	2	1	3	0	0
Brainard, p	3	2	2	3	0	0	0	0	0	0	1	2
Sweezy, 2d b	2	2	3	3	1	1	4	3	0	0	6	0
McVey, r.f.	5	0	0	0	0	0	0	2	0	2	0	0
TOTALS	33	7	10	12	4	7	9	15	4	26	14	6

ATLANTICS

	Batting Score						Fielding Score				
	0	R	1B	TB	E	L	B	F	LD		A	E
Pearce, ss	3	2	4	4	0	0	1	0	0	1	2	0
Smith, 3d b	3	2	2	4	1	0	0	2	0	2	0	2
Start, 1 b	3	3	3	5	0	0	8	6	0	14	1	0
Chapman, l.f.	4	0	0	0	1	1	0	2	0	2	0	0
Ferguson, c	3	1	2	2	0	1	0	2	2	4	0	7
Zettlein	5	0	1	1	0	0	0	2	0	2	1	0
Hall, c.f.	4	0	1	1	0	1	0	3	0	3	0	1
Pike, 2nd b	4	0	1	1	0	1	1	1	0	3	6	1
McDonald, r.f.	4	0	2	2	0	0	0	2	0	2	0	1
TOTALS	88	8	16	20	2	4	10	20	2	33	10	13

Willie Keeler played for the old Baltimore Orioles and for Brooklyn (1898–1902), alternately known then as the Trolley Dodgers, Bridegrooms, or Superbas. He had a lifetime batting average of .345 and is enshrined in the Hall of Fame at Cooperstown. But "Wee Willie" was a product of Brooklyn. Born in 1872 at 376 Pulaski Street in the Bedford section, he died in his house a few blocks away at 1010 Gates Avenue fifty years later.

THE FIELDS OF BROOKLYN

Burt Solomon

The weather in Brooklyn had been quirky since Christmas. The mercury had fallen the night before to thirteen degrees, the coldest of the winter so far, and snow had been predicted for this dying day of 1922. In its place came a heavy rain followed by hours of disarming sunshine and then a chilly wind.

"Wee Willie" Keeler, the famous old ballplayer, was propped up on pillows in his sickbed, looking wan and wasted. Though he was small, his features had been generous; now they seemed shriveled. The pain in his chest had been disabling at times, but his eyes still shone.

Charles Wuest, his doctor and friend, came by around noon. Willie invited him over for a quiet party that evening. "Well, I've got to have a New Year smoke and drink with old friends like you," Willie said. Even in illness and penury he seemed playful and kind. "I had a dream last night that we were all going to California to spend the winter."

He understood that he would never go. His brothers, Tom and Joe, and his closest friends had been told that the end was imminent. Willie had not: The patient never was. But surely he knew. No batsman had ever faced the twirlers with a keener eye.

He had already told Tom, his oldest brother, that he knew this was a fight he would lose. That night he spoke to his friends who had squeezed into his dim second-floor flat at 1010 Gates avenue. "You think that I am going to die," he said. "But I am not going to pass out this year. I am going to see the new year in."

Willie Keeler was only fifty, but what more was there to do? He had lost everything he loved when he left baseball. He had never married or fathered a child. He had been the first ballplayer to be paid $10,000 a year. Known as the Brooklyn Millionaire when he retired, now he was a pauper. At last he had found Clara, but only when it was too late.

He fell asleep as midnight neared. His guests went into the street to listen to the bells of Brooklyn, the City of Churches, ring in the new year. Willie lived in a row house with bow windows, a half-block on the wrong side of Broadway. On the other side, beyond the loud grimy el, stood the Victorian mansions of Bushwick. Willie's side was crowded with the children of immigrants—from Russia, Austria, Germany, France, Alsace, and most of all Ireland, where his parents had been born.

All over Brooklyn, sirens and bells were sounded as 1923 arrived. An eight-year-old girl in Bushwick sat in the rear window of her home and was shot in the forehead by a rifle fired in the air. (Dr. Wuest, a coroner's physician, conducted the autopsy.) On Gates avenue, the muffled sounds of celebration penetrated inside.

Suddenly there was a sound in the sickroom. Tom, who had stayed behind, rushed to his brother's bedside. He found Willie sitting up. A smile creased Willie's face as he shook a miniature cowbell.

"You see," he said, "the new year is here and so am I — still."

He exchanged good wishes with the others once they returned. He took a short smoke and a drink—"really medicine for him," Dr. Wuest said later. Willie finished and said to his friends: "I'm pretty tired. I feel like taking a good, long sleep." He dozed off.

He never awakened.

Within an hour Willie Keeler had breathed his last. Dr. Wuest looked at his watch. It was a quarter past one.

On the death certificate the doctor described the cause of death as chronic endocarditis, an inflammation of the lining of the heart. Willie had suffered from it for five years. There was also a report of dropsy, an excess of fluid between the cells, the sign of a failing heart.

The reaction to his death was intense. WILLIE KEELER STRUCK OUT BY THE GREAT UMPIRE, the *Brooklyn Daily Times* grieved. WILLIE KEELER, GREATEST OF ALL PLACE HITTERS, LEAVES BEHIND A BRILLIANT RECORD, ran the headline in the *Brooklyn Daily Eagle*. *The Sporting News* listed the records he still held. He had batted safely in forty-four consecutive games in a season. He had collected at least two hundred hits in each of eight straight seasons, and claimed to have once played an entire season without striking out. George Sisler had broken his record of 239 hits in a season only three years before. Willie's batting average of .424 back in 'ninety-seven was the second highest ever (next to Hugh Duffy's .440), other than in 'eighty-seven, the year that four strikes made an out and bases on balls counted as hits.

Even more than his individual achievements, Willie Keeler had helped change the face of the national game. The newspapers in Baltimore mourned the passing of the first of the Big Four who had played for the celebrated Orioles a quarter-century earlier. At the time, baseball had been a game of power and thick-bodied men. Then came the Orioles, scrappy and swift. In 'ninety-four they won the first of three pennants in a row. They used the hit-and-run, the bunt, the squeeze play, the cutoff play, the Baltimore chop — whatever was unexpected and put their opponents on edge. They never stopped thinking. Scientific baseball, it was called, or inside baseball, or — more than occasionally — dirty baseball.

Whatever the name, the national game would never be the same. Before Willie broke in, ballplayers customarily held the bat at the very end; he choked almost halfway up and chopped and thrust and poked at the ball. By his success, he changed what was right. In place of the slugging came speed and strategy and smarts. Even now, Ty Cobb and Rabbit Maranville were still slicing up the base-paths in the old Orioles' footsteps.

It was after Willie Keeler had returned to Brooklyn from Baltimore that a baseball scribe asked him for his secret of hitting. Willie had been thinking about it for years. "Keep your eye clear," he replied, "and hit 'em where they ain't."

He could see the rotation on the ball from the instant the pitcher released it. He had to use every advantage, for he was not much bigger than a batboy. Willie claimed to be five feet, four and one-half inches tall — and would never consent to be measured. The others of the Big Four — John McGraw, Hughey Jennings, and even Swaggering Joe Kelley — were not all that much bigger. They were brainy at bat and reckless on the base-paths and fearless in the field. Old-timers still talked of the afternoon in Washington that Willie had stuck his hand up through the barbed wire fence and prevented a home run. The great second baseman Johnny Evers, famed as a fielder himself, thought that no ballplayer had ever been a better judge of where a batter would drive a pitch.

Yet it was not only for his playing that Willie was eulogized. "The loveliest character in baseball," Brooklyn manager Wilbert Robinson, the catcher and captain of the old Orioles, murmured to a reporter on New Year's night. Among teammates who sharpened their spikes, Willie was known for his decency and gentlemanly demeanor.

From the start he had been amazed he was paid to do something he would have done for free. "I like playing ball so much," he once told the Orioles in their clubhouse, "I'd pay them for the privilege if that was the only way I could get into the ballpark."

Yet even while he was on the diamond, the air of innocence was fading fast. Baseball was not what it had once been. Monopoly and greed had transformed the national game and at last touched even Willie. "I am in baseball for all I can get out of it," he explained matter-of-factly when he jumped to the American League in 1903. "In baseball, as in any profession, business prevails over sentiment."

Ever since, things had only grown worse. The Black Sox scandal, when gamblers fixed the World Series of 1919, had shown baseball as something darker than a sport. In response — and panic — the ballclubs' owners had hired a tyrannical commissioner to save them from themselves. On the field the game was changing again. A borough away, a spindly legged strongman by the name of Babe Ruth was banging home runs and turning baseball into a game of sluggers again.

Nor was Brooklyn what it had been while Willie was growing up, just a dozen blocks from where he died. Brooklyn had never grown so fast. Where fields had been, now there were homes. Asphalt had replaced the cobblestones; the milk trucks no longer wakened the hard-of-hearing. A record number of new buildings had gone up in the previous year and more than a thousand miles of sewers twisted beneath its streets, instead of sixty, as just a decade before. Changes in zoning had spattered businesses among the narrow, unremitting homes. Willie had died beside a bank and over a branch office of the *Brooklyn Daily Eagle*. An undertaker labored a block away.

Willie Keeler's body lay in a plain oaken coffin by the bow window. He had died on a Monday and the funeral was arranged for Thursday morning. The mourners had started to gather by Wednesday. That night, two hundred members of the Brooklyn Lodge of the Elks, No. 22, passed through Willie's rooms to say their farewells to one of the lodge's most enduring members. Thomas Burns led the hymns and prayers, then every Elk filed silently past the casket and dropped a single red rose from his lapel.

Hundreds of people waited outside in the cold. In Willie's playing days they had been called "cranks" and were now known as "fans."

It snowed overnight, seven-and-a-half inches, the heaviest of the winter so far. It was also the prettiest. A covering of white concealed the grit of the streets. The plows had been out in the night so that by morning the trolleys could pass.

Several hundred people gathered again in the morning on Gates Avenue and stood with their heads bared in the sun. Police reserves from the Ralph Avenue station stood nearby.

Inside the tan brick house with the chocolate-colored cornice and the ornamental trim, the manager of the world champion New York Giants, one of the most celebrated men in America, stood by the open casket and stared at the face of his friend. John McGraw had known Willie Keeler for twenty-nine years. They had batted one-two in the Orioles' lineup. How many hundreds of times had Willie moved Mac along a base or more? They had wrestled with each other, the two bantams rolling around in the dirt. They had sat side by side at the vaudeville show and in church. After five glorious years as teammates they played on rival teams, then in rival leagues. When Willie's playing days were just about done, Mac hired him as a pinch hitter and a coach.

He gazed down on the casket for five minutes, which seemed as eternity. Mac was white-haired now. Once he had been the scrawny and fiery soul of a team. Now he was the little Napoleon, stocky and imperious, who could never admit to a doubt that he was right. How he had changed from when they were young.

Willie had not changed. To be sure, he had compromised with the ways of the world. He had allowed his innocence to turn into something else. But he had never really changed.

Only now he was dead.

McGraw started to weep. The *Eagle* said he broke down. He wailed so loudly, the Keeler family recounted later, that Joe Kelley — always spoiling for a fight — barged in from a room away and threw him out.

Other ex–Orioles had come to pay their respects — Hughey Jennings and Steve Brodie and Kid Gleason and Jack Doyle and the man at the center of the team, their brilliant strategist of a manager, Ned Hanlon. Every year the old teammates still gathered for a reunion. Usually they went to Baltimore, but recently they had been coming to New York, so that Willie could attend.

Now they had learned, on a side street in Brooklyn, that the bonds between them would last until death.

The flowers kept arriving, as they had all night. Colonel Jacob Ruppert and Colonel T. L. Huston, the owners of the Yankees, sent an enormous cluster of roses and pink carnations. A casket bouquet came from the Giants—the first big league ballclub Willie had played for, and the last. Flowers arrived from almost every major league club and from the leaders of the national game and from celebrated players of yore. It took two open motorcars to carry them all the four blocks to the church.

The neighborhood grew fancy. The row houses widened and had staircases with wrought-iron railings. The Gothic spire of the Church of Our Lady of Good Counsel, on Putnam avenue between Patchen and Ralph, rose like a guardian angel over a neighborhood in no evident need of one. Snow covered the steps of the brooding gray church; ice encased the bower of branches that wreathed the Crusader-arched doorway.

Hundreds of worshipers crowded inside. Charley Ebbets, the president of the Brooklyn ballclub, was traveling in Europe, and Wilbert Robinson, the portly Uncle Robbie, was at his winter home in Georgia (disappointing local sportswriters, who hoped to ask about the rumors of a trade). But many others had come. Charley Ebbets, Jr., and Ed McKeever represented the Brooklyn club.

A smaller crowd gathered again shortly before noon at Calvary Cemetery, just into Queens. Snow shrouded the hillside. Willie's father had purchased the plot when Willie was three years old, to bury a baby daughter and later a two-year-old son. He had come again to bury his beloved wife. For the past eleven years he had rested beside her, facing east across the quiet landscape, toward Ireland.

Now Willie, sweet Willie, would join them. Three tender pink roses gently rested on his casket, and John McGraw and Hughey Jennings and Wid Conroy each tossed on a spadeful of earth as it was lowered into the ground. Tears came into their eyes, not only for a teammate but for a time.

II. Early Innings

Overconfidence May Cost Dodgers Sixth Place

— Headline in *Brooklyn Eagle,* 1929

Charles Ebbets had worked for the Dodgers since the founding of the ball club in 1883. In 1902, when Ned Hanlon announced his plan to purchase available stock interests and move the club to Baltimore, Ebbets swore to "keep the Dodgers in Brooklyn." He borrowed the funds, made the purchase himself and became the new owner of the Dodgers.

History Lesson

Arthur Daley

[JANUARY 1, 1957:] The new home of the Dodgers—when, as and if it is constructed—will be the fifth ball park to house Brooklyn's entry in the National League. It is to be hoped that Walter O'Malley won't make the mistake that was made by his ancient predecessor as president of the Dodgers, Charlie Ebbets.

When Ebbets Field was opened with great fanfare in April 1913, the park was up-to-the-minute in every respect—except that Charlie forgot to install a press box. Posterity now recognizes the oversight as merely another illustration of the Brooklyn touch.

The borough was dotted with ball fields and populated by eager ballplayers more than a century ago. All this, however, was on an amateur scale. In 1869 the first professional team to be organized was the Cincinnati Red Stockings. They won all sixty-five of their games that season and whisked through twenty-seven more the next year. Then they were foolish enough to meet the Atlantics. Naturally enough, the Atlantics were from Brooklyn.

Into Overtime

The Atlantics were inordinately pleased to hold the famed invincibles to a 5–5 tie in nine innings. No one else had done that well in ninety-two games. They wanted to quit then and there.

"Nothing doing," snarled the Red Stockings. "We'll settle this in extra innings."

So the boys from Brooklyn beat the invincibles in the tenth. This was also known as the Brooklyn touch.

But it was not until 1883 that the Trolley Dodgers became Brooklyn's first professional team in organized baseball. They played at Washington Park, between Fourth and Fifth avenues and Third to Fifth streets. However, they shifted to East

New York after they entered the National League in 1890 and didn't fare well either financially or artistically. That made an unhappy man of Ebbets, the new and youthful president of the Brooks.

"We've got to get back to Washington Park," insisted Ebbets. "East New York isn't Brooklyn. It's a suburb of Brooklyn."

But by the time his idea gained acceptance, Washington Park's land had been sold. The undaunted Ebbets thereupon built a new Washington Park at Third and Fourth avenues, First to Third streets.

Another Move

Casey Stengel, then a rookie Brooklyn outfielder, still cherishes—if cherishes is the word—one memory of Washington Park.

"The mosquitoes was somethin' fierce," he recalls.

Although Ebbets, operating on a low budget, was able to show a profit, he knew by 1908 that his ball park was outmoded and inadequate. So he started to look around, personally tramping Brooklyn streets in his search for a suitable site. Only a man with imagination could have envisioned the spot he found in Flatbush.

It was a disreputable, ramshackle neighborhood known as Pigtown. The shanty dwellers used the yawning pit in its center as a garbage dump. Ebbets' friends told him he was crazy to think such a miserable location could be converted into a modern ball park. But Charlie persisted, quietly buying up parcels of land behind the disguise of a dummy corporation.

Such a move could not remain a secret forever. When the news leaked out, Ebbets had to pay outrageous prices for the last few parcels. Finally, he had every piece of land he needed except one. And the owner couldn't be found.

Long Search

The gumshoe boys employed by Ebbets traced the missing owner to California and lost him. They picked up the trail again and chased him to Berlin. But he'd gone to Paris. Then he came back to the United States to visit friends in New Jersey. And that's where Ebbets agents found him.

"You want to buy the property I own in Brooklyn?" said the owner with a careless laugh. "I'd even forgotten I owned it."

"How much do you want for it?" cautiously asked the agent.

"Would $500 be too much?" asked the man. No one ever received five hundred bucks faster. Ebbets had swung the deal. Yet he still didn't know what to call the new ball park.

"I suppose I'll call it Washington Park," he told a sports writer.

"That's silly," said the writer. "This has been your baby from the start. You dreamed it up. You fought for it. It should be called Ebbets Field."

"Okay," said Charlie reluctantly, "Ebbets Field it will be."

And Ebbets Field has been a richly historic site ever since.

Ebbets Field opened for play on April 9, 1913, with the Brooklyn Superbas taking on the Philadelphia Phils. A pitcher's duel between Tom Seaton of the Phils and the Brooklyn ace Nap Rucker resulted in a 1–0 Philadelphia win. The Brooklyn Daily Eagle *covered the game with this story on April 10, 1913, by Thomas Rice.*

SUPERBAS OPEN SEASON WITH A 1–0 SHUTOUT DEFEAT

Thomas Rice

Failure to Hit in the Pinches Proves Fatal to Our
Chances — Seaton Outgames Nap Rucker in
a Great Pitcher's Duel — Meyer Muffs
a Fly and Knabe Scores the Solitary Tally.

A GAZOOK with a wise and throbbing head has remarked that it is no time for mirth or laughter in the cold, gray dawn of the morning after, and thereby he expressed a great essential truth, for "it ain't" as they say in the dialect novels, and among some of our very best public school graduates.

On this afternoon or the afternoon after Ebbets Field saw its first championship game, there is admittedly no occasion for the well-known mirth or laughter, for the very simple reason that there is no reason for such frivolity. A chuckle might be evolved now and then by the true optimist, such as Billy Kelly, the president of all the letter carriers, because of the obvious strength of the Brooklyn team, but just ordinary white folk cannot but be depressed for a minute because our bold athletes were beaten yesterday on The Eagle special opening date, by the Phillies, and by 1–0.

Curses on the Luck

Baseball is baseball, wherefore we go to see the games. If everybody knew what everybody on the field were going to accomplish there would be no baseball. Thus the fan liveth from day to day and he who booteth today shall yell like blazes tomorrow. One of the sad incidents that make baseball, followed by another incident that makes baseball and also makes for the enriching of the language in forceful expression, came to pass yesterday, when Benny Meyer, the promising young stock drover

Originally published in the *Brooklyn Daily Eagle* April 10, 1913.

of Hermitite, Mo., dropped a foul from Lobert in the first inning, and wrought thereby a foul deed. It is historically true that Benny subsequently caught a foul from Lobert, but in such a place that Knabe was enabled to go from second to third on the play and eventually score. It is likewise a matter of sad comment that immediately after valorous catch of the fly from Lobert, Benjamin, the boy stock drover, dropped a fly from Sherwood Magee. Not only did he drop it, but he kicked it while it was down and called it out of its name, for which sinful action he was punished by seeing Knabe score with the only run of the game for the world's polar championship.

There Are Reasons

Making errors is one of the easiest things we know. We have seen some of our upright citizens fall down and then heard the judge say that he hated to do it, but would have to give them the limit. All flesh is prone to err, and in a survey of the outfield situation we find that outfielders are not proud flesh who refuse to follow the general rule.

Benny Meyer had a high sky and a higher wind on both of those subsequent and monumental muffs and fandom should not be harsh with him. On Monday the shiverers in the grandstand saw Hal Chase, who is esteemed a ball player of more than the average ability, whizz around after a fly at second base and thereby allow Charley Stengel to make a two-base hit on an infield fly. Manager Dahlen was interviewed after the game and said that Benny was human and the wind was strong. Next year he hopes to have superhuman outfielders and no wind at all, which will insure the team against similar mischances.

Wheat to the Fore

Zachary Wheat once more bulged to the front as a sure-footed runner in bad footing, when he took in a couple of difficult flies, upon which flies he might have fallen down without loss of honor. His best stunt was on a short offering from Luderus in the fourth inning. Luderus thought it was safe, and so did his playmates, but you never can tell about these aborigines, and when Wheat gathered the ball to his bosom we were entirely unaffected by astonishment.

Stengel Shows an Arm

Charley Stengel crimped the Phils in the very first inning with a throw that made them behave. Magee was on second when Dolan banged a clean single to center. The Magee person is rated one of the most dangerous base runners in the Philadelphia lineup and a fellow who is always willing to take a chance. He took one on that single, and attempted to go home from second on the wallop. Miller got the ball from Stengel so far ahead of the runner that he almost forgot to touch Magee as he came flopping into the plate. In view of Stengel's batting that strong-arm work as an additional asset made nobody from this town mad.

Wilbert Robinson became manager of Brooklyn in 1914 and stayed until 1931. He won pennants in 1916 and 1920, but lost the World Series both times. In 1916, in game two, Brooklyn was defeated 2–1 in 14 innings by a young left-hander named Babe Ruth.

UNCLE ROBBIE
AND THE BROOKS

Arthur Daley

[JANUARY 1, 1951:] The Brooklyn Dodgers will formally unveil a plaque to Wilbert Robinson at Ebbets Field a week from tomorrow. It is a nice gesture but totally unnecessary. Uncle Robbie is a more integral part of Brooklyn than Prospect Park. There probably never has been a baseball manager quite like the Falstaffian leader of the Brooks during the era when the Daffiness Boys were in their heyday. He ran the team with musical comedy overtones. If it wasn't good baseball, at least it was an awful lot of fun.

Diamond history indicates that managers inevitably attract or gather to them players who reflect their personalities. Never was it truer than in the case of Uncle Robbie, a simple, down-to-earth guy with such peculiar overtones to his nature that he seemed to draw under his capacious wing every gay irresponsible in the business.

To him baseball was a game involving a ball, a bat and a glove. Strategy and percentage play were a lot of nonsense. His idea was to get pitchers so big and so fast that they could propel the ball past enemy hitters before the bat could be swung around; and to get sluggers who could wallop the ball over the fence. A home run to him was a much better play than a squeeze bunt. He didn't do too badly considering the fact that he won two pennants and usually operated with discards the other fellows didn't want.

Everyone in the Act

When Uncle Robbie ran the team, everyone else was like Umbriaggo. They wanted to get into the act. The 300-pound manager of the Daffiness Boys would argue strategical concepts with taxi drivers. He let the waiters at Joe's pick his pitchers. He let baseball writers name his starting line-up. And he always listened to his beloved Ma Robinson, his wife.

26

Once he started a rookie pitcher against the Cubs and patiently waited until the Cubs had lashed him for twelve runs before yanking him. Then he walked over to the box where Ma was seated.

"I hope you're satisfied," he said bitterly. "I started the kid like you suggested and maybe you'll now do less second-guessin'."

One day he decided to start Oscar Roettger in the outfield and couldn't spell his name when he was writing out the line-up.

"What the hell!" he said in abject surrender. "Maybe I oughter start Dick Cox at that." He did, too.

Sheer Fantasy

The Brooks were so utterly fantastic during the reign of Uncle Robbie that they were perpetually straining credulity. There was, for instance, the time the Dodgers were in the midst of a rousing rally and Chick Fewster began to pound a bat on the dugout steps in baseball's best whooping-it-up tradition.

"Cut that out," snapped Robbie. Then noting Fewster's questioning gaze, Uncle Robbie nodded to the far end of the bench where Jess Petty was slumbering soundly.

"I don't want you to wake up old Jess," he said with dignity.

Robbie once flashed a bunt sign to Zach (Buck) Wheat. The outfield star ignored the sign and hit a home run.

"Atta way to hit 'em, Buck," roared Robbie, already forgetting that he'd ordered a bunt.

Signals usually so perplexed the Daffiness Boys that they became more confused than usual — which was something. It was Babe Herman who solved everything.

"Let's cut out signs, Robbie," he urged. "We don't get 'em anyway."

So they played without signs for a while until everything was complete chaos. Then Robbie got firm. He called a meeting.

Too Many Dumbbells

"Our trouble ain't signs," he announced. "It's having too many dumbbells who think they're smart managers. From now on I'm the only dumbbell giving signals around here."

However, Robbie was not dumb. He had an astonishing native shrewdness and knew everything that went on. He once had a heavy drinker who thought his imbibing was a well-kept secret. One day a mosquito made a three-point landing on the neck of the disciple of Bacchus.

"Lookit that mosquito," snorted the observant Robbie at the other end of the dugout. "He's got himself drunk on that guy's neck."

Uncle Robbie was tremendously fond of Babe Herman's son. The little fellow regularly would climb into his capacious lap. Once Robbie unceremoniously dumped him on the floor and the little chap looked up at his idol with hurt eyes.

"Why ain't your old man hittin'?" asked Robbie accusingly.

Wilbert Robinson was a priceless character and his imprint is so deeply stamped on the Dodgers that it never will be erased. He doesn't need a monument to perpetuate his memory. He left one in the Brooklyn Dodgers.

On May 1, 1920, at Braves Field in Boston, the Braves and the Brooklyn Robins hooked up in a twenty-six inning duel. It was to be the longest game ever played in the major leagues. Incredibly, both pitchers, Leon Cadore of Brooklyn and Joe Oeschger of Boston, pitched the entire game.

BROOKLYN V. BOSTON IN 26 INNINGS

Ralph D. Blanpied

Boston Braves and Brooklyn Robins
1–1 After 26 Innings

The Robins and the Braves celebrated May Day in this ordinarily peaceful city by staging a prolonged, heartbreaking struggle for twenty-six innings at Braves Field and bombing to bits all major-league records for duration of hostilities. When darkness drew its mantle over the scene, both teams were still on their feet, interlocked in a death clutch and each praying for just one more inning in which to get in the knockout blow.

As far as results in the chase for the pennant go the game was without effect, for the final score was 1–1. In the matter of thrills, however, the oldest living man can remember nothing like it, nor can he find anything in his granddad's diary worthy of comparison. Heart disease was the mildest complaint that grasped the spectators as they watched inning after inning slip away and the row of ciphers on the scoreboard began to slide over the fence and reach out into the Fenway.

Nervous prostration threatened to engulf the stands as the twentieth inning passed away in the scoreless routine and word went out from the knowing fans to those of inferior baseball erudition that the National League record was twenty-two innings, the Robins having beaten the Pirates by 6 to 5 in a game of that length played in Brooklyn on Aug. 22, 1917.

The twenty-second inning passed in the history-making clash, and then the twenty-third, with a total result of four more ciphers on the scoreboard and a new National League record.

Now the old-timers in the stands began to whisper that the big-league record was twenty-four innings, established in an American League game in the Hub on Sept. 1, 1906, on which occasion the Athletics downed the Red Sox by 4 to 1. The

Robins and the Braves didn't care. They didn't even know it. They simply went along in their sublime ignorance and tied this record, then smashed it, and by way of emphasis tacked on a twenty-sixth session.

At this stage of the proceedings Umpire McCormick yawned twice and observed that it was nearly bedtime. He remembered that he had an appointment with a succulent beefsteak and became convinced that it was too dark to play ball. Thereupon he called the game.

The fielding on both sides was brilliant in the crises. Olson saved Brooklyn in the ninth, when, with the bases filled and one out, he stopped Pick's grounder, tagged Powell on the base line and threw out the batter.

In the seventeenth inning one of the most remarkable double plays ever seen in Boston retired Brooklyn. The bases were filled and one was out when Elliott grounded to Oeschger. Wheat was forced at the plate, but Gowdy's throw to Holke was low and was fumbled. Konetchy tried to score from second and Gowdy received Holke's throw to one side and threw himself blindly across the plate to meet Konetchy's spikes with bare fist.

Joe Oeschger and Leon Cadore were the real outstanding heroes among a score of heroes in the monumental affray of this afternoon. The two twirlers went the entire distance, each pitching practically the equivalent of three full games in this one contest, and, *mirabile dictu*, instead of showing any sign of weakening under the prolonged strain, each of them appeared to grow stronger. In the final six innings neither artist allowed even the shadow of a safe bingle.

The Braves twirler had rather the better of the duel in some respects. Fewer hits were made from his delivery that from that of Cadore. Oeschger practically twirled three 3-hit games in a row, while Cadore pitched three 5-hit games in the afternoon's warfare. In only one inning, the seventeenth, did Oeschger allow two safe blows, and Cadore let the local batters group their hits only in the sixth and the ninth.

At the receiving end of the batteries, O'Neil gave way to Gowdy for the Braves before hostilities were concluded, and Elliott took Krueger's place behind the bat for Brooklyn.

Robbie's men got their tally in the fifth inning. Krueger was walked by Oeschger, who offended in this way very seldom this afternoon. Krueger went to second while Oeschger was fielding Cadore's little pat and getting his man at first. Ivy Olson slashed a line drive over Maranville's for a single, on which Krueger crossed home plate. Olson went to second on a wild pitch but was left there as Oeschger tightened up and fanned Neis and Johnston lined to Mann in left field.

The Braves tied the score in the succeeding inning, jamming over the final run of a game which was destined to go on for twenty scoreless innings thereafter, equaling the existing record in this respect. Cadore threw Mann out at first. Cruise came along with a mighty drive to the scoreboard for three bases. Holke popped up a short fly to left which Wheat caught. Boeckel delivered the goods with a single to center upon which Cruise tallied. Maranville followed with a double to center but Boeckel was caught at the plate in the effort to score on the Rabbit's blow, Hood, Cadore and Krueger participating in the put-out.

After this session, save for the Braves' flash in the ninth and the Robins' effort in the seventeenth, the two twirlers were entire masters of the situation.

The Line Score

Brooklyn	0	0	0	0	1	0	0	0	0	0	0	0	0	0	0	0	0	0	0	0	0	0	0	0	0	0	—1
Boston	0	0	0	0	0	1	0	0	0	0	0	0	0	0	0	0	0	0	0	0	0	0	0	0	0	0	—1

The lovable Babe Herman, Brooklyn's Babe, epitomized baseball in Brooklyn in the late 1920s and early 1930s. The era of the "Daffiness Boys" ... but how he could hit.

THE UNBELIEVABLE BABE HERMAN

John Lardner

Floyd Caves Herman, known as Babe, did not always catch fly balls on the top of his head, but he could do it in a pinch. He never tripled into a triple play, but he once doubled into a double play, which is the next best thing. For seven long years, from 1926 through 1932, he was the spirit of Brooklyn baseball. He spent the best part of his life upholding the mighty tradition that anything can happen at Ebbets Field, the mother temple of daffiness in the national game.

Then he went away from there. He rolled and bounced from town to town and ball club to ball club. Thirteen years went by before he appeared in a Brooklyn uniform again. That was in the wartime summer of 1945, when manpower was so sparse that the desperate Dodger scouts were snatching beardless shortstops from the cradle and dropping their butterfly nets over Spanish War veterans who had played the outfield alongside Willie Keeler. In the course of the great famine, Branch Rickey and Leo Durocher lured Babe Herman, then 42, from his turkey farm in Glendale, California, to hit a few more for the honor of Flatbush. A fine crowd turned out to watch the ancient hero on the first day of his reincarnation.

"It looks like they haven't forgotten you here, Babe," said one of the players, glancing around the grandstand.

Mr. Herman shook his head. "How could they?" he said with simple dignity.

And he went on to show what he meant. In his first time at bat he was almost thrown out at first base on a single to right field. The Babe rounded the bag at a high, senile prance, fell flat on his face on the baseline, and barely scrambled back to safety ahead of the throw from the outfield. The crowd roared with approval. Fifteen years earlier they would have booed themselves into a state of apoplexy, for that was a civic ritual at Ebbets Field—booing Herman. But this was 1945. You don't boo a legend from out of the past, a man who made history.

Before he went home to California to stay, a few weeks later, the Babe gathered

Reprinted with permission of Susan Lardner, Mary Jane Lardner, and John N. Lardner.

the younger players around his knee and filled them with blood-curdling stories about his terrible past.

"You know the screen on top of the right-field fence," he said. "They put that up there on account of me. I was breaking all the windows on the other side of Bedford Avenue."

Looking around to see if that had sunk in, he added: "There used to be a traffic tower on Bedford Avenue there. Once I hit one over the wall that broke a window in the tower and cut a cop's hand all to pieces. Wasn't my fault," said the Babe philosophically. "When I busted 'em, there was no telling where they'd go."

* * *

It's beyond question that Mr. Herman could bust them. He always admitted it. He used to be irritated, though, by the rumor that he was the world's worst outfielder and a constant danger to his own life. He was also sensitive about his base-running.

"Don't write fresh cracks about my running," he once told an interviewer, "or I won't give you no story. I'm a great runner."

He proceeded to tell why he stole no bases in 1926, his first year with Brooklyn, until the very end of the season. It seems that the late Uncle Wilbert Robinson, then managing the Dodgers, came up to Mr. Herman one day and said, sourly: "What's the matter, can't you steal?"

"Steal?" said the Babe. "Why, hell, you never asked me to."

So then he stole a couple of bases, to prove he could do everything.

One talent for which Babe never gave himself enough public credit was making money. He was one of the highest-salaried players of his time, year after year. He got these salaries by holding out all through the training season. Other players, starving slowly on the ball club's regular bill of fare in Southern hotels, used to go down the street to the restaurants where Herman, the holdout, ate, and press their noses against the window like small boys, watching the Babe cut huge sirloin steaks to ribbons. It wasn't just the food that kept Babe from signing early. Holding out is a common practice with good-hit-no-field men, like Herman, Zeke Bonura, and Rudy York, in his outfielding days. The reason is obvious. The longer they postpone playing ball in the spring (for nothing), the less chance there is of getting killed by a fly ball.

Mr. Herman had such ambitious ideas about money that one year, returning his first contract to the Brooklyn office unsigned, he enclosed an unpaid bill from his dentist for treatment during the winter. The ball club ignored the bill. After all, Herman didn't hit with his teeth.

The Babe, as a player, was a gangling fellow with spacious ears who walked with a slouch that made him look less than his true height, six feet, four inches. He was born in Buffalo in 1903. Leaving there for the professional baseball wars in 1921, Mr. Herman worked for eighteen different managers before he met up with Uncle Robbie, and for nine more after that. It is said that he broke the hearts of 45 percent of these gentlemen. The rest avoided cardiac trouble by getting rid of the Babe as fast as they could.

He came up from Edmonton, in the Western Canada League, to Detroit, in the year 1922, and was promptly fired by Ty Cobb, the Tigers' idealistic manager.

"The Detroit club," said the Babe, his feelings wounded, "has undoubtedly made some bad mistakes in its time, but this is the worst they ever made."

He was fired from the Omaha club later in the same year while batting .416. A pop fly hit him on the head one day, and the Omaha owner lost his temper. The owner and the manager began to argue.

"Much as I would like to," said the manager, "I can't send away a man who is hitting .416."

"I don't care if he's hitting 4,000!" yelled the owner. "I am not going to have players who field the ball with their skulls. Fire him!"

The Babe explained later that the incident was greatly exaggerated.

"It was a foul ball," he said, "that started to go into the stands. The minute I turned my back, though, the wind caught the ball and blew it out again, and it conked me. It could happen to anybody."

Just the same, Mr. Herman was fired.

The Babe tried baseball in Boston briefly, when Lee Fohl managed the Red Sox. He never played an inning there. Studying his form on the bench, Mr. Fohl fired him. The Babe was just as well pleased. He said the Boston climate did not suit him. He went to Atlanta, where Otto Miller, later a Brooklyn coach, managed the team. Every morning for five days in a row, Mr. Miller resolved to fire Mr. Herman. Every afternoon of those five days, Mr. Herman got a hit that drove in runs and changed Mr. Miller's mind for the night. On the fifth day, playing against Nashville, he had four hits in his first four times at bat. He was robbed of a fifth hit by a sensational catch by Kiki Cuyler. After the game, Mr. Miller told the Babe that they might have won the game but for Cuyler's catch. He meant it kindly, but Mr. Herman took it as a personal criticism of himself. He was hurt. He began a loud quarrel with Otto, and was traded to Memphis on one bounce.

The Brooklyn club bought the Babe for $15,000 a couple of years later, while he was causing nervous breakdowns and busting up ball games in Seattle. Then Brooklyn tried to get rid of him for nothing, and failed. This gross insult to the name of Herman occurred as follows: The Dodgers wanted a Minneapolis player of no subsequent consequence, named Johnny Butler. They traded Herman and eight other men to Minneapolis for Butler. Minneapolis took the eight other men, but refused to take Herman. Brooklyn was stuck with the Babe, and history began to be made.

Jacques Fournier, the Dodger first baseman, hurt his leg one day in the summer of 1926. Herman replaced him. He had a good season at bat that year and the Brooklyn fans began to take to the Babe, wide ears, chewing tobacco, and all. Uncle Robbie took to him some days. Other days gave him pause — like the day famous in ballad and prose when Mr. Herman smote a two-base hit that ended in a double play.

The bases were full of Brooklyns, with one out, when the Babe strode to the plate on that occasion, swinging his bat like a cane in his right hand. He was a phenomenon physically, a left-handed hitter with most of his power in his right arm. Scattered around the landscape before him were Hank DeBerry, the Brooklyn catcher, on third base; Dazzy Vance, the immortal Dodger fireball pitcher, on second; and Chick Fewster, an outfielder, on first. Mr. Herman swung ferociously and the ball hit the rightfield wall on a line. DeBerry scored. Vance, however, being a man who did not care to use his large dogs unnecessarily, hovered between second and third for a moment on the theory that the ball might be caught. When it rebounded off the wall, he set sail again, lumbered to third base, and made a tentative turn towards home. Then, deciding he couldn't score, he stepped back to third. This move confounded Fewster, who was hard on Vance's heels. Fewster started back toward second base. At that moment, a new character, with blond hair and flapping ears, came into their lives.

Mr. Herman has described himself as a great runner. What he meant was, he was a hard runner. He forgot to mention that he ran with blinkers on, as they say at the race track. He concentrated on running and ignored the human and animal life around and ahead of him. Passing Fewster like the Limited passing a whistle stop, the Babe slid into third just as Vance returned there from the opposite direction. Herman was automatically out for passing Fewster on the baseline, though nobody realized it at once but the umpire, who made an "out" sign. The third baseman, not knowing who was out, began frantically to tag Herman, who was already dead, and Vance, who stood perfectly safe on third base.

"What a spectacle!" observed Vance nonchalantly to Herman, as the third baseman looked in vain to the umpire for the sign of another out. Fewster, confused, stood a little distance away. His proper move was to go back to second and stay there, but Herman's slide had destroyed his powers of thought. Finally, the third baseman caught on. He began to chase Fewster, who ran in a panic and did not even stop at second, where he would have been safe. He was tagged in the outfield for the third out of the inning.

Cheap detractors may say what they like about Herman merely doubling into a double play. It's obvious that what he really did—the rule book to the contrary—was triple into a double play.

It is also obvious that Vance and Fewster were as much at fault as Herman. That is the old, true spirit of Brooklyn cooperation. But Vance regarded Herman as the star of the act. A few years afterward, when Chicago officials announced that they expected a Chicago pennant in 1933 to make things complete for the Century of Progress exposition, Vance announced his counter-plan for that year in Brooklyn. Instead of a Century of Progress, said Dazzy, they would feature "A Cavalcade of Chaos; or, the Headless Horsemen of Ebbets Field." Herman was to be the star. Unfortunately, by the time the year 1933 rolled into Brooklyn, Herman had rolled out of there, to quieter pastures.

Uncle Robbie's comment on the celebrated double play of 1926 was "#$&%$%!!" However, that was Robbie's comment on practically everything, and he meant it in a friendly way. He was tolerant of Herman, for he understood that criticism or scolding drove the Babe crazy. When 30,000 people booed him in unison—and that happened often enough in 1927, when his batting average slipped to .272, and 1929, when he led the league's outfielders in errors—the Babe would sulk for days. It took Robbie a little while, at that, to learn patience with Herman. He asked waivers on him in 1927, but changed his mind and kept the Babe when John McGraw, of the New York Giants, refused to waive. "If that crafty blank-blank McGraw wants him," reasoned Mr. Robinson, "there must be something in him."

As time went on, the Brooklyn crowds became more sympathetic too, That's understandable. After 1927, Herman hit for averages of .340, .381, .393, .313, and .326. In 1930, he had 241 hits for a total of 426 bases, including 35 home runs. He scored 143 runs and batted in 130. The fans barbecued him one moment and cheered him the next.

"Not only is that fellow a funny-looking blank-blank-blank," said the manager, "but he is blankety-blank unlucky. Other men, when they're on third base, can sometimes beat the outfielder's catch when they start home on a fly ball. But not this blankety-blank Herman. He always gets called for it."

The wailing and the keening were great in Brooklyn when the Babe, called by Rogers Hornsby, "the perfect free swinger," was traded to Cincinnati in December 1932, in a six-player deal. It was not a bad deal for Brooklyn, in a strictly practical way. Herman never hit in high figures again after that year, while some of the players from the main, never forgave Max Carey, who had replaced Uncle Robbie as manager, for sending Herman away. They didn't care about being practical. They wanted salt in their stew.

Removed from the choice Brooklyn atmosphere, where he flourished, the Babe began to bounce from place to place again as he had in the days of his youth. Managers resumed the practice of firing him to save their health. He went from Cincinnati to Chicago to Pittsburgh to Cincinnati to Detroit to Toledo to Syracuse to Jersey City, and finally, with a strong tail wind, clear out to the Pacific Coast. The slower he got as a player, the more money he asked, and the more loudly he asked for it. However, the Babe did not like the word "holdout." Once, in the early spring of 1934, he denounced the press of Los Angeles, near his home, for using that term to describe him.

"You got the wrong idea entirely," he told the reporters sternly. "I am not holding out. I just don't want to sign this ----------------contract the Cubs have sent me, because the dough ain't big enough."

* * *

On his second time around in Cincinnati, in 1936, Mr. Herman came into contact with baseball's leading genius, Leland Stanford MacPhail, who was the Reds' general manager. They were bound to get together sometime, even though the Babe left Brooklyn before MacPhail was ripe for the city. It was also inevitable that MacPhail should someday fine Herman, and someday fire him. They were not made to be soulmates. MacPhail fined him, and Paul Derringer, the pitcher, $200 each, one day in July. It was a true Herman episode. With hostile runners on first and third, Derringer made a balk. The runner on third went home, and the runner on first went to second. Herman, communing with nature in the outfield, missed the play completely. He thought there were still men on first and third. When the next hitter singled to the Babe on one bounce, he studied the stitches on the ball and lobbed it back to the infield. The runner on second scored standing up. MacPhail turned purple, and levied his fines on both the pitcher and the Babe.

It's a matter of record that Derringer got his fine canceled, by throwing an inkwell at MacPhail, which impressed the great man. Mr. Herman was less direct, and therefore less successful. He waited a few weeks after being fined. Then he demanded from MacPhail a cash bonus over and above his salary. It was an ill-timed request.

"A bonus!" yelled the genius. "Why, you're not even good enough to play on this team!" He added that Herman was fired. And he was.

Right to the end of his playing days, the Babe retained his fresh young affection for cash money. He was farming turkeys at his home in Glendale by the time he landed with the Hollywood club of the Pacific Coast League in the twilight of his career. One day in 1942 — just a short while before that final, nostalgic, wartime bow in Brooklyn — he arranged to have his turkeys advertised on the scorecards in the Hollywood ball park. He then announced that he was holding out. The holdout kept him home in comfort among the turkeys, but not so far away from Hollywood that he couldn't drive over from time to time to negotiate. When he finally got his price and signed up to play ball, the Babe was fat and his reflexes were slow. So he made his seasons' debut at a disadvantage.

Hollywood was playing a game with Seattle. The score was tied going into the tenth inning. Seattle's young pitcher, a kid named Soriano, had already struck out ten men. Hollywood filled the bases on him, with two out, in the last of the tenth, but the boy was still strong and fast. The manager asked Mr. Herman if he was in shape to go in and pinch-hit.

"I may not be sharp," said the Babe, reaching for a bat, "and maybe I can't hit him. But I won't have to. I'll paralyze him."

He walked to the plate. He glowered at the pitcher, and held his bat at a menacing angle. He never swung it. Five pitches went by — three of them balls, two of them strikes. Then Mr. Herman pounded the plate, assumed a fearful scowl, and made as though his next move would tear a hole in the outfield wall. The last pitch from the nervous Soriano hit the ground in front of the Babe's feet for ball four. A run was forced in, and the ball game was over.

"That's a boy with an education," said the Babe, as he threw away his bat. "I see he's heard of Herman."

When Larry MacPhail came to Brooklyn in 1938, he began a whirlwind four years in which he bought, sold, innovated and built a winner. One of his projects was night baseball. He installed lights at Ebbets Field and the first night game was played on June 15, 1938. A young left-hander with Cincinnati hurled his second consecutive no-hit game that night. How's that for planning?

THE FIRST NIGHT MAJOR LEAGUE GAME IN THE METROPOLITAN AREA

Roscoe McGowen

Last night they turned on the greatest existing battery of baseball lights at Ebbets Field for the inaugural night major-league game in the metropolitan area. A record throng for the season there, 40,000, of whom 38,748 paid, came to see the fanfare and the show that preceded the contest between the Reds and the Dodgers.

The game, before it was played, was partly incidental; the novelty of night baseball was the major attraction.

But Johnny Vander Meer, tall, handsome twenty-two-year-old Cincinnati southpaw pitcher, stole the show by hurling his second consecutive no-hit, no-run game, both coming within five days, and making baseball history that probably will never be duplicated. His previous no-hitter was pitched in daylight at Cincinnati last Saturday against the Bees (Braves), the Reds winning, 3–0. Last night the score was 6–0.

The records reveal only seven pitchers credited with two no-hitters in their careers and none who achieved the feat in one season.

More drama was crowded into the final inning than a baseball crowd has felt in many a moon. Until that frame only one Dodger had got as far as second base, Lavagetto reaching there when Johnny issued passes to Cookie and Dolf Camilli in the seventh. Vandy pitched out of that easily enough and the vast crowd was pulling for him to come through to the end.

Johnny mowed down Woody English, batting for Luke Hamlin; Kiki Cuyler and Johnny Hudson in the eighth, fanning the first and third men. When Vito Tamulis, fourth Brooklyn hurler, treated the Reds likewise in the ninth, Vandy came out for the crucial inning.

He started easily, taking Buddy Hassett's bounder and tagging him out. Then his terrific speed got out of control and, while the fans sat forward tense and almost silent, he walked Babe Phelps, Lavagetto and Camilli to fill the bases.

All nerves were taut as Vandy pitched to Ernie Koy. With the count one and one, Ernie sent a bounder to Lew Riggs, who was so careful in making the throw to Ernie Lombardi that a double play wasn't possible.

Leo Durocher, so many times a hitter in the pinches, was the last hurdle for Vander Meer, and the crowd groaned as he swung viciously, to line a foul high into the right-field stands. But a moment later Leo swung again, the ball arched lazily toward short center field and Harry Craft camped under it for the put-out that brought unique distinction to the young hurler.

It brought, also, a horde of admiring fans onto the field, with Vandy's teammates ahead of them to hug and slap Johnny on the back and then protect him from the mob as they struggled toward the Red dugout.

The fans couldn't get Johnny, but a few moments later they got his father and mother, who had accompanied a group of 500 citizens from Vandy's home town of Midland Park, N.J. The elder Vander Meers were completely surrounded and it required nearly fifteen minutes before they could escape.

The feat ran the youngster's remarkable pitching record to 18⅓ hitless and scoreless innings and a streak of 26 scoreless frames. This includes a game against the Giants, his no-hitter against the Bees and last night's game. Vander Meer struck out seven Dodgers, getting pinch hitters twice, and of the eight passes he issued two came in the seventh and three in the tense ninth.

Added to his speed was a sharp-breaking curve that seldom failed to break over the plate and at which the Dodger batsmen swung as vainly as at his fastball.

On the offense, well-nigh forgotten as the spectacle of Vander Meer's no-hitter unfolded, the Reds made victory certain as early as the third frame, when they scored four times and drove Max Butcher away.

Frank McCormick hit a home run into the left-field stands with Wally Berger and Ival Goodman aboard, while a pass to Lombardi and singles by Craft and Riggs added the fourth run.

Craft's third straight single scored Goodman in the seventh, the latter's blow off Tot Pressnell's right kneecap knocking the knuckleballer out and causing him to be carried off on a stretcher. Berger tripled off Luke Hamlin in the eighth to score Vander Meer with the last run.

Larry MacPhail brought Red Barber to Brooklyn in 1939 and began the radio broadcasts that would make Red and the Dodgers a legend.

THE OLE REDHEAD COMES TO BROOKLYN

Red Barber and Robert Creamer

General Mills, which made Wheaties, had become the dominant sponsor at Cincinnati, and they had cornered most of the major league market and a lot of the top minor leagues, too. They wanted to break into New York, and when Larry MacPhail went to Brooklyn they had their chance. I learned that there were to be two broadcasts in New York in 1939 — the Dodgers on one, and the Giants and Yankees alternately on the other. In other words, I discovered that there were two jobs open in New York, and I wanted one of them. I was constantly in touch with people at General Mills, but they were elusive. They filled me with stories that there were thirty or forty other fellows after the two jobs and that they hadn't made up their mind yet, though they said I was high up on their list. I was so intent on landing one of those spots with General Mills that I kept forgetting I had a very good friend named Mac-Phail, who was general manager of one of the clubs who would be broadcasting. Forgetting that cost me a good deal of money. When General Mills got to dickering with Larry about broadcasting he said, okay, he would go along with them and break the radio ban, but he wanted three things. He wanted seventy-five thousand dollars for the rights for the first year. He wanted a fifty-thousand-watt radio station. And he wanted Red Barber to do the announcing. He told me this several years later. General Mills agreed but they made him promise not to say anything to me about it so that I couldn't hold them up on the price. They kept talking to me about the thirty or forty fellows they were considering, and when they finally said they had decided on me for one of the jobs, I jumped at it, even though they offered me only eight thousand dollars a year.

I remembered we settled things in New York early in December 1938, the day the New York Giants and the Green Bay Packers met at the Polo Grounds for the National Football League championship. I came into New York on an overnight train and arrived on a Sunday morning. I went to the Waldorf, where the General Mills

Reprinted from *Rhubarb in the Catbird Seat* by Red Barber and Robert Creamer, by permission of the University of Nebraska Press. ©1968 by Walter L. Barber and Robert Creamer.

people were staying, and had breakfast in their room. We talked about the broadcasting job, and then we all went up to the Polo Grounds to see the football game. The conversation about the broadcast was brief. They said they still were not positive whether I'd be at New York or Brooklyn, but they said they would pay me eight thousand dollars the first year, ten thousand dollars the second, and twelve thousand dollars the third, though they had the option not to renew. Bill Corum wrote that I came for twenty-five thousand dollars, and he went to his grave swearing that I told him that. It was considerably less, and, as a matter of fact, it cost me money to come to New York. When Powell Crosley heard that I was leaving he called me into his office and told me he wanted me to stay in Cincinnati. He said he would guarantee me sixteen thousand dollars, or twice what I was going to New York for. If I could make more than sixteen thousand dollars with my basic salary at WLW and my outside work, fine. But he'd guarantee that I'd make at least sixteen thousand dollars. And he added, "I'll do something else. I'll create a job for you. I'll make you our sports executive, answerable only to the general manager. You'll be free to select and broadcast any sporting event you want."

I felt like crying. That was a magnificent offer. Crosley was a close-fisted man — the standard joke in Cincinnati was that WLW stood for World's Lowest Wages — and I was flattered and tempted. But I thanked him very much and told him no. He said, "I'm puzzled. I believe I have the right to ask why you're turning down my offer for a job that will pay you only half as much."

I said, "Mr. Crosley, I'm not turning down your offer. I want to go to New York. I want to go there for the same reason that you went broke six times before you came up with WLW." Which was a fact. In the world of mechanics, inventions and machines, Crosley had been a Don Quixote tilting at windmills. He kept trying things, and fooling with things, and losing money. And then he finally started messing around with a little radio station in the living room of his house and he kept fooling with it until he turned it into a great, great success.

When I said that to him, he stood up and smiled the most cordial, warm, genuine smile I have ever seen. He came around the desk and shook hands with me vigorously and said, "I completely understand. Good luck!"

Harold Parrott spent 45 years in and around major league baseball. He covered the Brooklyn Dodgers as a journalist for the Brooklyn Eagle *for 15 years. He then became the team's traveling secretary and publicist. His book,* The Lords of Baseball, *has a unique behind-the-scenes view of baseball from Mr. Parrott's intimate perspective.*

WHEN EBBETS FIELD WAS A BAD JOKE

Harold Parrott

Hunting material for my column and as a backup man for Holmes, I had poked around Ebbets Field enough to learn that you could find more action in Mme. Tussaud's Wax Museum. Some of the characters with the ball club, like "Judge" Steve McKeever, who held court daily in a specially constructed armchair in the last row of the grandstand behind home plate, looked ready for the waxworks, at that.

The Judge was one of the McKeevers who had helped build the Brooklyn Bridge and had been warring with the Ebbets family for control of the ball club for years. In his seventies and decked out in a black derby hat and gold-handled cane, he accepted daily homage from droves of police captains, fire inspectors, and ward-heel politicians, for he was the one who handed out passes to the Dodger games. The genial old gent also had a colostomy, and he gave demonstrations of this surgical novelty along with the Annie Oakleys, if you could stand it.

Old man McKeever was the only visible sign of a Dodger front office, except for a figurehead named Dave Driscoll who was allowed to do little else but worry. Once in a great while Joe Gilleadeau, a dapper hat manufacturer, or Jim Mulvey, who was into movie-making as Samuel Goldwyn's right-hand man, would surface. But they were from rival factions in the club ownership, and they would pass each other silently, as if embarrassed to be connected with a team that lost and lost and lost again.

On the field, things were run by a little round man with a tummy that looked as if somebody had shoved in a pillow to make him pass for a department store Santa. Uncle Robbie, as Wilbert Robinson was called by one and all, was more of a habit than a manager. He had been managing the team since 1914, and here we were in the thirties, and nobody had asked him to leave.

Robbie couldn't remember his players' names, much less spell them. But so many came and went, you couldn't blame the old fellow. The Dodgers picked up every bit of baseball flotsam that floated past on the waiver lists.

That was pretty much how that hopeless, hapless team was run from day to day. Yet the little round manager bubbled with endless enthusiasm. After six or seven straight losses he would grin and say, "Don't worry, men. Daz'll stop those guys tomorrow!" If the Robins—called that by most papers because of Robinson's long tenure—were steamrollered by ten runs in the first game of a double-header, Robbie would chirp, "The Babe'll hit a couple in the second game."

"Daz" was Dazzy Vance, a pitcher who could strike out just about anybody he pleased, and "the Babe" was Herman, the only authentic Babe as far as Brooklyn was concerned, the Yankees' Ruth notwithstanding.

Vance was a late-blooming pitcher who had been pushed off on the Dodgers because every scout in the game had said the big guy with the windmill windup would never overcome his wildness. He led the National League seven straight times in strikeouts; but the Brooklyns were strictly sixth place in an eight-club league most of the time, except in 1924, when Vance did a Hercules number and lifted the whole team into a shot at the pennant. He won twenty-eight and lost only six that year, and they might have won the whole thing had the Dazzler agreed to pitch in cracker-box Baker Bowl in Philadelphia. But he would never take his turn there. "Might hurt my record," he would say, in all honesty. And Uncle Robbie would not order him to pitch, for he was Robbie's pet.

Never mind! Vance became a household word in Greenpernt and Gowanus and Lon Guyland (Long Island), as Dan Parker kiddingly called the Dodger precincts in his column in the *Mirror*. Vance was still pitching for the Bums, as they got to be called, at forty-five years of age; which should give you an idea of how Flynn's, the bar across the street, preserved Ebbets Field's heroes in those days. Two more years on the mound and the Dazzler would have been stuffed and put on exhibit in the famous Brooklyn Museum over on Eastern Parkway.

As it was, Dazzy barely missed the coming of MacPhail, and the Dodger Resurrection, in 1937.

But in the years just before MacPhail arrived on his white horse, the rest of the owners surely must have winked at the downhill slide of what should have been one of the richest franchises in the National League, where they should all have been picking up fat visiting-club checks.

They ignored it because in this setup they could shove their own rejects off on the defenseless Dodgers at holdup prices. There was no general manager in the nonexistent Brooklyn front office to stop this sort of thing, and Uncle Robbie was a patsy. He once traded a fine pitcher, Jess Petty, for a shortstop the Dodgers needed badly. But only after Glenn Wright arrived in Brooklyn was it discovered that he had hurt himself and was in fact a one-armed ballplayer. He could not throw across a room, much less an infield. But the fraud went uncorrected. Pittsburgh got away with Petty Larceny. And the Dodgers were stuck again.

Branch Rickey, who had seven hundred ballplayers in the minors, knew his lemons, and he selected some of the ripest for the Dodgers. One was Long Tom Winsett, who came to Brooklyn at a fancy price, billed as "the next Babe Ruth," amid terrific ballyhoo. Nobody thought to ask why Rickey didn't keep Winsett for his own Cardinals if he was that good.

During batting practice, the other ballplayers stopped whatever they were doing to stare at Winsett's beautiful swing, a classic stroke that was as much admired as Sam Snead's is in golf today. Not only that, but the Dodger rookie pumped ball after ball out of Ebbets Field, across Bedford Avenue into a parking lot where he created a windshield crisis until the attendants started parking the cars backward. Some of the balls were hit so high and far they vanished in the general direction of Canarsie.

But that was in batting practice. Once the game started, poor Tom couldn't get the bat and ball together.

To the ballplayers, Winsett was known as a "two o'clock hitter." All the games were in the afternoon then, and they started at three to get the "Wall Street crowd." Batting practice, where Long Tom put on his daily show was at two.

Curious, I asked Rickey about Winsett's problem the next time the old horse-trader came to Brooklyn to peddle another junk ballplayer. I had grown friendly with Branch because of some magazine pieces I had written about his St. Louis dynasty.

Mr. Rickey — as even his veteran employees addressed him — swore me to secrecy and explained.

"Watch that beautiful swing, my boy," he chuckled, "Mr. Winsett sweeps the bat in the same plane every time, no matter where the ball is pitched!"

Rickey let that sink in and then went on.

"Woe unto the pitcher who throws the ball where the Winsett bat is functioning," Branch said, sounding every bit like the psalm-singer the writers pictured him to be, "but throwing it almost anywhere else in the general area of home plate is safe!"

Safe indeed! The pitchers grew to love Long Tom, who hit only eight home runs in almost five hundred at bats during three years of high hopes in Brooklyn.

One of those who held those high hopes until the bitter end was Max Carey, who had become the manager when Uncle Robbie's comic term ended in 1932.

Carey was a God-fearing, college-educated man out of Concordia Seminary, and the warring McKeever-Ebbets factions one day got together in a civil conversation that lasted long enough for them to agree on him.

Max had played sixteen glorious seasons for the Pittsburgh Pirates, but then wound up with the Dodgers, as all broken-down ballplayers seemed to. Even though his legs had started to go, Carey stole thirty-two bases in his first full year with the Brooklyns, and they hadn't had anybody who could move that fast unless it was the Ebbets heirs, who had to keep ducking the sheriff.

But most of all, Max was well-scrubbed and polite, and didn't chew tobacco, so he was given the job of banishing buffoonery and imparting some decorum to this undisciplined crew. It just didn't work. One of the first problems Carey had to wrestle with was Hack Wilson, and Max flunked badly. But then Wilson might have defeated anybody, including Billy Graham, Savonarola, and a whole platoon of Alcoholics Anonymous.

Wilson had been nicknamed after Hackenschmidt, the famous wrestler. Hack was a barrel-chested little (5 foot, 6 inch) two hundred-pound outfielder with the muscled arms of a smithy and the feet (size 5) of a ballet dancer. This cameo Hercules had hit fifty-six home runs and driven in the unheard-of total of one hundred ninety runs for the clouting Chicago Cubs in 1930, just two years before, and that is a record that may stand forever. Where Wilson himself seemed to stand forever was at the handiest bar. He guzzled booze day and night, and as soon as he started to slip, the Cubs shipped him to—where else?—Brooklyn.

Carey, the preacher, tried a few fire-and-brimstone talks, but his words seemed to roll right off fun-loving Hack's back. So Max called a meeting of the entire team. A hitter as good as this—even hung over, Wilson was hitting .300 for the Dodgers and pumping out homers—had to be saved somehow! So Carey tried the psychological approach: health, doctors' warnings, and all that.

As he called the player meeting to order, Max stood at a table on which he had placed two glasses and a plate of live angleworms. One glass was filled with water, the other with gin, Wilson's favorite elixir.

With a flourish, the manager dropped a worm in the glass of water. It wriggled happily.

Now Max plunged the same worm into the gin; it stiffened and expired. A murmur ran through the room, and some of the players were obviously impressed.

Not Wilson. Hack didn't even seem interested.

Carey waited a little. Hoping for some delayed reaction from his wayward member. When none came, he provided: "That mean anything to you, Wilson?"

"Sure, Skipper," answered the sawed-off tree trunk of a man, anxious to oblige. "It proves if you drink gin you'll never have no worms!"

Wilson burned out almost as fast as Max's demonstration worm. He was washed up at thirty-four after three rollicking seasons with the Dodgers, and dead at forty-eight.

Max Carey's reform ideas weren't working, and the looting of the Dodgers continued, as the other owners shoved off on the Brooklyn team all the over-the-hill ballplayers they had.

This made for pretty grim reporting in the *Eagle*, and for McCullough's paper, too, for he was drinking heavily, and I had to cover for him most of the time. Many people tried to talk some sense into Bill, for he was a pleasant fellow, and they felt sorry for his embarrassed wife.

On one of his frequent visits from the Cardinals' base at Brandenton to the Dodger camp, Branch Rickey, a teetotaler himself, talked McCullough into taking the pledge.

A week later Rickey was back again, peddling another lemon, and he sought out Gladys McCullough. "Bill isn't drinking anymore?" he asked hopefully.

Gladys though a minute and then said, "No, Mr. Rickey, but not any less, either!"

With Carey's head obviously on the chopping-block although his contract still had a full season to run, there wasn't one of the twelve reporters in the Dodger camp who had the foggiest notion of who his successor would be. For a solid month I did two headline stories a night: one for the *Eagle*, and a completely different second-day angle for the *Times* under McCullough's name. I was just as proud of my handiwork for the rival paper as I was of what appeared under my byline.

McCullough was nice about it, too. When copies of his paper caught up with us at training camp, he often complimented me on stories that he saw under his name. But as long as Bill knew he had me as a pinch hitter, he drank more and more and wrote less and less.

The Dodgers were so dull under Carey that they helped drive more than McCullough to drink. Brooklyn fans had shown they could forgive errors in the field and incompetence, but they wouldn't stand for dullness, and Carey had no color, no flair as a leader. The fans were clamoring for a return to the rollicking days of Uncle Robbie.

Names, big baseball names, were bandied about by all the writers like confetti in a wind tunnel. I would give one of them the inside track for the job when I wrote my piece for the *Eagle*. Later that night, when I ghosted for McCullough, I would nominate somebody entirely different in the *Times*. Who would it be? We were all guessing.

One morning while he was still sober, McCullough got a penny postcard from Glendale, California. The message on it was just, "Leaving for Brooklyn on business." It was signed by Casey Stengel, whom Bill knew very well from his daffy days as a playing Dodger, when Casey let the bird out from under his baseball cap at home plate to ridicule an umpire.

Bill didn't bother to show me this postcard, and I thought it was odd that he wrote his own story that night. It was the first time in a week I hadn't had to pinch hit.

McCullough had been smart enough to put two and two together. He went out on a limb with a story in his Brooklyn *Times* saying Stengel would be named to succeed Carey as Dodger manager in a day or two.

When Casey did indeed get the job, it was a clean beat for McCullough and the *Times*, and all hell broke loose at the embarrassed *Eagle*.

For a while, it looked as if Mrs. Parrott would get her wish, and her little boy Harold would be saved from the pitfalls of the sinful newspaper game, his journalistic career at an end. I should have been fired.

But I was saved by Harris Crist.

I was still Crist's pet.

In 1938 a hurricane blew in from Cincinnati; in four tumultuous years he made the Dodgers champions. The hurricane was named Larry MacPhail.

Hurricane Larry

Donald Honig

The fortunes of the Brooklyn Dodgers were at this point at their lowest ebb. Ford Frick, at that time president of the National League, was becoming increasingly concerned about the franchise, once one of the league's strongest. Deciding to take a hand, Frick went to the board and urged them to hire a new general manager, someone not only with a track record but a person with flair and initiative.

"Like whom?" he was asked.

"Larry MacPhail," Frick said.

Larry MacPhail was not a breath of fresh air. He was a hurricane. He was a man in motion, aggressive, dynamic, brimming with ideas. A showman. Forty-eight years old when he took over in Brooklyn in January 1938, MacPhail had been a college athlete, a lawyer, a successful businessman, a captain in the First World War (his most famous caper was an attempt to kidnap the German Kaiser after the war, an attempt that came ridiculously close to succeeding). Brought into baseball by Branch Rickey in 1930 to run the Columbus club of the American Association, Larry was a huge success and soon went on — as was his wont — to better things.

A few years later he was running the Cincinnati club for Powell Crosley. Taking a moribund, near-bankrupt franchise, MacPhail began putting together the team that would eventually win pennants in 1939–40. In 1935 he introduced night baseball to the major leagues. He also began broadcasting Cincinnati's home games. The man he hired for the job was a smooth, articulate, honey-voiced Southerner named Walter (Red) Barber. The years in Cincinnati were like a trial run for what MacPhail was to do in Brooklyn.

MacPhail's arrival virtually coincided — it was almost symbolic — with the death of Steve McKeever, the last of the old guard. McKeever's stock passed to his daughter, Mrs. James Mulvey. But that hardly mattered. MacPhail was running the club, and everybody was giving him plenty of room. More importantly, the Brooklyn Trust Company was lending him whatever he needed. In spite of the team's mounting debt to the bank, the president, George V. McLaughlin, believed in MacPhail and was willing to go along with him.

From *The Brooklyn Dodgers: An Illustrated Tribute* by Donald Honig. Reprinted by permission of St. Martin's Press, LLC. ©1981 by Donald Honig.

MacPhail spent several hundred thousand dollars refurbishing Ebbets Field, repairing and painting the stands, replacing broken seats, cleaning up the rest rooms and clubhouses. He also announced that henceforth Dodger games would be broadcast by Red Barber, who was only too happy to join Larry in Brooklyn. The decision to broadcast broke what had been a gentleman's agreement between the three New York clubs not to "give away their games for nothing" over the airwaves. The Giants and Yankees were upset by the decision, but there was nothing they could do about it.

What interested the fans most, however, was what Larry was going to do to improve the club. Less than two months after taking over, MacPhail gave them an inkling—he bought first baseman Dolph Camilli from the Phillies for $50,000. A flashy fielder with a potent bat, Camilli gave the Dodgers the power hitter they sorely needed. Camilli was MacPhail's primary player acquisition that first year, because there were limits on the amount of cash the bank would advance, and much of it—something like $100,000—was going into the light towers that Larry was building on the roof of Ebbets Field. Night baseball was coming to New York—another innovation of MacPhail's that the Yankees and Giants thought foolish and unnecessary.

The first night game in New York history was played on June 15, 1938, against the Cincinnati Reds. With a bit of timing that showed that the gods were for the time being on MacPhail's side, pitching for the Reds was a wild, exceedingly quick young left-hander named Johnny Vander Meer, who just four days before had no-hit the Braves.

Fan response to the first night game was overwhelmingly favorable. Too favorable, as a matter of fact. The place was packed, and the fire department finally had to close the gates. MacPhail gave night baseball in Brooklyn a gaudy send-off with a pregame show that included Olympic champion Jesse Owens starring in foot races. But the night belonged to Vander Meer, who under Brooklyn's glowing arc lights achieved something that had never been done before, or been done since—a second consecutive no-hitter.

The club finished seventh in 1938, but attendance, stimulated by night baseball, jumped nearly 200,000. There was a new air of optimism and excitement about the ball club now, and the energy center was MacPhail, who knew he had been hired to build a winner and was hell-bent upon doing it.

Not long after the 1938 World Series, MacPhail announced that Burleigh Grimes was being let out as manager of the Dodgers. It had been expected. What had not been expected was the name of his replacement, the team's shortstop, Leo Durocher.

MacPhail couldn't have picked a more apt man. Durocher was pure New York, the city where he had begun his big-league career as a utility infielder on the 1928 Yankees. The Massachusetts-born Durocher was always sharp and brash, with an astute baseball mind that had long been apparent. A tactical genius with an abrasive personality that could rub a marble statue raw, Leo was the man to cohere and motivate a team; he would provoke the opposition, arouse the fans, stimulate the press.

Durocher's only real problem in Brooklyn—aside from building a winner—was MacPhail. The stormy personalities and bustling egos of the two men were dangerously similar. MacPhail would "fire" Leo countless times over the next few years, but the firings—though quite emphatic at the moment—were so ephemeral that he never even bothered to hire Durocher back. It was MacPhail's way.

In 1939 the Dodgers' twin dynamos swung into action. Their early moves did not seem spectacular at first but were to prove extremely shrewd. They drafted a big right-hander from Memphis named Hugh Casey. MacPhail bought from the minor leagues a seemingly washed-up former American League pitcher named Whitlow Wyatt. After a desultory career with the Tigers, White Sox and Indians, the thirty-two-year-old Wyatt was considered through. Returning to the minors, however, he learned to throw a devastating slider and with it was able to work his way back to the major leagues, with Brooklyn. A gentle, soft-spoken Georgian, Wyatt was a picture of style and grace on the mound, and a more cold-blooded competitor never pitched.

In July 1939 MacPhail picked up another supposedly washed-up American Leaguer, an outfielder named Fred (Dixie) Walker. At one time he had been a promising outfielder with the Yankees in the early thirties, but a series of shoulder injuries had curtailed Walker's effectiveness and he had drifted through the league for several years, always hitting well but apparently injury-prone. MacPhail got him at the waiver price from the Tigers, and Dixie reported to Ebbets Field.

It was love at first sight for the Dodger fans. Whatever it is that gives a ball player charisma, Walker surely had it in abundance for the people of Brooklyn. No more popular player ever put on a Dodger uniform. Recognizing the affinity, the writers soon dubbed the new right fielder "The People's Cherce."

The Dodgers finished the '39 season in third place. Attendance jumped to close to a million, and the club was beginning to pay back some of its debts. There was drama and excitement and a certain raucous joy on the grounds at Ebbets Field now. A team was beginning to come together.

In 1938 Branch Rickey was presiding over a vast St. Louis Cardinal farm system that at one time included fifty teams and nearly a thousand players. Rickey had to do a lot of manipulating of contracts to keep all of his players protected. (The Cardinals even had two teams playing in the same league here and there.) Rickey's sharp practices were coming more and more under the intense scrutiny of baseball's stern and unforgiving commissioner, Judge Kenesaw Mountain Landis. Finally exasperated by Rickey's machinations, Landis "liberated" over one hundred players from the Cardinal farm system and gave them free agency.

One of those youngsters, the jewel of the Cardinal organization and the finest young ball player in the land, was a nineteen year old from St. Louis named Harold Patrick Reiser, called by one and all "Pistol Pete" because of a youthful affinity for Wild West movies.

It broke Rickey's heart to lose Reiser, who could hit with power from either side of the plate, play infield and outfield with equal skill and zest, and run with blinding speed. MacPhail went after Reiser, gave him a $100 bonus, and signed the handsome kid to a contract. (It later developed that MacPhail had agreed to "hide" the kid in the Dodger farm system for several years and then deal him back to the Cardinals, as a favor to old friend Rickey. Given the dimensions of Reiser's talent, however, it would have been easier to hide the Washington Monument. Pistol Pete was simply too good, and MacPhail had no choice but to renege on the deal.)

Reiser joined the club midway through the 1940 season, the same year the Dodgers acquired a twenty-one-year-old baby-faced shortstop named Harold (Pee Wee) Reese, a youngster of impressive skills and with impeccable baseball instincts born into him.

Reese was playing for Louisville in the American Association, a club then controlled by the Red Sox. Reese was obvious major league material to all who saw him — except Red Sox player-manager Joe Cronin, who just happened to be a shortstop himself. The story was that Cronin, a powerful hitter but mediocre shortstop, was unwilling to move to make room for the kid. Cronin was able to impress his opinion on Red Sox owner Tom Yawkey, who promptly sold the youngster to MacPhail. Player-manager Leo Durocher was also a shortstop. When he took one look at Reese, however, he knew his career was over.

Almost manically, MacPhail continued putting together the pieces. On June 12, 1940, he made a startling announcement: The Dodgers had acquired Joe Medwick from the Cardinals for the huge sum of $125,000 and four players. Along with Medwick, the Dodgers obtained a veteran side-wheeling right-hander, Curt Davis.

The twenty-eight-year-old Medwick had been the league's top hitter through the thirties, a right-handed powerhouse who swung at anything and ripped vicious line drives in all directions. Sullen, individualistic, quick with his fists, he was the left fielder the Dodger needed.

Brooklyn fans were delirious with joy, but not for long. A week after the trade, the Cardinals were in town. With Medwick at the plate, the Cardinal pitcher, right-hander Bob Bowman, let fly a high fastball that Medwick momentarily lost. The ball crashed against his head, and Joe went down and lay sickeningly still.

A moment later pandemonium broke out on the field. The charge was led by Durocher, who claimed the beaning had been deliberate — there was known to be bad blood between Bowman and Medwick.

MacPhail, seething in the press box, later demanded Bowman be barred from baseball for life and tried to have the pitcher indicted for attempted murder. The Cardinals spirited Bowman out of town that night to spare him the wrath of Dodger fans, an excitable species even under normal circumstances.

Medwick recovered — he was back in the lineup in less than a week — but he never was the same hitter again. Lost forever was that aggressive confidence he had always brought to bat with him.

The Dodgers made a run at Cincinnati for the pennant that season, but their tank went dry in late summer. They finished in second place, their highest notch since 1924.

That familiar Brooklyn cry of relentless optimism, "Wait till next year," was to find fulfillment in 1941. It was a long, hard-fought, at times bitter season, with feuds, brawls, spikings, beanball wars. Durocher seemed to go out of his way to antagonize the opposition; Brooklyn was the most hated team in the league, and Leo seemed to prefer it that way.

MacPhail had put the final pieces in place. In need of another starting pitcher, he bought strong-armed, fast-balling right-hander Kirby Higbe from the Phillies. In need of a catcher he bought a hustling, battling Mickey Owen from the Cardinals.

Only second base remained a problem, and this was taken care of in early May with the purchase of one of the best, Billy Herman, from the Cubs.

The club was now set. It was a marvelously weighed and balanced machine. Camilli was to lead the league in home runs and runs batted in, and ended up being voted Most Valuable Player. What Camilli didn't lead in, Reiser did — doubles, triples, runs scored, slugging average, total bases, batting average. The youngster was proving to be as great as everyone said, and his future seemed unlimited. Reese, playing shortstop like a veteran, Herman at second, and Lavagetto at third gave Brooklyn, along with Camilli an outstanding infield. Walker and Medwick, flanking Reiser in center field, batted .311 and .318 respectively. Owen was as steady as a rock behind the plate.

The pitching was superb. Wyatt and Higbe topped the league with twenty-two wins each; Curt Davis won thirteen; Hugh Casey, starting and relieving, won fourteen. Thirty-nine-year-old Fred Fitzsimmons, pitching in spots, turned in a 6–1 record.

It was a glorious summer to live in Brooklyn, be a Dodger fan, and have fifty-five cents for a bleacher seat. The battle was waged against a hungry, rugged aggregate of St. Louis Cardinals. These two splendid teams left the rest of the league in shadows as they clawed and scrambled through the season.

On September 25 Wyatt shut out the Braves in Boston, and the pennant was clinched. The final margin was two and a half games. After twenty-one years of wandering in the wilderness, the Dodgers had come home.

Waiting for them in the World Series was a great Yankee team, in the midst of reeling off seven pennants in eight years. The Yankees were led by Joe DiMaggio, who was backed up by Charlie Keller, Bill Dickey, Tommy Henrich, Joe Gordon, and Phil Rizzuto, and although the pitching was not as formidable as the rest of the club, it included steady winners like Red Ruffing, Ernie Bonham, Marius Russo, and Spud Chandler. It was the first of seven World Series meetings between these two clubs over the next fifteen years. One man, Pee Wee Reese, would play in all of them.

The first two games were rather quiet and uneventful, Ruffing beating Davis 3–2 in the opener, Wyatt beating Chandler by the same score the next day.

The third game was played at Ebbets Field. Fitzsimmons and Russo dueled tenaciously in a scoreless tie into the top of the seventh. Then a line drive off the bat of Russo struck Fitz on the knee, and he had to leave the game. Casey came in, gave up two runs in the top of the eighth, and Russo held on for a 2–1 win. Brooklyn felt they had gotten a bad break, losing Fitz, who had been pitching so well. But that was nothing compared to what happened the next day, October 5, 1941, destined to stand as the darkest day in Dodger history until Bobby Thomson came to bat in the bottom of the ninth ten years minus two days later.

With Hugh Casey pitching strongly in relief, the Dodgers carried a 4–3 lead into the top of the ninth. Casey retired the first two men easily. The next batter was Tommy Henrich. The count went full. Casey broke off a wicked curve — some say it was a spitter — and Henrich swung and missed. The pitch had so much on it, however, that Owen was unable to hold onto it, and the ball rolled away to the right of the plate. The alert Henrich made it to first. (Owen later claimed that it had not been a spitter but rather the best curveball Casey ever threw. Henrich said the ball "exploded" when it got to the plate and broke with incredible sharpness, to the extent that he was actually trying to check his swing.)

Now Henrich was on first, and Casey was fuming. Instead of going out and talking to his pitcher, as he later conceded he should have, Durocher remained in the dugout, as incredulous as everyone else.

What happened next, in very short order, was brutal. DiMaggio lined a single to left. Keller doubled against the right-field wall for two runs. Dickey walked. Gordon doubled to left for two more runs. It was now 7–4, which was the final score.

The next day — "We couldn't have beaten a girls' team," Billy Herman said ruefully — Bonham allowed but four hits, and the Dodgers went quietly, 3–1, wasting a creditable performance by Wyatt.

By the time the 1942 season rolled around, the country was at war. Cookie Lavagetto joined the Navy, and MacPhail replaced him by swinging a deal with Pittsburgh for their great shortstop, Arky Vaughan, who was installed at third base. Otherwise the team was pretty much the same as the year before, perhaps even stronger, with the addition of veteran pitchers Larry French, Johnny Allen, and youngster Ed Head. The team had six winners in double figures and overall won 104 games, enough for a pennant anytime — except in 1942. A relentless Cardinal team was not to be denied, coming from ten and a half games behind in August to win 106 games and the pennant.

There was no question but that the Dodgers lost the pennant on July 19, in St. Louis. With the score tied in the eleventh inning of the second game of a doubleheader, Enos Slaughter hit a shot out to deep center field. Reiser, playing with the reckless zeal that he always did, tracked the ball at top speed and ran full force into the center-field wall. The ball popped out of his glove, and Slaughter circled the bases for a home run. Reiser, hitting near .390 at the time, suffered a severe concussion and fractured skull. It was recommended that he not play anymore that season. Durocher, however, mesmerized by the youngster's abilities, unwisely reinserted him into the lineup a few days later. But not even Pistol Pete could play with headaches and blurred vision. By season's end his average had sunk to .310. "I cost us the pennant," Reiser later said. But the guilt lay elsewhere, with Durocher and MacPhail, for letting the youth play. Not only was he costing the team games, but he was probably risking his life. Future injuries, in particular another violent collision with a wall in Brooklyn in 1947, were to sap his blazing talents and deny Pete Reiser a place among the game's immortals. Some starry-eyed romantic later dubbed him, "the John Keats of baseball."

The Dodgers had given their fans the two most exciting years in the club's history. But now it was over, and nothing was ever going to be the same again. The nation, indeed, the entire world, was falling deeper into the flames of war. After the 1942 season, ballplayers began entering the armed services in wholesale numbers. Among the first to go were Reese, Reiser, Casey, and French. After the 1943 season, Herman and Higbe went off to war. Vaughan voluntarily retired, and during the '43 season Medwick was dealt to the Giants. Camilli was also dispatched to the Giants in a midseason deal, but Dolph, a Dodger loyalist to the core, retired rather than report.

There was another change after the 1942 season. MacPhail, no doubt feeling that the war could not be won without him, resigned from the Dodgers to accept a commission in the Army.

The man chosen to replace MacPhail was Larry's opposite in many ways. Where MacPhail had a flair for the bright lights, gambling, booze, hectic melodrama, Branch Rickey led a quiet, orderly life. Religious, scholarly, a teetotaler, Rickey did not even use profanity, the nearest he came to it being the exclamation, "Judas priest!"

But one thing the two men did have in common was a grim determination to do things their way. Perhaps the most intellectual man ever to come into baseball, Rickey had been a ballplayer — a poor one — and had managed the Browns and Cardinals. His biggest impact on the game, however, had come during his years as general manager of the Cardinals in the twenties and thirties. While he did not invent the farm system, Rickey perfected it. Those were Rickey's teams that had made life miserable for Dodger fans these past few years, almost every member of those teams being a home-grown product, signed for a pittance, nurtured through the farm system, and finally brought to the big leagues after undergoing baseball's most exciting winnowing process.

In a tightfisted era, Rickey had the most tenacious grip on a dollar. "He would go into the vault to give you change for a nickel," one of his players said. But he was also the shrewdest appraiser of ball-playing talent ever to squint at a field full of hopefuls.

Rickey's method was to sign any kid who showed a glimmer of talent. In those pre-bonus-player days, youngsters were only too eager to sign a ninety-dollar-a-month contract for the opportunity to play pro ball. When he got to Brooklyn, Rickey continued in this style. He sent his scouts out across the country with orders to sign any likely-looking youngster. He knew that one day the war would be over, and things would return to their proper perspective; and when that happened he wanted to have as many of the bright young ballplayers under contract as he could.

The war years were dismal ones for Brooklyn baseball. Like everyone else, the Dodgers were trying to make do, marking time, filling their roster with shopworn veterans and untried youngsters, most of whom had no business in the major leagues. Baseball was doing its best in response to President Roosevelt's request that the game go on in spite of the war, as a morale builder for the nation and its servicemen.

The Dodgers had a few bona fide big leaguers during those dreary years, including Eddie Stanky, Augie Galan, Curt Davis, and Dixie Walker, who helped lift the gloom with a batting championship in 1944, hitting .357. In 1944 forty-one-year-old Paul Waner played alongside sixteen-year-old Tommy Brown and seventeen-year-old Eddie Miksis. In 1945 a caretaker of Brooklyn's past, Babe Herman, was brought out of retirement and employed as a pinch hitter. The forty-two-year-old Babe hit a respectable .265. Among the many faces that ducked in and out of Brooklyn during the war years was nineteen-year-old Gil Hodges, who went zero for two in 1943 before going off to war.

In 1943 they finished third. In 1944, with fifty-three different men in uniform at one time or another, they finished seventh. In 1945 they were third.

The war ended in the summer of '45. Baseball was looking ahead to 1946, hoping to pick up where it left off in 1942. But it was not going to be business as usual. Branch Rickey had already seen to that. The sixty-four-year-old boss of the Dodgers was about to drag the conservative old game screaming and kicking into a new era.

The first of a string of World Series defeats for the Dodgers at the hands of the Yankees began in 1941. In game three there was the injury to pitcher Fred Fitzsimmons. And in game four, the famous dropped third strike.

OWEN DROPS THIRD STRIKE

Harold Parrott

[OCTOBER 5, 1941:] ONE GAME GUY — Mickey Owen was pouring out his heart. He wasn't sullen or sniveling. He spoke from down deep. You knew he meant it.

"I don't mind being the goat, Harold," he said, "but the tough part is that it costs these other fellows money. I'm square with myself. I knew I gave it everything I had, although I can't tell you, for the life of me, how that ball got away in the ninth. Honest, I wouldn't mind being the goat every day — if we won! Even if it was just my loss I wouldn't mind. But these fellows…"

A few moments earlier, when the newsmen had crowded around him, Mickey spoke out in a way that made you like him, too. He knew the fellows he was facing had already "hung the horns" on him, as ballplayers say. He knew that even then upstairs in the press box, where the lights were beginning to twinkle, fellows with facile typewriters were writing his name indelibly into baseball history. Writing it in painfully beside Fred Snodgrass, whose 1912 World Series "skull" is a classic from sandlots to stadia, and alongside Hack Wilson, whose outfield staggers in 1929 blew an 8–0 lead in the eighth inning, opened the floodgates for 10 Athletic runs and a crushing victory — that led to a World Series blackout of the Cubs.

And Mickey didn't alibi. "I really can't tell you how it happened, fellows," he had said, "because I don't know. It was a good pitch, maybe the best curve ball Casey threw all afternoon. It spurted out of my glove somehow. Why, I don't know. I do know I'm a better catcher than that!"

The Dodgers seemed to shout assent, without making a sound. It was a curious thing. They felt worse for Mickey than for the $2,000 that was slipping out of their pockets, you sensed. Owen wasn't in THEIR doghouse.

LIP SILENCED — Just across from Owen, Hugh Casey was toweling himself. Casey, Saturday's goat, who had come back to pitch, as Durocher said, "a whale of a game."

Casey was a picture of dejection. "I can lose 'em every way in the book and a few others," he sighed. "Balk 'em away, throw 'em away — ."

Originally published in the *Brooklyn Eagle*, October 5, 1941. Reprinted with permission of Historical Briefs, Inc.

Durocher was speechless with bitterness and chagrin, although 20 minutes had past since the blowup. Twenty minutes in which the Dodgers tried to come out of their haze before letting the reporters into the room.

At first, when asked who'd pitch tomorrow, Durocher said, "You've got me." Later he said, "Wyatt." Then he pointed to a bottle on the table. "Know what that ballgame was?" he said. "It was like the Yankees catching lightning in a bottle. They did it. And beat us out of a game!"

Talking seemed to bring the Lip's health back. "Those cops!" he exploded. "Did you see 'em rushing out of our dugout on that final play? They might have stopped Owen from making a play on that ball. I'll tell you they won't be in there tomorrow. I'll see to that."

WHAT NEXT?— Dixie Walker, never one to squawk, was insisting the Yankees were the luckiest team baseball had ever seen. "Every break in the book went to them," he sighed. "Why, even in that big ninth-inning rally that ball that Keller hit fiddled around on top of that concrete wall and let DiMaggio go home with the second, or winning run. Not that it would have meant anything as things turned out, you understand," added Dixie, "but it just shows you. That ball stayed up there on the fence like somebody was holding it. Those lucky Yankees…"

"They've been lucky for ten years, those guys," stuck in Johnny Allen, and old Yank and an old Yank hater.

A few seconds later Allen went popeyed as that Marvelous MacPhail came in, started to "needle" a newspaperman as an anti–Dodger and then got the whole club out of the doldrums by promoting a laugh or two.

A few minutes before we had heard a grinning Joe DiMaggio explain that ninth-inning whirlwind finish: "Well, they say everything happens in Brooklyn!"

To which Allen, watching MacPhail's antics, might have added: "Yea, brother!" Johnny, only recently initiated as a Dodger, did mumble a perplexed "What next?"

I wonder.

Following the Japanese attack on Pearl Harbor on December 7, 1941, President Franklin Delano Roosevelt sent his now-famous "green-light" letter to baseball, urging that, in the interest of the morale of the American people, baseball continue to be played. That same winter, Larry MacPhail, representing the Brooklyn Dodgers, issued a stern challenge to the major leagues.

BASEBALL GOES TO WAR

Frank Graham

On February 1, 1942, at the annual dinner of the New York Chapter of the Baseball Writers' Association at the Commodore Hotel in New York, the Dodgers, as personified by Larry MacPhail, stole the show. President Franklin D. Roosevelt had given the by now celebrated "green light" to baseball in his letter to Clark Griffith, which expressed his personal wish that the sport continue during the war; but the brass hats of the game still were muddling about, not knowing quite what to do. That night, at the dinner, MacPhail showed them the way.

He began by saying, in a speech that, although it came near the end of the long evening of entertainment and oratory, held his listeners' attention closely:

"There will be some who will interpret the President's green light signal to go ahead as relieving baseball from some of its duties and obligations in the greatest crisis our country has ever faced.

"We can't adopt any 'business as usual' slogan for baseball. There is no business in this country so dependent upon the good will of the public as baseball. We are expected to do more than provide recreation for twenty million workers. We are expected to work out a definite program of unselfish co-operation with agencies of government needing help. If we keep the faith, the workers will agree with the President that baseball has its place in an all-out effort to win the war."

He outlined the program he had drawn up for presentation at the joint meeting of the National and American League club owners the following day. It suggested that:

1. Everyone in baseball, "from Commissioner Landis to the peanut vendor," take part of his pay in war bonds or stamps.
2. Two all-star games be played, so that an extra $250,000 might be raised as a fund for athletic equipment for the armed forces.
3. The regular all-star game, scheduled for Ebbets Field in July, be moved to the Polo

Reprinted from *The Brooklyn Dodgers: An Informal History* by Frank Graham, with permission of Frank Graham, Jr. ©1945.

Grounds because of the greater seating capacity of the Giants' park, and the second game be played by the winner of the first against a picked team of major league stars in service.

4. A small part of every admission to a major league game be put into a pool for the purchase of a four-motored bomber to be turned over to the Army or Navy.

He delivered his speech with characteristic MacPhailian vigor, and at the finish, snapped:

"No club that doesn't sign up one hundred percent with this program should be allowed to open its gates."

The response of his audience was enthusiastic. Morning newspapermen, knowing that Larry was going to speak but having no idea what his subject would be, and not provided with copies of the speech, scribbled their notes hastily and rushed to telephones to give the story to their papers. It developed later no copies of the speech had been made, and but for the enterprise of Harold Parrott of the *Eagle*, the original would have been lost. After the dinner, Parrott asked Larry for a copy and Larry said:

"Copy? I haven't any copy. But if you want it the way I wrote it, I'll give it to you."

He fumbled in the pockets of his dinner jacket.

"Oh, hell," he said. "I remember. I left it on the table. Go up there and comb it out of Landis' hair — or maybe it's around the microphone somewhere."

Parrott salvaged the sheets, some of them stained with Scotch-and-soda or strawberry ice cream, and they have been preserved in the files at the *Eagle* office. It was a memorable and, to baseball, important speech, and the program that Larry outlined was carried out almost to the letter. Ballplayers and park employees subscribed heavily to war bonds and stamps. Two all-star games were held, one at the Polo Grounds, the other at Cleveland, with a service team opposing the American League team, victors in New York, in the second game. The bomber was never purchased, but in other ways, major and minor leagues contributed $1,294,958.67 to Army and Navy funds.

The very next day the club owners of both leagues, spurred to action by MacPhail's speech, were formulating a workable, helpful wartime campaign, the wisdom of Larry's deal for Vaughan was emphasized. The president of the Dodgers received a wire from Oakland, California, which read:

"I am joining the Navy today. So long for the duration. Good luck."

It was signed: "Harry Lavagetto."

The first break had been made in the championship infield.

In 1942 the Dodgers took spring training in Havana, Cuba. Billy Herman remembers this spring for more than baseball.

HAVANA: 1942

Donald Honig

[SPEAKER:] Billy Herman
Infielder, Brooklyn Dodgers

That was some season (1942), beginning with spring training. We took spring training in Havana that year. We had a lot of hell-raisers on that club. It was a wild time. Why, MacPhail had detectives trailing some of the guys.

You know, Ernest Hemingway lived in Havana at that time, and I spent a night with him I'll never forget. Hemingway liked to hang around with ballplayers, and one day he invited a few of us out to this gun club where he and his wife were members. Hemingway took a lot of pride in all this manly stuff, guns and boozing and fighting, things like that. He was a big, brawny man and when he'd had a few drinks, he got mean, real mean.

So he invited Hugh Casey, Larry French, Augie Galan, and myself out to the gun club. Believe me, this was no Coney Island shooting gallery. It was a real fancy place. You had a guy with a portable bar following you around. You'd get up, take your shots, and there'd be a drink ready for you. This went on from three o'clock in the afternoon until dark. At that point Hemingway said, "Ah, the hell with this. Come on up to the house, and let's have a few drinks."

So we all went up to his house. He had a big beautiful home. He took us into a huge dining room–living room combination, with all terrazzo floors, and told us to make ourselves comfortable while he went and got the drinks.

He came back with an enormous silver tray, with all the bottles, the mixers, the glasses, the ice, the whole works. He set it up on this little bookstand in the middle of the floor. And we started drinking. Hemingway was a real great host. He couldn't do enough for you. He gave each of us an autographed copy of *For Whom the Bell Tolls*, his book about the Spanish Civil War.

We talked a lot about the war. The war had just started, in December, and this was in March. Hemingway started talking about the Japanese and how far they were

From *Baseball When the Grass Was Real* by Donald Honig, by permission of the University of Nebraska Press. ©1975 by Donald Honig.

going to go. And you know, events proved him right. He said they were going to go down the Malay Peninsula, that they were going to take Burma, and this island and that island. He'd been a foreign correspondent in different parts of the world and knew a hell of a lot about a lot of things, and it was fascinating.

We had quite a bit to drink; then he laid out some food. After we ate, we had a few more drinks. It was getting pretty late now, and Mrs. Hemingway excused herself and went to bed. Hemingway was good and loaded by this time.

Now Hugh Casey was a very quiet man, and he wasn't saying much. Hugh never said much. But he was a drinker. I'd say that of everybody in the room, Hugh and Hemingway were feeling the best. But everything was still serious, with talk about the war and one thing and another. Then out of a clear blue sky Hemingway looked over at Casey, sort of sizing him up. Hemingway had this funny little grin; I assumed it was friendly, but then again it might not have been.

"You know, Hugh," he said, "you and I are about the same size. We'd make a good match."

Casey just grinned.

"Come on," Hemingway said. "I've got some boxing gloves. Let's just spar. Fool around a little bit."

Casey grinned and shrugged his shoulders. Hemingway went and got the boxing gloves. He came back and slipped on a pair of gloves and handed Casey the other pair. As Hugh was pulling his gloves on, Hemingway suddenly hauled off and belted him. He hit him hard too. He knocked Casey into that bookstand and there goes the tray with all the booze and glasses smashing over the terrazzo floor. It must have echoed all through the house because Hemingway's wife came running out.

"What happened?"" she asked.

"Oh, it's all right, honey," he said. "Hughie and I are just having a little fun. You go back to bed."

She looked at him, looked at Casey, looked at the mess on the floor, and then went back to bed.

Casey didn't say anything about the sneak punch. He just got up and finished putting the gloves on. Then they started sparring. Hemingway didn't bother to pick up the tray or anything, and they were moving back and forth across the broken glass and you could hear it cracking and crunching on the terrazzo floor whenever they stepped on it.

Boom, Casey starts hitting him. And hitting him. Then Casey started knocking him down. Hemingway didn't like that at all. Then Casey belted him across some furniture, and there was another crash as Hemingway took a lamp and table down with him. The wife came running out again, and Hemingway told her it was all right, to go back to bed, that it was all in fun. She went away, but this time she was looking a little bit doubtful about the whole thing.

Hemingway was getting sore. He'd no sooner get up then Hugh would put him down again. Finally he got up this one time, and made a feint with his left hand, and kicked Casey in the balls.

That's when we figured it had gone far enough. We made them take the gloves off. Then everything was all right.

"Let's have another drink," Hemingway said.

But it was getting very late now; we had to be back at the hotel at twelve o'clock. We told him that.

"Well," he said, "I'm too drunk to drive you back to Havana. I'll have my chauffeur drive you."

As we were going to the door, he grabbed Casey by the arm.

"Look," Hemingway said, "you stay here. The chauffeur'll take them. You stay here. Spend the night. Tonight we're both drunk. But tomorrow morning we'll wake up, we'll both be sober. Then you and me will have a duel. We'll use swords, pistols, whatever you want. You pick it." And he's dead serious about it. He wanted to kill Casey. Hughie'd got the better of him, and Hemingway wanted to kill him.

"Unh-unh," Casey said, shaking his head. He didn't want any part of it. So we left.

The next day Hemingway's wife brought him down to the ball park. You never saw a man so embarrassed, so ashamed. He apologized to everybody. "Don't know what got into me," he said. Well, I can tell you what got into him. About a quart.

In August 1945 a Dodger scout brought an uncertain Jackie Robinson to 215 Montague Street, the Dodger executive office in downtown Brooklyn. This was the historic first meeting between the ballplayer and the preacher.

WARM-UPS

John C. Chalberg

August 1945 was a month of seismic shocks. On August 6 an atomic bomb obliterated Hiroshima. Three days later Nagasaki was hit with the same terrible weapon. Hiroshima and Nagasaki ... the names of those two Japanese cities immediately became part of the permanent vocabulary of people everywhere, for what happened on those two devastating August days guaranteed a rapid end to the second great war of the twentieth century. It also provided a very unsettling start to what would soon prove to be a postwar filled with shocks and aftershocks all its own.

A few weeks later a bombshell of a different sort reached an advanced state of readiness in an American city far removed from the carnage of war. On August 28, 1945, a scout for the Brooklyn Dodgers baseball team escorted an intriguing, if not exactly youthful, prospect into the intriguing, if not exactly welcoming, office of a veteran baseball man who had already revolutionized the sport at least once. Jackie Robinson met Branch Rickey.

What exactly happened in that cluttered room over the course of the next few hours has long since passed into American folklore. By definition, folklore exists in a realm at least one step removed from the historical record. But what is beyond dispute is that this meeting set in motion changes in major league baseball and in the nation, changes that would echo long after the postwar became the Cold War. At least one of the participants suspected as much at the moment, if only because he alone knew exactly what he had in mind to do.

It might have begun with a handshake, but in all probability it didn't. Most likely, the host simply motioned for his guest to sit down. Common politeness aside, this gesture implied that their meeting would not be a short one — or at least indicated that the visitor had better be seated before hearing what he was about to hear. Certainly the rest of the country would need to be so situated when it finally learned the results of this encounter. Two months would pass before the results were made public. This delay made the announcement no less jarring to much of white America, and no less shocking in its own way for many black Americans as well. Branch Rickey could have predicted as much. In fact, he even suspected, even feared, as much for a very long time. But never once did he come close to changing his course or his mind. If anything, his suspicions and fears gave him all the more reason to proceed — so long as he could be sure that he had the right man to carry out his plan. And that was the point of this historic meeting.

Though Rickey knew that the first steps would be the most treacherous, he knew much more than that: he knew that he was doing the right thing. It was right for the younger man who faced him; and it was right for their country, their sport, and for what would soon be *their* team (although not necessarily in that order).

"We first endure," Branch Rickey liked to say. "Then we pity. Finally we embrace." The aphorism was not his— it was actually penned by an Englishman named Alexander Pope and can be found in his "Essay on Man"— but Rickey had long since embraced it as his own.

There would be no embrace between Rickey and Robinson during or after their marathon meeting. But well before — and forever after — their initial encounter each man embraced an ideal. At the heart of that ideal was a color blind America, an America of genuine equality of opportunity, an America in which character counted for everything and achievement was possible for everyone.

But on this warm day in late August ideals could wait. First things first. The Brooklyn Dodger executive knew that his prospect could play baseball. For weeks, Dodger scout Clyde Sukeforth had been trailing Robinson and sending detailed reports back to Brooklyn. But why was he scouting a black ballplayer? If Sukeforth had reason to wonder, his boss had a reasonable answer. The official word was that Rickey was organizing a new team (the Brooklyn Brown Dodgers) to compete in a new Negro league (to be called the United States League). The unannounced idea was to add to the Dodgers' profit margin by plugging more home dates onto the team's Ebbets Field calendar. Other major league teams rented their ball parks to Negro League teams. Why not the Dodgers as well? Baseball, after all, *was* a business, and no one understood that better than Branch Rickey.

In truth, "Mr. Rickey" (as he was called by virtually everyone, at least by virtually everyone in his presence) had something else in mind when he concocted the Brown Dodgers story. Branch Rickey generally had more than a few things on his mind at the same time, not to mention multiple motives. In this case, a desire to make money and win baseball games (not necessarily in that order) provided most of the motivation he needed. When it came to his sport both goals *always* topped his list of things to accomplish. But in preparing for this meeting he had something else on his mind as well.

As of 1945, the sixty-three-year-old Rickey had already made his share of money. Moreover, his teams, whether the Cardinals of St. Louis or the Dodgers of Brooklyn, had generally won more than their share of games. Some might call that luck. Mr. Rickey would not. "Luck," Branch Rickey liked to say, was nothing more than "the residue of design."

Whether Clyde Sukeforth knew it or not, their was a design to this scouting mission. And certainly there was a mission behind Branch Rickey's design. The proposed

Brooklyn Brown Dodgers were a small piece of Rickey's design, but they were never part of his mission. In fact, this paper "team" was nothing more than a ruse. In all likelihood Sukeforth didn't know that. Neither did the ballplayer he had been assigned to scout more thoroughly than any other.

Though twenty-six, Jackie Robinson was only in his rookie season in Negro League baseball. But he was far from a novice at the game. He had played college ball, semi-pro ball, and during World War II he had also played army ball. Following his discharge from the military, Robinson was not ready to put baseball entirely behind him. Hence his decision to play for the Kansas City Monarchs during the 1945 campaign. By August of that year, he had not only established himself as the Monarchs' regular shortstop, but he was clearly a rising star in the Negro Leagues.

Throughout that 1945 season, Branch Rickey was keeping close tabs on a number of Negro League players, but he had more than one good reason to keep an especially close watch on Robinson's progress. Everything he had read and heard about both Robinson the man and Robinson the player impressed him, everything, that is, except a measure of concern about the shortstop's arm. Was it strong enough for the major leagues? There was total agreement within the Dodger organization that Robinson could run, hit and field. But what about his right arm? Could he get the ball to first base from deep in the hole at shortstop, and could he get it there with "something on it?" To get the definitive answer to that question Rickey instructed Sukeforth to approach Robinson before a game at Chicago's Comiskey Park and ask him to throw the ball from the hole — and to throw it often and throw it hard.

Robinson declined. Not only was he currently "riding the bench," but he wasn't throwing at all. It seems that he had fallen on his right shoulder a few days earlier. The injury was not thought to be serious, but he did expect to be out of the lineup for at least another week. Another scout might have packed his bags and returned to Brooklyn on the spot. But Clyde Sukeforth was not just another scout. He was Branch Rickey's most reliable and most resourceful agent. As it turned out, Clyde Sukeforth wasn't the only one who packed his bags, and he didn't ride the train back east alone. With Robinson temporarily on the shelf, Sukeforth saw the opportune time for that face-to-face meeting that Mr. Rickey had mentioned to him on more than one occasion. Sukeforth knew that Robinson was at the top of his boss's list of candidates for those Brown Dodgers.

When Sukeforth and Robinson arrived in Brooklyn, "Mr. Rickey" was ready for them. In truth, the Dodger executive had been planning for this day for a long while: certainly ever since he had taken over the Dodgers after the 1942 season, and possibly as long ago as 1903, when a much younger Branch Rickey was coaching his college baseball team. But for all of his plotting and designing the Dodger president could never have imagined that he would have quite this compelling a prospect on his hands, suspect arm or no. To add to the drama, Jackie Robinson was also a very intriguing human being. Rickey was certainly going to relish the next few hours. As least Clyde Sukeforth suspected as much. After all, Rickey's marching orders to his scout had been clear: if Robinson would not come to him, he would come to Robinson.

Thanks to Sukeforth's initiative, Rickey could remain ensconced in his office at

215 Montague Street in the New York borough of Brooklyn. And what an office it was that a wary Jackie Robinson entered on the morning of August 28. The place had even acquired a nickname, courtesy of Rickey's friends and enemies among baseball reporters. And to friend and enemy alike, it was the "cave of the winds," within which visitors could expect to be subjected to extended rhetorical gusts. The most prominent feature within this dark, paneled room (aside from its terminally "windy" occupant) was a large, illuminated goldfish tank. It entertained Rickey when he was alone and served to distract visitors from whatever business was at hand when he wasn't. Just as distracting was the clutter strewn across Rickey's oversized mahogany desk, a mess that belied the clarity of its creator's mind.

Weighing down at least some of the debris were two well-thumbed volumes, specifically a massive dictionary and a copy of *Bartlett's Quotations*. Behind the desk was a well-worn swivel chair that had as many moves as its regular occupant had ideas. Behind all of that were pictures of the two non-baseball men Rickey admired beyond all others (Winston Churchill and Abraham Lincoln), and a few of his baseball protégés (including Dodger manager Leo Durocher). Somewhere among this select gallery were these framed words:

> *He that will not reason is a bigot*
> *He that cannot reason is a fool*
> *He that dares not reason is a slave.*

Off to the side stood an imposing globe. Stretched across an entire side wall was a massive blackboard containing the names of every player at every level in the Dodger organization. Might it have begun to dawn on Robinson that his name would one day appear on that blackboard?

For the moment, all was silent. Behind his bushy eyebrows and trademark bow tie, the host simply stared at his guest. Robinson had no choice but to stare right back. Still maintaining his silence, Rickey reached for a cigar before settling deeper into his chair. Only then did he signal to Robinson and Sukeforth that it was time to take their seats. Then came words, mostly from Rickey's mouth, mostly in the form of questions, and mostly in sudden torrents.

"Do you have a girl?" Rickey asked.

Robinson hesitated before answering. In the first place, he wasn't all that confident of the status with the girl that he did indeed have. Secondly, he didn't quite know what Rickey wanted to hear. When Robinson finally did respond he offered only a equivocal "I'm not sure." His interrogator seemed perplexed. Robinson nervously tried to explain that, yes, he did have a girl, but that he wasn't certain he could count on her. At this point Rickey's confusion seemed to give way to disappointment. So Robinson tried again. What he meant to say was that he saw no reason why anybody should count on him, what with all the traveling ballplayers had to do. Hearing that, Rickey was mildly encouraged. At least he was encouraged enough to press on. So pressed, Robinson finally said what Rickey wanted to hear: If he had a choice in the matter, he'd marry the girl in question. Hearing that, Rickey was openly ecstatic.

Branch Rickey was never one to keep his advice to himself. If Jackie Robinson had found the right girl, he should marry her — and sooner rather than later, because he would need all the help he could get in the months and years to come. This bit of counsel led the Dodger boss directly to the question that placed him one step away from revealing his entire hand.

"Do you know why you were brought here?" he asked.

Robinson started to shake his head. All he knew was that Clyde Sukeforth had asked him to come. Maybe to play for the Brown Dodgers, came the cautious reply.

"No," Rickey interjected. "That isn't it. You were brought here to play for the Brooklyn organization." "And not for the Brown Dodgers," he quickly added. Robinson's first stop would be the International League and the Dodgers' top farm team, the Montreal Royals. This was minor league baseball at its highest level. If he performed well there, he would be brought up to the parent Brooklyn Dodgers to begin a career as a major league player.

Robinson was speechless. The increasingly garrulous Rickey was not. Before Robinson could even ask why, Rickey told him: "I want to win a pennant and we need ballplayers!" he roared. Suddenly reflective, Rickey went into a full swivel as he took his new prospect on a historical tour of his recent search for black ballplayers. A final turn once again brought him face to face with Robinson. And one more question brought Robinson up short: "Do you think you can do it?"

Robinson could still say nothing. As Sukeforth remembered it, "Jack waited, and waited, and waited before answering."

"Yes, if … if I got the chance," he finally stammered.

Jackie Robinson may have thought that this response would signal the end of the interrogation. Instead, he quickly discovered that Branch Rickey was just warming up.

"I don't know how you play, but my scouts do," he hedged. It was true that prior to this meeting Rickey had never seen Jackie Robinson on or off a baseball diamond, but he surely knew that his prospect was a superb baseball player. Under normal circumstances, Branch Rickey would have done his own scouting of a player of Robinson's potential. As a young ballplayer, Rickey had been far enough above average himself to make it to the major leagues, at least for a few years. And as a baseball executive, he had acquired a deserved reputation as a keen judge of baseball talent. What's more, even at his age he still enjoyed being on the road watching ball games. Major league or minor league, it didn't matter. It was baseball, and baseball was at the heart of most everything that Branch Rickey loved in this world.

But these were not normal circumstances. As such, they required something other than the full truth. Or perhaps Rickey genuinely believed that he could grasp a player's potential only after he had personally seen him in action. Still, in this case he had no real choice but to operate on the basis of secondhand information. After all, had *the* Branch Rickey been seen at Negro League games, the whispers alone would have been enough to scotch his plan before he could so much as begin to hatch it. Besides, Clyde Sukeforth was his best scout. With a nod in Sukeforth's direction, Rickey confirmed as much for Robinson with this bit of praise: "If he says you're a good ballplayer, I'll take his word for it."

Now it was Rickey's turn to scout his prospect. "I know you're a good ballplayer," Rickey went on. "What I don't know is whether you have the guts."

His manhood on the line, Robinson readied an angry reply when Rickey cut him off—and set him straight—all at once: "I'm looking for a ballplayer with guts enough *not* to fight back." With that he whacked his desk and began to pace about the room. Returning to Robinson, he pointed a finger at him and exclaimed, "You've got to do this job with base hits and stolen bases and fielding ground balls, Jackie. Nothing else!"

Before a stunned Robinson could respond to this latest surprise, Rickey stripped off his sports coat and assumed the first of a series of roles, each one more offensive than the last. On his own makeshift stage, Rickey played the part of a white hotel clerk refusing to give Robinson a room. Then he posed as a haughty waiter denying him service before ordering him to leave the restaurant. Next he was a rival player cursing everything from his race to his family. Still not through, he took on the demeanor of a racist sportswriter. Closing in on Robinson, Rickey then pretended to jostle him in imaginary hotel lobbies and railroad stations. Finally, he was a vindictive base runner coming out of a spikes-up slide shouting, "How do you like that, nigger boy?"

To clinch his point and ease the tension, Rickey added, "What I am saying to you, Jackie, is that you will have to be more than a good ballplayer." After another interval of silence Robinson finally spoke: "Mr. Rickey, I think I can play ball, and I promise you that I will do the second part of the job, although I can't be an obsequious, cringing fellow."

"Obsequious," "cringing" ... if Branch Rickey had harbored any remaining doubts, they were dispelled when he heard those words. Obviously, this young man could find his way around more than just a baseball diamond. And just as obviously, Rickey was now thoroughly convinced that sitting before him was the right man to break baseball's invisible, but nonetheless impenetrable, color line.

Rickey suddenly grew reflective. With an unlit cigar locked in his mouth, he leaned heavily back in his chair, all the while still staring directly at Robinson. In measured, but fatherly words, he warned Robinson of the "tremendous load" he was about to bear. From somewhere on his desk he fished out a book, Giovanni Papini's *The Life of Christ*. "Ever hear of it?" Rickey asked.

"No" Robinson replied.

Rickey then began to read aloud:

> *There are three answers that men can make to violence: revenge, flight, turning the other cheek. The first is the barbarous principle of retaliation.... Flight is no better than retaliation.... Turning the other cheek means not receiving the second blow. It means cutting the chains of the inevitable wrongs at the first link. Your adversary is ready for anything but this.... Every man has an obscure respect for courage in others, especially if it is moral courage, the rarest and most difficult sort of bravery.... To answer blows with blows, evil deeds with evil deeds, is to meet the attacker on his own ground, to proclaim oneself as low as he is.*
> *...Only he who has conquered himself can conquer his enemies.*

As he finished, Rickey set the book back adrift in the sea of papers on his desk. Turning directly to Robinson, he asked, "Can you do it?" Could he promise to turn the other cheek — and not just for a week or two, but for at least three years? "Three years — can you do it?"

Rickey knew that Robinson was a devout Christian and an intense competitor. When it came to Christianity, Rickey could not imagine anyone being too devout. But when it came to competition, he understood that one could easily be too intense. Hence Rickey's decision to risk the question: "What will you do when they call you a black son of a bitch?"

At this point the only noise in the "cave of the winds" came from a lone electric fan whirring away in the corner, this single concession to what had become a hot August afternoon doing little to cool off a perspiring, agitated Rickey. Now on his feet, Rickey prowled purposefully around the edge of his desk. As he approached Robinson, he curled his gnarled right hand into a fist. Without warning, the older man unloaded a swing in the general direction of the younger man's head. It missed, but the accompanying words did not.

"What do you do?" Rickey shouted while still hovering over his target.

Before the startled Robinson could summon an answer, Rickey let him know exactly what he could *not* do. Above all, "you cannot strike back," he lectured. On the baseball diamond Robinson might be filled with righteous anger. He might have stored up any number of reasons to unleash a few right hand jabs of his own. Each might have been intended to reach its target. And each of his reasons — and his jabs — might have been justifiably summoned and delivered. But he had to resist everything his mind and heart told him to do. No matter what, he must not fight, Rickey counseled. If he did, everything that the designing Dodger president had plotted would come to nothing. The experiment would fail. The color line would be restored. And what then? Jackie Robinson might go down in history as the first black man to play major league baseball in the modern era. But his career would be brief, and no member of his race would follow him any time soon.

"So what do you do?"

"Mr. Rickey," the younger man finally replied, "I've got two cheeks. Is that it?"

It was. The interrogation was finally over. Now it was time to do a little business. And business, especially baseball business, was never very far down the list of Mr. Rickey's things to do.

Did Robinson have a contract with the Monarchs?

"No sir," was the reply.

"Do you have any agreements — written or oral — concerning how long you will play for them?"

"No sir, none at all. I just work payday to payday."

Was he under any obligation of any kind to the Monarchs?

"None whatever," Robinson shot back.

That was all an exhausted Rickey wanted to hear. He may have had sweat dripping off his brow. He may have been still trying to catch his breath. But he was not too tired to ask Robinson to put in writing what he had just said. Robinson complied. Rickey then set before Robinson an agreement that would bind him to play baseball for the Dodger organization — that would be the Brooklyn Dodgers— not the Brooklyn Brown Dodgers. Specifically this agreement called for Robinson to play for the Montreal Royals. If he signed, he would be paid an immediate bonus of $3,500. His monthly salary would be $600. This time Rickey was neither expecting nor desiring a reply. None was forthcoming. Ballplayers, black or white, rookies or veterans, didn't negotiate contracts with Branch Rickey or with anyone else among his generation of baseball owners. They simply signed them. Which is exactly what Jackie Robinson did.

Oh, yes, there was one more thing. Until they were told otherwise, neither Robinson nor Sukeforth could tell anyone anything about this meeting. To make certain that his point was completely understood, Rickey pledged both to secrecy. With that, the Dodger boss restored the cigar to its rightful place, glanced at his watch, and ushered his veteran scout and newest employee out of the office.

Better than three hours had passed. Not bad for a partial day's work, especially considering that a little history was in the making. But a lot more history was yet to be made, and a lot more fireworks were set to explode. Once word of Robinson's signing escaped that office, there was no way of knowing how explosive things would become.

Robinson kept his part of the bargain. He told no one of the meeting or his signing, though he immediately telephoned his girl to say that "something wonderful" had happened, something that would "affect us both." Then he returned to Kansas City and the Monarchs. His original absence had gone unexcused and unexplained. It remained just that. Monarch management learned only that Robinson had gone to New York City. The team's starting shortstop then punctuated his return by declaring that he intended to end his season early. He let it be known that he would play only until September 21, at which point he planned to return home to California.

The owner of the Monarchs, J.L. Wilkinson, was one of the few white men in Negro League baseball. White or black, Negro League owners had precious little control over their players. Contract jumping was the order of the day. Such leaps took place within individual Negro Leagues and between them. Now Wilkinson faced the additional complication of having his players jump to an entirely new league (to be headlined, as announced by Rickey, by the Brooklyn Brown Dodgers). Little did Wilkinson know as of early September 1945 just how complicated Branch Rickey was about to make his baseball life. Wilkinson knew nothing about Rickey's larger agenda. And he certainly did not know that Robinson's departure was a permanent one, one that would ultimately destroy the future of all Negro League teams. The issue at hand, therefore, was an irritant, not a major concern. And Wilkinson could only deal with the problem as he understood it. Robinson wanted to go home early; Robinson had to be stopped. But what leverage did he have? All he could do was issue a threat of his own. Through his son, Richard, Wilkinson chose a Monarch team meeting to respond to Jack's request: Robinson would play "all the remaining games or none." The younger Wilkinson went on to inform Jack that if he left the Monarchs before the end of the season he would never again play in the Negro Leagues. Robinson was unfazed. Given the agreement that he had just signed with Rickey, he had reason to think that his future extended beyond Kansas City and Negro League baseball. In fact, he was so confident of that future that he didn't bother complaining or protesting. He simply kept his mouth shut, called Wilkinson's bluff, and promptly left the Monarchs for California and home.

Once again surrounded by his family, Robinson couldn't resist dispensing broad hints about his baseball future to his mother, brothers, sisters, and friends. No one really wanted to listen to him, much less believe him. As far as they were concerned, white people were untrustworthy at best and downright sinister at worst. But Jack's world was no longer his family's world. To be sure, he had dealt with his share of racist cops and exploitative coaches. But as an athlete he had come to understand that dependence was a two-way street. White coaches did have plenty of power, especially when it came to taking advantage of their black players. But they also offered opportunities to be seized. A veteran of collegiate and professional sport, Jack knew all of that — and more. After all, he had been around long enough to realize that white coaches and athletic directors needed him as much as he needed them.

All that said, Jackie Robinson had never met anyone quite like Branch Rickey. Following their marathon meeting, Robinson had not dropped all of his considerable guards. Nonetheless, it is safe to conclude that Rickey had greatly impressed the not-so-easily impressed Robinson. No white man had ever seemed so sincere, so committed to racial justice, so full of passion on the twin subjects of winning baseball games and making history. To be sure, Rickey had not dispelled all of Robinson's doubts about the white power structure that controlled major league baseball. But for the time being, at least, he was willing to give Branch Rickey the benefit of the doubt.

For his part, Rickey had to believe that he had been taken at his word. His more immediate worry was not that Robinson would think that he was the victim of a cruel publicity stunt, but how to control the public relations of what he had done and intended to do. The brief fireworks in the Monarchs' clubhouse were small fare compare to those yet to explode. At the time, Rickey knew nothing of the Wilkinsons' threat to their star shortstop. Nor did Robinson think it necessary to inform Rickey of it. But the Dodger president could be certain that there would be aftershocks aplenty once the white baseball world learned of his true intentions. Therefore, he wanted to control as much of the process as possible. Luck may have been the residue of design, but no one, not even Branch Rickey, could design what was to come in the months and years ahead.

If you were there in 1945, you would have opened your Brooklyn Daily Eagle *and read an account of the following event. The announcement of the signing of Jackie Robinson by the Brooklyn Dodgers had monumental repercussions that would only now begin to unfold.*

NEGRO ACE OUTSTANDING PROSPECT

Harold C. Burr

Dodgers Scouted Robinson for Big-League Role

Deal Made in August — Jackie to Train in Fla. with Flock, Royals

[BROOKLYN EAGLE—OCTOBER 24, 1945:] President Branch Rickey of the Brooklyn Dodgers has broken through the color line in signing the first Negro ball player to appear in Organized Baseball in the 70 years of its life. The player who enters through the opened door is Jackie Robinson, shortstop and UCLA football star.

During the 1945 season, Robinson was a member of the Kansas City Monarchs, hitting .340. He came to the Monarchs after serving as a second lieutenant in the army. He was quietly brought to Brooklyn in August. Rickey explained what he had in mind and Jackie agreed to sign Nov. 1.

Robinson was carefully scouted by Tom Greenwade, George Sisler and Clyde Sukeforth, the Rickey bird dogs. The boy was signed yesterday to a Montreal bonus contract, the Brooklyn club's double-A International League farm. But in reality he was scouted as a major league prospect. Robinson will go to the Dodger and Montreal combined training camp at Daytona Beach, Fla., in the Spring.

Jackie previously had received a tryout at Fenway Park, Boston, by the Red Sox. Of the three Negroes tried out on that occasion, Robinson received the most favorable attention from manager Joe Cronin. But the Red Sox made no attempt to sign him and the Dodger scouts took over and reported to Rickey that he was the best of the Negro prospects.

Originally published in the *Brooklyn Eagle,* October 24, 1945. Reprinted with permission of Historical Briefs, Inc.

May Cost Club Players

"Mr. Racine and my father," Branch Jr. said, "will undoubtedly be severely criticized in some sections of the country where racial prejudice is rampant. They are not inviting trouble, but they won't avoid it if it comes. Robinson is a fine type of young man, intelligent and college-bred."

Young Rickey admitted that the move might cost the Dodgers a number of players.

"Some of them, particularly those who come from certain sections of the South, will steer away from a club with a Negro player on its roster. Some players now with us may even quit, but they'll be back in baseball after they work a year or two in a cotton mill."

Racine, whose Montreal team won the International League's regular season championship, said he expected no opposition either from the league or from fans. "Negros fought alongside whites and shared the foxhole dangers," he said, "and they should get a fair trial in baseball."

Jack Roosevelt Robinson is 26 years old. He weighs 190 pounds, stands 5 feet, 11½ inches tall.

At UCLA, Robinson received numerous nominations for All-American honors in 1940 and again in 1941. He played in the 1942 All-Star game at Soldier Field, Chicago, and went to Honolulu for another All-Star game, and took part in about a dozen pro football games in the Coast League. He went into the army as a private in April 1942, attended Officers' Training School and was commissioned a second lieutenant in Nov. 1942. Early this year, he was given an inactive status.

The signing of Robinson produced a wave of wild reports. Among them was a yarn that the Dodgers had 25 other Negro prospects in mind. The Mahatma made haste to enter his denial.

Will Continue to Scout

"I haven't 25 prospects," declared Mr. Rickey. "The number I have in mind is nowhere comparable to that figure. I will continue to scout Negro talent. I know of no reason why I shouldn't go after any ball players regardless of color. If I thought it would hurt the Negro, or our players, I wouldn't have done it."

Mr. Rickey was asked about the problem of living and traveling while the Royals are on the road.

"The boy himself answered that question. 'I wouldn't want to go where I'm not welcome,' was the way he put it."

The president of the Dodgers explained why he hadn't broken ground before.

Blasts Griffith

"When I was in St. Louis Negroes were not allowed in the grandstand. Hence I could not arrange for tryouts. If I was in authority, I would have changed that. I got the idea when I came to Brooklyn after watching Negroes play at Ebbets Field. Baseball is a game played by human beings, regardless of color, and I want to have winning baseball."

President Clark Griffith gave out a statement in Washington condemning Rickey for raiding an organized professional league. Rickey came back with a hot retort.

"The Negro leagues, as they are today constituted, are in the nature of a racket and Griffith knows that. History will record that Mr. Griffith introduced Negro ball in the major leagues. I want to help the Negro leagues organize. I'm doing this in spite of outside interests and pressure groups who are exploiting the Negro rather than helping him."

Rickey said he had a heavy telegram reaction, mostly favorable.

In 1942 the Dodgers finished with a record of 104–50, but the St. Louis Cardinals won 106 games and the pennant. During the remainder of the war, Brooklyn finished 3rd, 7th, and 3rd again in 1945. Then, in the first season following the war, the Dodgers tied with the Cardinals and set the stage for the first National League play-off in history.

1946: SEASON OF TUMULT

William Marshall

As the nation's industries retooled and the service sector returned to peacetime pursuits, baseball was encouraged to do the same. J.G. Taylor Spink, editor of the *Sporting News*, predicted that the game would far exceed its prewar stature and would lead the nation through a postwar sports boom of unprecedented magnitude. He called for night baseball, renovated and freshly painted ballparks, and the creation of an atmosphere that would prove attractive to the female fans who were drawn to the game during the war. "Without them," he wrote, "the game no longer can exist."

One owner who did not require Spink's urgings was Larry MacPhail. He presided over a series of renovations that made Yankee Stadium the most modern in baseball and increased its capacity to 80,000. Moreover, inspired by Commissioner Chandler's policy of allowing unlimited night games, the Yankee president installed a lighting system capable of generating twice the illumination of any other stadium. Bathed in new paint—"Robin's egg blue, cerulean blue, blue, light greens and dark greens, orange and henna, overlays of silver paint everywhere, (and) chromium plating to great profusion," Yankee Stadium, more than any other park, became a symbol of baseball's renewal.

New lights were also added to Braves Field in Boston, and, only a short time before opening day, the grandstand was painted. Unfortunately, the new paint failed to dry and part way through the Braves' opener, fans, who discovered they had green paint on their hair, eyebrows, and clothes, were taking their complaints to the Braves' office. Issuing an official apology, the team received good publicity from their offer, and, as Braves president Lou Perini noted, "Nobody can say that it wasn't a colorful opening."

The physical condition and rusty baseball skills of returning veterans was a far greater concern than refurbishing ballparks. In a similar situation during World War I, several players, including Ernie Shore, Dutch Leonard, Hank Gowdy, and Grover Cleveland Alexander, failed to duplicate their prewar successes. Players who returned

Reprinted from *Baseball's Pivotal Era, 1945–1951* by William Marshall, by permission of the University Press of Kentucky. ©1999.

in 1945, such as Phil Marchildon of the Athletics, Hugh Mulcahy of the Phillies, and the Senators' Cecil Travis, had already demonstrated the difficult transition from soldier to civilian. Only Virgil Trucks, Bob Feller, Buddy Lewis, and Hank Greenberg showed signs of their prewar abilities. On the basis of what he had seen of wartime ball in 1945, Greenberg felt that the veterans should not be too worried. "They aren't going to find the opposition too great," he commented.

Spring training in Florida and California in 1946 was nothing like many players had envisioned or remembered before the war. First, there was an unprecedented rush on hotel space as war-weary tourists took their first vacations in years. They willingly paid prices that escalated daily. Ball clubs, which made advance arrangements, suddenly found themselves caught in the rush. Four players were often squeezed into one room. Moreover, wartime food scarcities continued. Butter was almost impossible to locate, and brown sugar was commonly substituted for white. Restaurant and hotel service was often poor, and dirty dishes were a common complaint. Prewar wages no longer appealed to waiters, waitresses, and chambermaids. The housing and hotel shortage also led teams to warn players against bringing their families to spring training. Many ex-servicemen ignored the advice. "I didn't see my wife and kids for two years while I was serving in the Pacific theater," announced St. Louis Browns pitcher Fred Sanford, "and I intend (on) seeing something of them now. They'll be at Anaheim."

Training camps were swollen as returning veterans vied with their wartime replacements for roster places. In many cases, teams were forced to train in two locations instead of one. More than a thousand players competed for just four hundred jobs. Baseball agreed to expand the rosters. To allow veterans more time to round into shape, five additional players could be carried by each team until June 15 of the 1946 season. This enabled teams to evaluate personnel and ensured that veterans had every opportunity to earn back their jobs.

On the field itself, it was evident that months and years with little opportunity for exercise or play at major-league levels had eroded the skills of many veterans. While the 1946 season might have been memorable solely for its overcrowded camps and the challenges presented by labor unrest and the Mexican League raids, it was also an exciting year on the field. In the National League, the heavily favored and talent-laden Cardinals edged out the Dodgers in a surprisingly close race by defeating them in the first-ever league playoff series. In the American League, the Red Sox battered their way to a pennant over the defending champion Detroit Tigers.

The National League Pennant Race

The National League pennant race was a battle between the Brooklyn Dodgers, who held first place from the end of May until the beginning of September, and the St. Louis Cardinals. The Dodgers' season began with a bang, as World War II veteran Ed Head pitched a no-hitter against the Braves on April 23. The Brooklyn club reflected the aggressive spirit of their manager, Leo Durocher. The team was led by the superb double-play combination of team captain and shortstop, Harold "Pee

Wee" Reese (.284-5-60) and second baseman Eddie Stanky (.273-0-36), nicknamed "The Brat." Whereas Reese served as the team's stabilizing influence, Stanky often provided the spark that ignited the Dodgers. A selective hitter with great bat control, Stanky led the National League with an on-base percentage of .436 in 1946. Branch Rickey lauded Stanky when he noted, "If there is a way to beat a team, you may depend on Stanky finding it." Outfielder Fred "Dixie" Walker (.319-9-116) also had an outstanding year for the Dodgers. Nicknamed "The People's Cherce," Walker was easily the most popular player in Brooklyn.

The Dodgers made the 1946 pennant race much closer than the talented Cardinals had anticipated. Rice University athletic great Eddie Dyer, whose personal style of managing was popular with his players, replaced St. Louis manager Billy Southworth. The team was paced by young superstar Stan Musial (.365-16-103), who led the league in batting average, runs scored (124), hits (228), doubles (50), and triples (20) and in the process won his second National League Most Valuable Player Award. Musial reluctantly switched from the outfield to first base — a position he was to hold for the next ten years. Third base was manned by George "Whitey" Kurowski (.301-14-89). A courageous, hard-working player, Kurowski overcame a deformed right arm that was described by one teammate as containing more "gristle" than bone below the elbow. Teammates marveled at his throwing ability and the fact that his disability actually allowed him to become a better pull hitter.

The Cardinals also had a superb double-play combination in Marty Marion and Red Schoendienst. Shortstop Marion, who possessed great range, sure hands, and a fine arm, rarely made an error in clutch situations and always made the big play. Second baseman Red Schoendienst was adept at fielding sharply hit balls and ended up leading the league in fielding percentage (.948) at his position. In the outfield the Cardinals had the incomparable Terry Moore (.263-3-28), who was considered to be one of the best defensive center fielders in the game. Unfortunately, Moore returned from the service with two bad knees, which diminished his production. Right field was occupied by the hustling North Carolinian Enos Slaughter (.300-18-130), a throwback to a bygone era. Nicknamed "Country" by his former manager Burt Shotton because of his mannerisms and attire, Slaughter ran hard on every play.

Cardinal pitching was deep, but with the loss of Max Lanier and Fred Martin to Mexico, the ineffectiveness of former twenty-game winner Red Barrett, and Johnny Beazley's injured arm, it needed to be. The team was paced by Murry Dickson (2.88, 15-6), Howie Pollet (2.10, 21-10), Harry Brecheen (2.49, 15-15), Al Brazle (3.29, 11-10), and Ted Wilks (3.41, 8-0). Dickson, nicknamed the "Great Houdini of the Mound," was a trick pitcher who liked to experiment when he was ahead in the count. The right-hander was adept at nibbling at the corners and refused to give in to hitters.

Howie Pollet was a stylish left-hander who relied on control, a moving fast ball, and an outstanding change-up. A wiry Oklahoman, Harry "The Cat" Brecheen earned his nickname because of his fielding quickness. Although not overpowering, the left-hander had a sneaky fastball, threw an outstanding screwball, and liberally employed the brush-back pitch as a weapon. He would often yell "Look out!" at the hitter as he was releasing the ball.

The Dodgers finally relinquished the lead to the Cardinals in mid–August. From that point forward, the two teams vied with one another for the top spot as the suspense mounted. On the last day of the season, the teams were deadlocked at ninety-six wins and fifty-eight losses, forcing the first best-two-out-of-three playoff series in National League history. St. Louis beat the Dodgers 4–2 in the first game, behind Howie Pollet, who pitched a complete game victory even though his left arm was heavily taped because of a torn muscle. Rookie catcher Joe Garagiola, who had three hits on the day, knocked in two runs as the Cardinals chased Dodger starter Ralph Branca in the third inning. Rumors and newspaper stories, which predicted long lines before the contest, apparently scared fans away. In the second game, the Cardinals scored an 8–4 triumph behind Murry Dickson to capture the National League pennant. The Dodgers rallied for three runs in the ninth inning but fell short when relief pitcher Harry Brecheen struck out Eddie Stanky and pinch-hitter Howie Schultz with the bases loaded.

The first hurdle for Jackie Robinson after signing with the Dodgers was winning the accep-tance of his teammates. This would prove to be more difficult than Branch Rickey had anticipated. The spring of 1947 brought another problem.

THE PETITION

Harold Parrott

Durocher had made no bones about wanting Robinson as a player on his Dodger varsity right from the very first moment he saw Jackie in spring training with the minor league Montreal farm club in the spring of 1946.

Why? Was there perhaps a hidden streak of humanitarianism running through this strange man who had been case-hardened in the school of hard knocks and the pool halls of Hartford?

No, nothing like that. Leo probably wouldn't have been able to spell "equality," much less preach it. He would be the first to tell you that all men were *not* created equal, and that Robinson was indeed a superman.

Then it was because the Lip had close Negro friends like Sammy Davis, Jr., Bojangles Robinson, and Nat King Cole?

Don't you believe it.

Money, that was the reason, pure and simple. Right from the very first time he saw this black man run wild on the bases and get up to rip the ball after they knocked him down with a duster, Leo had Jackie Robinson tabbed as a winner. The Lip figured Jackie could put them all in the World Series, the big dough, the endorsements and commercials, and all that went with winning.

I heard him bark this at his unhappy Dodger players in a bizarre midnight meet-ing in an army barracks in Panama, where we had gone to play exhibition games against Robinson and the rest of the Montreal squad in the spring of 1947. We were there because we daren't bring this black-and-white show into any of the Southern states.

By now it was a cinch that the Negro was too good to be kept off the Dodgers. When would he be brought up? That was the question.

Bobby Bragan and Dixie Walker and a few more of the hominy-grits boys decided to beat Rickey to the punch. They made up a petition saying they would not play on the same team with a Negro, and were trying to get a few patsies like Carl

Reprinted from *The Lords of Baseball* by Harold Parrott, by permission of the Bonfire Foundation and Tod Par-rott. ©1976.

Furillo to take it around and get others to sign it. The only south in Furillo's background was southern Italy; he wouldn't have known Mason and Dixon from the Smith Brothers.

Kirby Higbe, a strongarm pitcher, didn't like the aroma of the whole thing, even though he was from South Carolina. He tipped me off over a few beers in a Panama bar one night.

I phoned Rickey in Brooklyn, and the Old Man jumped into a plane within the hour, heading to Panama to quell the rebellion.

Rickey wasn't needed this time. Durocher handled the whole thing.

When I told Leo about the plot, he had exploded. He called the midnight meeting in the barracks, and I can still hear him as he challenged the mutineers. He was wrapped in a yellow bathrobe, and he looked like a fighter about to enter the ring. He stared down Walker and Bragan and started punching out the words.

"I don't care if the guy is yellow or black, or if he has stripes like a fuckin' zebra," Durocher rasped, glaring around the room. "I'm the manager of this team, and I say he plays. What's more, I say he can make us all rich." After a pause, the Lip added, "An' if any of you can't use the money, I'll see that you're traded!"

Money, that was it. Money to spend on clothes, beautiful women, horses, cards. Leo never had enough of the stuff. I remembered, as I listened that night in the barracks, how Leo had snorted when one New York writer had suggested in his column that the dandy little manager might retire rather than haggle with Rickey over a new contract. Durocher was rich now, insisted Arch Murray of the New York *Post*, and could make a career out of going on radio with Milton Berle and Jack Benny and Fred Allen.

"What's that Murray been smokin' lately?" Lippy had barked, tossing the offending newspaper into my lap. "Me, rich? Ain't he found out yet that I always spend more than I make?"

Leo hadn't meant it as a wisecrack, either.

There had been dollar signs dancing in Durocher's eyes from the very first day he saw Robinson. Leo wanted the black man right then. He thought Jack could ring the cash register for us all.

But Rickey had stuck to his carefully planned timetable: slow, slow, get the boy ready with a full year in the International League.

Now, as 1947 opening day approached, Durocher was gone, sawed off by Unhappy Chandler.

Robinson was not to forget that. He had to face a tough year backed only by Rickey, who was way up in the front office, where you couldn't hear half of what they were saying.

Then, when Rickey himself was thrown out in a power struggle with O'Malley after the 1950 season, Robinson was left very much alone on the Dodgers. Oh, there were other blacks by then, but Campanella and Newcombe were pussycats, too timid to be openly pally with a hot potato like Robinson.

All these things fed the demon that was inside Jackie. Then, in 1953, he had to watch the same gang guillotine Charley Dressen, whom he liked very much and always called his favorite manager.

Pete Reiser came up to the Dodgers in 1940. Years later Leo Durocher had this to say: "No doubt about it. He was the best I ever had, with the possible exception of Mays. At that, he was even faster than Willie."

THE ROCKY ROAD
OF PISTOL PETE

W.C. Heinz

"Out in Los Angeles," says Garry Schumacher, who was a New York baseball writer for 30 years and is now assistant to Horace Stoneham, president of the San Francisco Giants, "they think Duke Snider is the best center fielder they ever had. They forget Pete Reiser. The Yankees think Mickey Mantle is something new. They forget Reiser, too."

Maybe Pete Reiser was the purest ballplayer of all time. I don't know. There is no exact way of measuring such a thing, but when a man of incomparable skills, with full knowledge of what he is doing, destroys those skills and puts his life on the line in the pursuit of his endeavor as no other man in his game ever has, perhaps he is the truest of them all.

"Is Pete Reiser there?" I said on the phone.

This was last season, in Kokomo. Kokomo has a population of about 50,000 and a ball club, now affiliated with Los Angeles and called the Dodgers, in the class D Midwest League. Class D is the bottom of the barrel of organized baseball, and this was the second season that Pete Reiser managed Kokomo.

"He's not here right now," the woman's voice on the phone said. "The team played a double-header yesterday in Dubuque, and they didn't get in on the bus until 4:30 this morning. Pete just got up a few minutes ago and he had to go to the doctor's."

"Oh?" I said. "What has he done now?"

In two and a half years in the minors, three seasons of army ball and ten years in the majors, Pete Reiser was carried off the field 11 times. Nine times he regained consciousness either in the clubhouse or in hospitals. He broke a bone in his right elbow, throwing. He broke both ankles, tore a cartilage in his left knee, ripped the

From *What a Time It Was: The Best of W.C. Heinz on Sports* by W.C. Heinz. ©2001 by W.C. Heinz. Reprinted by permission of William Morris Agency, Inc., on behalf of the author, and by permission of Perseus Books Publishers, a member of Perseus Books, L.L.C.

muscles in his left leg, sliding. Seven times he crashed into outfield walls, dislocating his left shoulder, breaking his right collarbone and, five times, ending up in an unconscious heap on the ground. Twice he was beaned, and the few who remember still wonder today how great he might have been.

"I didn't see the old-timers," Bob Cooke, who is sports editor of the New York *Herald Tribune,* was saying recently, "but Pete Reiser was the best ballplayer I ever saw."

"We don't know what's wrong with him," the woman's voice on the phone said now. "He has a pain in his chest and he feels tired all the time, so we sent him to the doctor. There's a game tonight, so he'll be at the ball park about 5 o'clock."

Pete Reiser is 39 years old now. The Cardinals signed him out of the St. Louis Municipal League when he was 15. For two years, because he was so young, he chauffeured for Charley Barrett, who was scouting the Midwest. They had a Cardinal uniform in the car for Pete, and he used to work out with the Class C and D clubs, and one day Branch Rickey, who was general manager of the Cardinals then, called Pete into his office in Sportsman's Park.

"Young man," he said, "you're the greatest young ballplayer I've ever seen, but there is one thing you must remember. Now that you're a professional ballplayer you're in show business. You will perform on the biggest stage in the world, the baseball diamond. Like the actors on Broadway, you'll be expected to put on a great performance every day, no matter how you feel, no matter whether it's too hot or too cold. Never forget that."

Rickey didn't know it at the time, but this was like telling Horatius that, as a professional soldier, he'd be expected someday to stand his ground. Three times Pete sneaked out of hospitals to play. Once he went back into the lineup after doctors warned him that any blow on the head would kill him. For four years he swung the bat and made the throws when it was painful for him just to shave and to comb his hair. In the 1947 World Series he stood on a broken ankle to pinch hit, and it ended with Rickey, then president of the Dodgers, begging him not to play and guaranteeing Pete his 1948 salary if he would just sit the season out.

"That might be the one mistake I made," Pete says now. "Maybe I should have rested that year."

"Pete Reiser?" Leo Durocher, who managed Pete at Brooklyn, was saying recently. "What's he doing now?"

"He's managing Kokomo," Lindsey Nelson, the TV sportscaster, said.

"Kokomo?" Leo said.

"That's right," Lindsey said. "He's riding the buses to places like Lafayette and Michigan City and Mattoon."

"On the buses," Leo said, shaking his head and then smiling at the thought of Pete.

"And some people say," Lindsey said, "that he was the greatest young ballplayer they ever saw."

"No doubt about it," Leo said. "He was the best I ever had, with the possible exception of Mays. At that, he was even faster than Willie." He paused. "So now he's on the buses."

The first time that Leo ever saw Pete on a ball field was in Clearwater that spring of '39. Pete had played one year of Class D in the Cardinal chain and one season of Class D for Brooklyn. Judge Kenesaw Mountain Landis, who was then Baseball Commissioner, had sprung Pete and 72 others from what they called the "Cardinal Chain Gang," and Pete had signed with Brooklyn for $100.

"I didn't care about money then," Pete says. "I just wanted to play."

Pete had never been in a major-league camp before, and he didn't know that at batting practice you hit in rotation. At Clearwater he was grabbing any bat that was handy and cutting in ahead of Ernie Koy or Dolph Camilli or one of the others, and Leo liked that.

One day Leo had a chest cold, so he told Pete to start at shortstop. His first time up he hit a homer off the Cards' Ken Raffensberger, and that was the beginning. He was on base his first 12 times at bat that spring, with three homers, five singles and four walks. His first time against Detroit he homered off Tommy Bridges. His first time against the Yankees he put one over the fence off Lefty Gomez.

Durocher played Pete at shortstop in 33 games that spring. The Dodgers barnstormed North with the Yankees, and one night Joe McCarthy, who was managing the Yankees, sat down next to Pete on the train.

"Reiser," he said, "you're going to play for me."

"How can I play for you?" Pete said. "I'm with the Dodgers."

"We'll get you," McCarthy said. "I'll tell Ed Barrow, and you'll be a Yankee."

The Yankees offered $100,000 and five ballplayers for Pete. The Dodgers turned it down, and the day the season opened at Ebbets Field, Larry MacPhail, who was running things in Brooklyn, called Pete on the clubhouse phone and told him to report to Elmira.

"It was an hour before game time," Pete says, "and I started to take off my uniform and I was shaking all over. Leo came in and said: 'What's the matter? You scared?' I said: 'No. MacPhail is sending me to Elmira.' Leo got on the phone and they had a hell of a fight. Leo said he'd quit, and MacPhail said he'd fire him — and I went to Elmira.

"One day I'm making a throw and I heard something pop. Every day my arm got weaker and they sent me to Johns Hopkins and took X-rays. Dr. George Bennett told me: 'Your arm's broken.' When I came to after the operation, my throat was sore and there was an ice pack on it. I said: 'What happened? Your knife slip?' They said: 'We took your tonsils out while we were operating on your arm.'"

Pete's arm was in a cast from the first of May until the end of July. His first two weeks out of the cast he still couldn't straighten the arm, but a month later he played ten games as a left-handed outfielder until Dr. Bennett stopped him.

"But I can't straighten my right arm," Pete said.

"Take up bowling," the doctor said.

When he bowled, though, Pete used first one arm and then the other. Every day that the weather allowed he went out into the back yard and practiced throwing a rubber ball left-handed against a wall. Then he went to Fairgrounds Park and worked on the long throw, left-handed, with a baseball.

"At Clearwater that next spring," he says, "Leo saw me in the outfield throwing left-handed, and he said: 'What do you think you're doin'?' I said: 'Hell, I had to be ready. Now I can throw as good with my left arm as I could with my right.' He said: 'You can do more things as a right-handed ballplayer. I can bring you into the infield. Go out there and cut loose with that right arm.' I did and it was okay, but I had that insurance."

So at 5 o'clock I took a cab from the hotel in Kokomo to the ball park on the edge of town. It seats about 2,200, 1,500 of them in the white-painted fairgrounds grandstand along the first base line, and the rest in chairs behind the screen and in bleachers along the other line.

I watched them take batting practice; trim, strong young kids with their dreams, I knew, of someday getting up where Pete once was, and I listened to their kidding. I watched the groundskeeper open the concession booth and clean out the electric popcorn machine. I read the signs on the outfield walls, advertising the Mid-West Towel and Linen service, Basil's Nite Club, the Hoosier Iron Works, UAW Local 292 and the Around the Clock Pizza Café. I watched the Dubuque kids climbing out of their bus, carrying their uniforms on wire coat hangers.

"Here comes Pete now," I heard the old guy setting up the ticket booth at the gate say.

When Pete came through the gate he was walking like an old man. In 1941 the Dodgers trained in Havana, and one day they clocked him, in his baseball uniform and regular spikes, at 9.8 for 100 yards. Five years later the Cleveland Indians were bragging about George Case and the Washington Senators had Gil Coan. The Dodgers offered to bet $1,000 that Reiser was the fastest man in baseball, and now it was taking him forever to walk to me, his shoulders stooped, his whole body heavier now, and Pete just slowly moving one foot ahead of the other.

"Hello," he said, shaking hands but his face solemn. "How are you?"

"Fine," I said, "but what's the matter with you?"

"I guess it's my heart," he said.

"When did you first notice this?"

"About eleven days ago. I guess I was working out too hard. All of a sudden I felt this pain in my chest and I got weak. I went into the clubhouse and lay down on the bench, but I've got the same pain and I'm weak ever since."

"What did the doctor say?"

"He says it's lucky I stopped that day when I did. He says I should be in a hospital right now, because if I exert myself or even make a quick motion I might go—just like that."

He snapped his fingers. "He scared me," he said. "I'll admit it. I'm scared."

"What are you planning to do?"

"I'm going home to St. Louis. My wife works for a doctor there, and he'll know a good heart specialist."

"When will you leave?"

"Well, I can't just leave the ball club. I called Brooklyn, and they're sending a replacement for me, but he won't be here until tomorrow."

"How will you get to St. Louis?"

"It's about 300 miles," Pete says. "The doctor says I shouldn't fly or go by train, because if anything happens to me they can't stop and help me. I guess I'll have to drive."

"I'll drive you," I said.

Trying to sleep in the hotel that night I was thinking that maybe, standing there in that little ball park, Pete Reiser had admitted out loud for the first time in his life that he was scared. I was thinking of 1941, his first full year with the Dodgers. He was beaned twice and crashed his first wall and still hit .343 to be the first rookie and the youngest ballplayer to win the National League batting title. He tied Johnny Mize with 39 doubles, led in triples, runs scored, total bases and slugging average, and they were writing on the sports pages that he might be the new Ty Cobb.

"Dodgers Win on Reiser HR," the headlines used to say. "Reiser Stars as Brooklyn Lengthens Lead."

"Any manager in the National League," Arthur Patterson wrote one day in the New York *Herald Tribune*, would give up his best man to obtain Pete Reiser. On every bench they're talking about him. Rival players watch him take his cuts during batting practice, announce when he's going to make a throw to the plate or third base during outfield drill. They just whistle their amazement when he scoots down the first base line on an infield dribbler or a well-placed bunt."

He was beaned the first time at Ebbets Field five days after the season started. A sidearm fast ball got away from Ike Pearson of the Phillies, and Pete came to at 11:30 that night in Peck Memorial Hospital.

"I was lying in bed with my uniform on," he told me once, "and I couldn't figure it out. The room was dark, with just a little night light, and then I saw a mirror and I walked over to it and lit the light and I had a black eye and a black streak down the side of my nose. I said to myself: 'What happened to me?' Then I remembered.

"I took a shower and walked around the room, and the next morning the doctor came in. He looked me over, and he said: 'We'll keep you here for five or six more days under observation.' I said: 'Why?' He said: 'You've had a serious head injury. If you tried to get out of bed right now, you'd fall down.' I said: 'If I can get up and walk around this room, can I get out?' The doc said: 'All right, but you won't be able to do it.'"

Pete got out of bed, the doctor standing ready to catch him. He walked around the room. "I've been walkin' the floor all night," Pete said.

The doctor made Pete promise that he wouldn't play ball for a week, but Pete went right to the ball park. He got a seat behind the Brooklyn dugout and Durocher spotted him.

"How do you feel?" Leo said.

"Not bad," Pete said.

"Get your uniform on," Leo said.

"I'm not supposed to play," Pete said.

"I'm not gonna play you," Leo said. "Just sit on the bench. It'll make our guys feel better to see that you're not hurt."

Pete suited up and went out and sat on the bench. In the eighth inning it was tied, 7–7. The Dodgers had the bases loaded, and there was Ike Pearson again, coming in to relieve.

"Pistol," Leo said to Pete, "get the bat."

In the press box the baseball writers watched Pete. They wanted to see if he'd stand right in there. After a beaning they are all entitled to shy, and many of them do. Pete hit the first pitch into the center-field stands, and Brooklyn won, 11–7.

I could just barely trot around the bases," Pete said when I asked him about it. "I was sure dizzy."

Two weeks later they were playing the Cardinals, and Enos Slaughter hit one and Pete turned in center field and started to run. He made the catch, but he hit his head and his tail bone on that corner near the exit gate.

His head was cut, and when he came back to the bench they also saw blood coming through the seat of his pants. They took him into the clubhouse and pulled his pants down and the doctor put a metal clamp on the cut.

"Just don't slide," he told Pete. "You can get it sewed up after the game."

In August of that year big Paul Erickson was pitching for the Cubs and Pete took another one. Again he woke up in a hospital. The Dodgers were having some pretty good beanball contests with the Cubs that season, and Judge Landis came to see Pete the next day.

"Do you think that man tried to bean you?" he asked Pete.

"No sir," Pete said. "I lost the pitch."

"I was there," Landis said, "and I heard them holler: 'Stick it in his ear.'"

"That was just bench talk," Pete said. "I lost the pitch."

He left the hospital the next morning. The Dodgers were going to St. Louis after the game, and Pete didn't want to be left in Chicago.

Pete always says that the next year, 1942, was the year of his downfall, and the worst of it happened on one play. It was early July and Pete and the Dodgers were tearing the league apart. In a four-game series in Cincinnati he got 19 for 21. In a Sunday double-header in Chicago he went 5 for 5 in the first game, walked three times in the second game and got a hit the one time they pitched to him. He was hitting .381, and they were writing in the papers that he might end up hitting .400.

When they came into St. Louis the Dodgers were leading by ten and a half games. When they took off for Pittsburgh they left three games of that lead and Pete Reiser behind them.

"We were in the twelfth inning, no score, two outs and Slaughter hit it off Whit Wyatt," Pete says. "It was over my head and I took off. I caught it and missed the flagpole by two inches and hit the wall and dropped the ball. I had the instinct to throw it to Pee Wee Reese, and we just missed getting Slaughter at the plate, and they won, 1–0.

"I made one step to start off the field and I woke up the next morning in St. John's Hospital. My head was bandaged, and I had an awful headache."

Dr. Robert Hyland, who was Pete's personal physician, announced to the newspapers that Pete would be out for the rest of the season. "Look, Pete," Hyland told him. "I'm your personal friend. I'm advising you not to play anymore baseball this year."

"I don't like hospitals, though," Pete was telling me once, "so after two days I took the bandage off and got up. The room started to spin, but I got dressed and I took off. I snuck out, and I took a train to Pittsburgh and I went to the park.

"Leo saw me and he said: 'Go get your uniform on, Pistol.' I said: 'Not tonight, Skipper.' Leo said: 'Aw, I'm not gonna let you hit. I want these guys to see you. It'll give 'em that little spark they need. Besides, it'll change the pitching plans on that other bench when they see you sittin' here in uniform.'"

In the fourteenth inning the Dodgers had a runner on second and Ken Heintzelman, the left-hander, came in for the Pirates. He walked Johnny Rizzo, and Durocher had run out of pinch hitters.

"Damn," Leo was saying, walking up and down. "I want to win this one. Who can I use? Anybody here who can hit?"

Pete walked up to the bat rack. He pulled out his stick. "You got yourself a hitter," he said to Leo.

He walked up there and hit a line drive over the second baseman's head that was good for three bases. The two runs scored, and Pete rounded first base and collapsed.

"When I woke up I was in a hospital again," he says. "I could just make out that somebody was standin' there and then I saw it was Leo. He said: 'You awake?' I said: 'Yep.' He said: 'By God, we beat 'em! How do you feel?' I said: 'How do you think I feel?' He said: 'Aw, you're better with one leg and one eye than anybody else I've got.' I said: 'Yeah, and that's the way I'll end up — on one leg and with one eye.'

"I'd say I lost the pennant for us that year," Pete says now, although he still hit .310 for the season. "I was dizzy most of the time and I couldn't see fly balls. I mean balls I could have put in my pocket, I couldn't get near. Once in Brooklyn when Mort Cooper was pitching for the Cards I was seeing two baseballs coming up there. Babe Pinelli was umpiring behind the plate, and a couple of times he stopped the game and asked me if I was all right. So the Cards beat us out the last two days of the season."

The business office of the Kokomo ball club is the dining room of a man named Jim Deets, who sells insurance and is also the business manager of the club. His wife, in addition to keeping house, mothering six small kids, boarding Pete, an outfielder from Venezuela and a shortstop from the Dominican Republic, is also the club secretary.

"How do you feel this morning?" I asked Pete. He was sitting at the dining-room table, in a sweat shirt and a pair of light-brown slacks, typing the game report of the night before to send it to Brooklyn.

"A little better," he said.

Pete has a worn, green 1950 Chevy, and it took us eight and a half hours to get to St. Louis. I'd ask him how the pain in his chest was and he'd say that it wasn't bad or it wasn't so good, and I'd get him to talking again about Durocher or about his time in the Army. Pete played under five managers at Brooklyn, Boston, Pittsburgh and Cleveland, and Durocher is his favorite.

"He has a great mind and not just for baseball," Pete said. "Once he sat down to play gin with Jack Benny, and after they'd played four cards Leo read Benny's whole hand to him. Benny said: 'How can you do that?' Leo said: 'If you're playin' your cards right, and I give you credit for that, you have to be holding those others.' Benny said: 'I don't want to play with this guy.'

"One spring at Clearwater there was a pool table in a room off the lobby. One night Hugh Casey and a couple of other guys and I were talking with Leo. We said: 'Gee, there's a guy in there and we've been playin' pool with him for a couple of nights, but last night he had a real hot streak.' Leo said: 'How much he take you for?' We figured it out and it was $2,000. Leo said: 'Point him out to me.'

"We went in and pointed the guy out and Leo walked up to him and said: 'Put all your money on the table. We're gonna shoot for it.' The guy said: 'I never play like that.' Leo said: 'You will tonight. Pick your own game.' Leo took him for $4,000, and then he threw him out. Then he paid us back what we'd gone for, and he said: 'Now, let that be a lesson. The guy is a hustler from New York. The next time it happens I won't bail you out.' Leo hadn't had a cue in his hands for years."

It was amazing that they took Pete into the Army. He had wanted to enlist in the Navy, but the doctors looked him over and told him none of the services could accept him. Then his draft board sent him to Jefferson Barracks in the winter of 1943, and the doctors there turned him down.

"I'm sittin' on a bench with the other guys who've been rejected," he was telling me, "and a captain comes in and says: 'Which one of you is Reiser?' I stood up and I said: 'I am.' In front of everybody he said: 'So you're trying to pull a fast one, are you? At a time like this, with a war on, you came in here under a false name. What do you mean, giving your name as Harold Patrick Reiser? Your name's Pete Reiser, and you're a ballplayer, aren't you?' I said: 'I'm the ballplayer and they call me Pete, but my right name is Harold Patrick Reiser.' The captain says: 'I apologize. Sergeant, fingerprint him. This man is in.'"

They sent him to Fort Riley, Kansas. It was April and raining and they were on bivouac, and Pete woke up in a hospital. "What happened?" he said.

"You've got pneumonia," the doctor said. "You've been a pretty sick boy for six days. You'll be all right, but we've been looking you over. How did you ever get into this Army?"

"When I get out of the hospital," Pete was telling me, "I'm on the board for a discharge and I'm waitin' around for about a week, and still nobody there knows who I am. All of a sudden one morning a voice comes over the bitch box in the barracks. It says: 'Private Reiser, report to headquarters immediately.' I think: 'Well, I'm out now.'

"I got over there and the colonel wants to see me. I walk in and give my good salute and he says: 'Sit down, Harold.' I sit down and he says: 'Your name really isn't Harold, is it?' I say: 'Yes, it is, sir.' He says: 'But that isn't what they call you where you're well known, is it? You're Pete Reiser the ballplayer, aren't you?' I say: 'Yes, sir.' He says: 'I thought so. Now, I've got your discharge papers right there, but we've got a pretty good ball club and we'd like you on it. We'll make a deal. You say nothing, and you won't have to do anything but play ball. How about it?' I said: 'Suppose I don't want to stay in?'

"He picked my papers up off his desk," Pete was saying, "and he tore 'em right up in my face. I can still hear that 'zip' when he tore 'em. He said: 'You see, you have no choice.'

"Then he picked up the phone and said something and in a minute a general came in. I jumped up and the colonel said: 'Major, this is Pete Reiser, the great Dodger ballplayer. He was up for a medical discharge, but he's decided to stay here and play ball for us.'

"So, the general says: 'My, what a patriotic thing for you to do, young man. That's wonderful. Wonderful.' I'm sittin' there, and when the general goes out the colonel says: 'That major, he's all right.' I said: 'But he's a general. How come you call him a major?' The colonel says: 'Well, in the regular Army he's a major and I'm a full colonel. The only reason I don't outrank him now is that I've got heart trouble. He knows it, but I never let him forget it. I always call him major.' I thought: 'What kind of an Army am I in?'"

Joe Gantenbein, the Athletics' outfielder, and George Scharein, the Phillies' infielder, were on that team with Pete, and they won the state and national semipro titles. By the time the season was over, however, the order came down to hold up all discharges.

The next season there were 17 major-league ballplayers on the Fort Riley club, and they played four nights a week for the war workers in Wichita. Pete hit a couple of walls, and the team made such a joke of the national semipro tournament that an order came down from Washington to break up the club.

"Considering what a lot of guys did in the war," Pete says, "I had no complaints, but five times I was up for discharge, and each time something happened. From Riley they sent me to Camp Livingston. From there they sent me to New York Special Services for twelve hours and I end up in Camp Lee, Virginia, in May of 1945.

"The first one I meet there is the general. He says: 'Reiser, I saw you on the list and I just couldn't pass you up.' I said: 'What about my discharge?' He says: 'That will have to wait. I have a lot of celebrities down here, but I want a good baseball team.'"

Johnny Lindell, of the Yankees, and Dave Philley, of the White Sox, were on the club and Pete played left field. Near the end of the season he went after a foul fly for the third out of the last inning, and he went right through a temporary wooden fence and rolled down a 25-foot embankment.

"I came to in the hospital, with a dislocated right shoulder," he says, "and the general came over to see me and he said: 'That was one of the greatest displays of courage I've ever seen, to ignore your future in baseball just to win a game for Camp Lee.' I said: 'Thanks.'

"Now it's November and the war is over, but they're still shippin' guys out, and I'm on the list to go. I report to the overseas major, and he looks at my papers and says: 'I can't send you overseas. With everything that's wrong with you, you shouldn't even be in this Army. I'll have you out in three hours.' In three hours, sure enough, I've got those papers in my hand, stamped, and I'm startin' out the door. Runnin' up to me comes a Red Cross guy. He says: 'I can get you some pretty good pension benefits for the physical and mental injuries you've sustained.' I said: 'You can?' He said: 'Yes, you're entitled to them.' I said: 'Good. You get 'em. You keep 'em. I'm goin' home.'"

When we got to St. Louis that night I drove Pete to his house and the next morning I picked him up and drove him to see the heart specialist. He was in there for two hours, and when he came out he was walking slower than ever.

"No good," he said. "I have to go to the hospital for five days for observation."

"What does he think?"

"He says I'm done puttin' on that uniform. I'll have to get a desk job."

Riding to the hospital I wondered if that heart specialist knew who he was tying to that desk job. In 1946, the year he came out of the Army, Pete led the league when he stole 34 bases, 13 more than runner-up Johnny Hopp of the Braves. He also set a major-league record that still stands, when he stole home eight times.

"Nine times," he said once. "In Chicago I stole home and Magerkurth hollered: 'You're out!' Then he dropped his voice and he said: '_____, I missed it.' He'd already had his thumb in the air. I had nine out of nine."

I suppose somebody will beat that some day, but he'll never top the way Pete did it. That was the year he knocked himself out again trying for a diving catch, dislocated his left shoulder, ripped the muscles in his left leg and broke his left ankle.

"Whitey Kurowski hit one in the seventh inning at Ebbets Field," he was telling me. "I dove for it and woke up in the clubhouse. I was in Peck Memorial for four days. It really didn't take much to knock me out in those days. I was comin' apart all over. When I dislocated my shoulder they popped it back in, and Leo said: 'Hell, you'll be all right. You don't throw with it anyway.'"

That was the year the Dodgers tied with the Cardinals for the pennant and dropped the play-off. Pete wasn't there for those two games. He was in Peck Memorial again.

"I'd pulled a charley horse in my left leg," Pete was saying. "It's the last two weeks of the season, and I'm out for four days. We've got the winning run on third, two outs in the ninth and Leo sends me up. He says: 'If you don't hit it good, don't run and hurt your leg.'

"The first pitch was a knockdown and, when I ducked, the ball hit the bat and went down the third base line, as beautiful a bunt as you've ever seen. Well, Ebbets Field is jammed. Leo has said: 'Don't run.' But this is a big game. I take off for first, and we win and I've ripped the muscles from my ankle to my hip. Leo says: 'You shouldn't have done it.'

"Now it's the last three days of the season and we're a game ahead of the Cards and we're playin' the Phillies in Brooklyn. Leo says to me: 'It's now or never. I don't think we can win it without you.' The first two up are outs and I single to right. There's Charley Dressen, coachin' at third, with the steal sign. I start to get my lead, and a pitcher named Charley Schanz is workin' and he throws an ordinary lob over to first. My leg is stiff and I slide and my heel spike catches the bag and I hear it snap.

"Leo comes runnin' out. He says: 'Come on. You're all right.' I said: 'I think it's broken.' He says: 'It ain't stickin' out.' They took me to Peck Memorial, and it was broken."

We went to St. Luke's Hospital in St. Louis. In the main office they told Pete to go over to a desk where a gray-haired, semistout woman was sitting at a typewriter. She started to book Pete in, typing his answer on the form.

"What is your occupation, Mr. Reiser?" she asked.

"Baseball," Pete said.

"Have you ever been hospitalized before?"

"Yes," Pete said.

In 1946 the Dodgers played an exhibition game in Springfield, Missouri. When the players got off the train there was a young radio announcer there, and he was grabbing them one at a time and asking them where they thought they'd finish that year.

"In first place," Reese and Casey and Dixie Walker and the rest were saying. "On top" ... "We'll win it."

"And here comes Pistol Pete Reiser!" the announcer said. "Where do you think you'll finish this season, Pete?"

"In Peck Memorial Hospital," Pete said.

After the 1946 season Brooklyn changed the walls at Ebbets Field. They added boxes, cutting 40 feet off left field and dropping center field from 420 to 390 feet. Pete had made a real good start that season in center, and on June 5 the Dodgers were leading the Pirates by three runs in the sixth inning when Culley Rikard hit one.

"I made my turn and ran," Pete says, "and, where I thought I still had that thirty feet, I didn't."

"The crowd," Al Laney wrote the next day in the New York *Herald Tribune*, "which watched silently while Reiser was being carried away, did not know that he had held onto the ball.... Rikard circled the bases, but Butch Henline the umpire, who ran to Reiser, found the ball still in Reiser's glove.... Two outs were posted on the scoreboard after play was resumed. Then the crowd let out a tremendous roar."

In the Brooklyn clubhouse the doctor called for a priest, and the Last Rites of the Church were administered to Pete. He came to, but lapsed into unconsciousness again and woke up at 3 A.M. in Peck Memorial.

For eight weeks he couldn't move. After three weeks they let him out, and he made that next western trip with the Dodgers. In Pittsburgh he was working out in the outfield before the game when Clyde King, chasing a fungo, ran into him and Pete woke up in the clubhouse.

"I went back to the Hotel Schenley and lay down," he says. "After the game I got up and had dinner with Peewee. We were sittin' on the porch, and I scratched my head and I felt a lump there about as big as half a golf ball. I told Peewee to feel it and he said: 'Gosh!' I said: 'I don't think that's supposed to be like that.' He said: 'Hell, no.'"

Pete went up to Rickey's room and Rickey called his pilot and had Pete flown to Johns Hopkins in Baltimore. They operated on him for a blood clot.

"You're lucky," the doctor told him. "If it had moved just a little more you'd have been gone."

Pete was unable to hold even a pencil. He had double vision and, when he tried to take a single step, he became dizzy. He stayed for three weeks and then went home for almost a month.

"It was August," he says, "and Brooklyn was fightin' for another pennant. I thought if I could play the last two months it might make the difference, so I went back to Johns Hopkins. The doctor said: 'You've made a remarkable recovery.' I said:

'I want to play.' He said: 'I can't okay that. The slightest blow on the head can kill you.'"

Pete played. He worked out for four days, pinch hit a couple of times and then, in the Polo Grounds, made a diving catch in left field. They carried him off, and, in the clubhouse he was unable to recognize anyone.

Pete was still having dizzy spells when the Dodgers went into the 1947 Series against the Yankees. In the third game he walked in the first inning, got the steal sign and, when he went into second, felt his right ankle snap. At the hospital they found it was broken.

"Just tape it, will you?" Pete said.

"I want to put a cast on it," the doctor said.

"If you do," Pete said, "they'll give me a dollar-a-year contract next season."

The next day he was back on the bench. Bill Bevens was pitching for the Yankees and, with two out in the ninth, it looked like he was going to pitch the first no-hitter in World Series history.

"Aren't you going to volunteer to hit?" Burt Shotton, who was managing Brooklyn, said to Pete.

Al Gionfriddo was on first and Bucky Harris, who was managing the Yankees, ordered Pete walked. Eddie Miksis ran for him, and when Cookie Lavagetto hit that double, the two runs scored and Brooklyn won, 3–2.

"The next day," Pete says, "the sports writers were second-guessing Harris for putting me on when I represented the winning run. Can you imagine what they'd have said if they knew I had a broken ankle?"

At the end of that season Rickey had the outfield walls at Ebbets Field padded with one-inch thick foam rubber for Pete, but he never hit them again. He had headaches most of the time and played little. Then he was traded to Boston, and in two seasons there he hit the wall a couple of times. Twice his left shoulder came out while he was making diving catches. Pittsburgh picked Pete up in 1951, and the next year he played into July with Cleveland and that was the end of it.

Between January and September of 1953, Pete dropped $40,000 in the used-car business in St. Louis, and then he got a job in a lumber mill for $100 a week. In the winter of 1955 he wrote Brooklyn asking for a part-time job as a scout, and on March 1, Buzzy Bavasi, the Dodger vice-president, called him on the phone.

"How would you like a manager's job?" Buzzy said.

"I'll take it," Pete said.

"I haven't even told you where it is. It's Thomasville, Georgia, in Class D."

"I don't care," Pete said. "I'll take it."

At Vero Beach that spring, Mike Gaven wrote a piece about Pete in the New York *Journal American.*

"Even in the worn gray uniform of the Class D Thomasville, Georgia, club," Mike wrote, "Pete Reiser looks, acts and talks like a big leaguer. The Dodgers pitied Pete when they saw him starting his comeback effort after not having handled a ball for two and a half years. They lowered their heads when they saw him in a chow line with a lot of other bushers, but the old Pistol held his head high…."

The next spring, Sid Friedlander, of the New York *Post,* saw Pete at Vero and wrote a column about him managing Kokomo. The last thing I saw about him in the New York papers was a small item out of Tipton, Indiana, saying that the bus carrying the Kokomo team had collided with a car and Pete was in a hospital in Kokomo with a back injury.

"Managing," Pete was saying in that St. Louis hospital, "you try to find out how your players are thinking. At Thomasville one night one of my kids made a bad throw. After the game I said to him: 'What were you thinking while that ball was coming to you?' He said: 'I was saying to myself that I hoped I could make a good throw.' I said: 'Sit down.' I tried to explain to him the way you have to think. You know how I used to think?"

"Yes," I said, "but you tell me."

"I was always sayin': 'Hit it to me. Just hit it to me. I'll make the catch. I'll make the throw.' When I was on base I was always lookin' over and sayin': 'Give me the steal sign. Give me the sign. Let me go.' That's the way you have to think."

"Pete," I said, "now that it's over, do you ever think that if you hadn't played it as hard as you did, there's no telling how great you might have been or how much money you might have made?"

"Never," Pete said. "It was my way of playin'. If I hadn't played that way I wouldn't even have been whatever I was. God gave me those legs and the speed, and when they took me to the walls that's the way it had to be. I couldn't play any other way."

A technician came in with an electrocardiograph. She was a thin, dark-haired woman and she set it up by the bed and attached one of the round metal disks to Pete's left wrist and started to attach another to his left ankle.

"Aren't you kind of young to be having pains in your chest?" she said.

"I've led a fast life," Pete said.

On the way back to New York I kept thinking how right Pete was. To tell a man who is this true that there is another way for him to do it is to speak a lie. You cannot ask him to change his way of going, because it makes him what he is.

Three days after I got home I had a message to call St. Louis. I heard the phone ring at the other end and Pete answered. "I'm out!" he said.

"Did they let you out, or did you sneak out again?" I said.

"They let me out," he said. "It's just a strained heart muscle, I guess. My heart itself is all right."

"That's wonderful."

"I can manage again. In a couple of days I can go back to Kokomo."

If his voice had been higher he would have sounded like a kid at Christmas.

"What else did they say?" I said.

"Well, they say I have to take it easy."

"Do me a favor," I said.

"What?"

"Take their advice. This time, please take it easy."

"I will," he said. "I'll take it easy."

If he does it will be the first time.

Some of Brooklyn's fans were as well known as the players. Perhaps the most famous fan of the 1940s and 1950s was Hilda Chester. She and her cowbell were known all over the ballpark.

Hilda, Leo, and Pistol Pete

Donald Honig

PETE REISER: Anyway, the Dodgers called me up on June 22, 1940. I felt great. I rode the bus all night into New York. Couldn't sleep a wink, I was so excited. The first game was a night game, and afterwards I'm leaving the ball park, and some big guy hits me on the shoulder.

"Hey, Pete," he says in this deep voice.

Here was the meanest-looking son of a bitch you ever saw. I asked myself, "What the hell does *he* want?"

"You don't know me, do you?" he says.

"No, I don't think so," I said.

"Well, I know you."

"From where?"

"Elmira," he says.

"Oh, you from Elmira?" I asked.

"No," he says. "I'm from Brooklyn. But you and the Elmira Pioneers came up there last year and played an exhibition game at the prison. Listen," he says, "I just got out. And I want to tell you I appreciate things like that from you athletes. Listen, anybody gives you trouble in this town, I want you to know I'm gonna be out there every ball game. You just whistle up to me. Anybody gives you trouble, they're dead."

Welcome to Brooklyn!

You know, I saw that guy out there as long as I played in Brooklyn. I'd walk out to center field, and he'd stand up and yell, "Everything all right, Pete?" "Great, buddy," I'd yell back.

You know, that Ebbets Field was a hell of a place to play ball. Some of those fans were unbelievable. And they were out there day after day. You got to know them. One who still stands out in my mind is Hilda Chester. She never missed a game, it

From *Baseball When the Grass Was Real* by Donald Honig. Reprinted by permission of the University of Nebraska Press. ©1975 by Donald Honig.

seemed. She'd sit out in the bleachers yelling in a foghorn voice and ringing this big cowbell she always carried. I remember one time, it was either '41 or '42; we were in the seventh inning of a game. I was going out to take my position in center field, and I hear that voice: "Hey, Reiser!" Hilda. There could be 30,000 people there yelling at once, but Hilda was the one you'd hear. I look up, and she's dropping something onto the grass. "Give this note to Leo," she yells. So I pick it up and put it in my pocket. At the end of the inning I start heading in.

Now MacPhail used to sit in a box right next to the dugout, and for some reason he waved to me as I came in, and I said, "Hi, Larry," as I went into the dugout. I gave Hilda's note to Leo and sat down. Next thing I know he's getting somebody hot in the bullpen; I think it was Casey. Meanwhile, Wyatt's pitching a hell of a ball game for us. In the next inning the first guy hits the ball pretty good and goes out. The next guy gets a base hit. Here comes Leo. He takes Wyatt out and brings in Casey. Casey got rocked a few times, and we just did win the game, just did win it.

Leo had this rule that after a game you didn't take off your uniform until he said so. Usually he didn't invoke it unless we lost a tough one. But this day he goes into his office and slams the door without a word. We're all sitting there waiting for him to come out. Finally the door opens and out he comes. He points at me.

"Don't you *ever* give me another note from MacPhail as long as you play for me."

"I didn't give you any note from MacPhail," I said. "That was from Hilda."

"From Hilda," he screams. I thought he was going to turn purple. "You mean to say that wasn't from MacPhail?"

I'd never even looked at the note, just handed it to him. Leo had heard me say something to MacPhail when I came in and figured the note was from Larry. It seems what the note said was: "Get Casey hot, Wyatt's losing it." So what you had was somebody named Hilda Chester sitting in the center-field bleachers changing pitchers for you. You talk about oddball things happening at Ebbets Field, you're not exaggerating.

There was a guy named Eddie, used to come out to all the games. He owned some apartment houses in Brooklyn. He was a real rabid fan. He came up to Boston with us in '41 when we clinched the pennant, and naturally he came back on the train with the team. Well, there was a big mob to meet us at Grand Central that night and the reporters are interviewing everybody who comes off the train. Somebody asks Eddie how he feels about it. He says, "I'm so happy about this I'm going to put all new toilet seats in my apartment buildings."

There really was no place like Brooklyn.

In his book Brooklyn's Dodgers, *Carl E. Prince, a professor of history at New York University, explored the cultural and sociological aspects of the borough and its baseball team. The following chapter describes the ethnicity of Brooklyn and how it relates to the Brooklyn Dodgers.*

THE DODGERS AND BROOKLYN'S ETHNIC ISOLATION

Carl E. Prince

Isolation was no stranger to the borough of Brooklyn. In the era before bridges and subways connected Brooklyn to Manhattan, geography imposed a quarantine on what was first a village and eventually a city. After those physical links were in place, cultural segregation persisted, extending Brooklyn's inward-looking tradition. From the late nineteenth century on, immigrants and their children generally stayed with their own. For its ethnic residents, Brooklyn was a borough of marbleized ghettos. The isolation was reflected in attitudes outside the borough. Brooklyn was not really thought to be part of New York City by "genuine" New Yorkers. There were the *New York Yankees,* and the *New York Giants* after all, but the *Bums* were the Brooklyn Dodgers. A corollary to this was the frequently confrontational nature of ethnic relationships in the borough, a hostility within that matched the sense of isolation without. The Dodgers formed an ameliorating force for unity in Brooklyn, but the team's local mystique did not miraculously bring all the people to love each other. Still, the Dodger presence helped.

As new neighborhoods rolled east from Brooklyn Heights, they reflected the realities of a ghettoization common generally to late nineteenth and early twentieth-century American cities. While the fashionable Heights, in the shadow of Brooklyn Bridge, remained generally bedrock elite, native, and protestant, the rest of Brooklyn was solidly ethnic: mainly Irish, Italian, and Jewish, with smaller groups of Scandinavians, Greeks, and Poles in the mix. By the end of the Second World War, a growing African American influx into what became Bedford-Stuyvesant augmented a small black community of long standing.

This was a remarkably diverse and equally tense cultural mix in a geographically contained area, and the Dodger ball club provided the major unifying focus amid this Joseph's Coat of a population. The degree to which this was true may be measured by the Dodgers' central place in the distinct language of Brooklyn. Overt class consciousness seemed to run higher in Brooklyn than elsewhere in the city, and the Dodgers' presence helped maintain an easy truce among ethnic groups. The comforting melting-pot notion of the American immigrant experience, with its emphasis on shared American values and a growing commonality of interests, has largely gone by the boards among American historians. The realities of immigrant differences dominated everyday life, as the Brooklyn experience yet again demonstrated. The Dodgers, in this tense setting, formed a social force for acculturation, perhaps an example of the larger role baseball has played in shaping American commonality in the twentieth century.

The borough's cultural isolation was accentuated, literally, by "Brooklynese," a dialect a shade deeper than common New York accents. It was closely identified in New York and the nation with "dem Bums." In fact the cartoon symbol of the Dodger Bum bespoke not only a scrappy and idiosyncratic baseball team but, in broader terms, the lower-middle-class origins of its ethnic fans. Because of Brooklyn's cultural isolation, both within the borough itself and as a distinct part of greater New York, the sense of class inferiority common to most first-and second-generation immigrants could only have been enhanced.

While the Dodger Bum was a visual symbol of some weight, through radio and movies in the 1930s and '40s, Brooklyn's harsh accents became even more nationally known as a signifier of the borough's apartness. That déclassé symbol was fixed deeply in the public mind during the Second World War. Because of William Bendix's starring role in *Wake Island*, a 1942 propaganda movie that hit home emotionally for many Americans after that island's capture by the Japanese, Americans related the "Brooklyn accent" to the Dodger team, and not incorrectly. After Bendix, the tough-talking Brooklyn fan became a stock character of war films.

Brooklyn became the butt of aggressive satire. When borough president John Cashmore was asked why the very name of Brooklyn would make people smile (or sometimes snicker), Cashmore replied, "It may be the whole world is pleased there is such a fine place as this." Cashmore's deft answer notwithstanding, he and many other Brooklyn denizens felt the sting of the intended ridicule. "Everybody was laughing at us," one said. "If you listened to a radio quiz program and a contestant said he came from Brooklyn, you heard a clamor of laughter from the studio audience." And you expected the contestant to lose, he added. Yankee manager Casey Stengel said on the eve of his only World Series loss to the Dodgers, "Trouble with Brooklyn, it's been insulted too long."

The Society for the Prevention of Disparaging Remarks Against Brooklyn was founded during the war, to respond wherever and whenever it came upon offensive slights of the borough. This was not some tongue-in-cheek invention, but an organization driven by an educational mission. By 1946, it claimed, with a good deal of exaggeration, 40,000 members. They culled 3000 slanders in the media that year alone. If this appears to be an excessive claim, note that H.L. Mencken saw it happening. In his 1948 edition of *The American Language,* he concluded that "the vulgar speech of New York City, once known as Boweryese, [is] now generally called Brooklynese." A good part of parodied English fixed on the Dodgers, and much of that reflected outsiders' perceptions of what they took to be semi-literate lower-class Brooklyn street talk. The language of "baseballese" (for example, Casey Stengel's popularized version), which in the borough cross-fertilized "Brooklynese," salted the latter with large doses of baseball lingo, as we shall see.

This satirical language, so widely ridiculed, coincided with the 1940s popularization of cartoonist Willard Mullins's Dodger Bum, the pictorial incarnation of the Dodgers' scrappy reputation. It was also an affirmation for many of the lower-class reputation of the borough. Leo O'Mealia, commemorating the Dodgers' 1955 World Championship, built his famous "Whose a Bum!" cartoon around Mullins's drawing. The "Bum" was never meant to denigrate the lowly. It represented at heart a lingering Depression mentality that exalted the virtue that it wasn't what you had that mattered, but how you looked at things. In this way, it was a Dodger-focused, widely understood symbol of working-class pride; the emphasis is on class here, for one of the Bum's roles was to mock perceived "upper class" pretensions.

Stephen King, a Brooklyn native, grew up a Dodger fan. In a youthful poem he remarked on "the faceless fans who cry down juicy vowels." Juicy they were. Recalling his first taste of Ebbets Field, Carl Erskine told of being spotted as he arrived at the Ebbets Field rotunda carrying his Fort Worth Cats duffel. "Hey, there's Oiskine. From Fort Woith. Hi, Oisk. "Oisk" he was forevermore, orally and all too often in print.

New York Post columnist Jimmy Cannon wrote ironically of Red Barber in 1952: "You notice they want someone to speak English on the radio they don't get no guy from Brooklyn. They get a guy from down South. It goes to prove they don't even like to hear themselves talk, don't it, when you got to get a yamer to speak for you." Was a "yamer" someone who ate yams? Someone who "yammers" for a living? Take your pick. Barber, columnist Steve Jacobson said years later, gave Brooklynites "tone and flavor and [new] expressions to mangle."

Establishment types habitually and, some might say, comically reinforced the propriety of the distinctive rules of grammar that touched Dodger-freighted Brooklynese. "The speechways of Dodger fans enriched the language," John Lardner wrote. "It was from this that philologists learned that the plural of 'ya bum, ya!' is 'yez bums, yez!'" The New York City Board of Education was asked to comment on the grammatical correctness of Charley Dressen's famous 1953 comment that "the Giants is dead." A Brooklyn board member responded, thinking naturally of the impressionable young: "Of course," the educator explained, "if one member of the Giants were alive, like Maglie, you could not say the Giants *is* dead. But if every member of this entity is dead, hence the Giants *is* too."

The language of the Brooklyn streets brought an irresistible urge to parody even fellow Brooklynites. William Poster, in "Twas a Dark Night in Brownsville," recounts how a suddenly self-conscious Brooklyn boy responded to an outsider's query on his turf: "Where ya from? ... Ahah! Dat's in Brahnsvil, hah, hah, Brahnsvil. Noo? Howz Peetkin Avenue?"

Brooklynites' sensitivity to these seemingly endless satires ran deep, and language was only part of the problem. They were often defensive. Dodger fans knew they had a winner in the great team Branch Rickey put together after World War II. But continuing heart-wrenching losses to "New York" ball clubs hurt. The Yankees won the World Series with sodden regularity, and the Giants' "miracle" in 1951 was devastating, reinforcing the star-crossed feeling in Brooklyn that "we never win it all."

It was as much a class thing as it was cultural isolation. "It ties up with a sort of social neurosis," sportswriter Joe Williams said, "an elegant, smug New York versus a plain, provincial Brooklyn." Compared with mainland baseball fans, "Dodger fans are vulgar," one Manhattanite characteristically commented. Arthur Daley of the *New York Times* put the stereotype succinctly in 1949: the Dodgers had become a great team, he concluded, but the Brooklyn fan "has the brashness and ostentation of the nouveau riche while the Yankee fan has the conservatism and slightly disdainful superiority of the born aristocrat." This cultural isolationism and its accompanying defiance of the world had another side: Brooklyn's "specialness" was also a source of pride. Both sides of that lower-class archetype that passed for a Brooklyn fan in the public prints were equally present in a patronizing poem Grantland Rice, an elder statesman among sports columnists, wrote in lieu of his usual *New York Sun* column. It was meant to be complimentary; it wasn't:

> He's a neolithic throwback to the past....
> As he concentrates upon the vocal blast....
> But he's hooked up with an outfit
> that can feed him daily thrills,
> Which is something millionaires can never buy.

The *Times*'s sportswriters in particular repeatedly exploited the perception of class gulf that separated Brooklyn from Manhattan. They rarely visited Ebbets Field, as if they felt uncomfortable there. But a descriptive, class-based column deliberately blurring the line between the borough and the team was apparently accepted as insightful. For example, Arthur Daley wrote in 1953 that "because of Brooklyn's raffish past a Yankee fan automatically assumes an air of aristocratic superiority on the eve of any World Series." On another occasion he cited nameless "baseball people" for this quote: "Dodger fans were insufferable enough when they had nothing. They'll be completely unbearable now when they have everything." In another anonymous "it's been said" representation, John Lardner described the Dodger appeal as "brash, low, even buffoonish." This comment came late, in 1956, when the Dodgers were the reigning world champions. Lardner added there is a "school of thought [again anonymous] that has always associated the Brooks with déclassé phenomena like El lines, cobblestones and walk-up rooming houses." Throwaway remarks like these were bald allusions to perceived class differences that distanced Brooklyn from "New York."

Peter Golenbock, with great insight, catches this class consciousness, revealing that "The Bums" and the borough alike were interchangeable within the web of lower-middle-class outsiders' perceptions. His oral histories are laced with examples of outside-imposed class consciousness, whether referring to the team or the town. The 1955 World Series win over the Yankees meant to one representative Brooklyn native that "a whole city ... now can raise its head, look across the river ... and say, 'We're number one.'" The price of class ran very high, psychologically and otherwise, as it turned out.

The déclassé image of Dodger fans was deeply ingrained in the larger New York culture. Even *Psychology Today*, a later icon of the educated upper middle class, unconsciously picked up the existing stereotype of Brooklyn fans in a 1978 article on why people root for certain teams. The author noted in passing that a six-year-old became a Yankee fan because his mother bought him a Yankee cap from a street display featuring three New York teams. The mother, the author said, picked the Yankee hat because "Dodger blue was too bold." It was in fact a stylish navy blue, so memory seems quirky here, psychologist's credentials notwithstanding. But the point is his conclusion: "My mother was a woman of taste and class," so the Dodger cap was out.

Class differences were not the same as ethnic differences in Brooklyn. Ethnics in Brooklyn were largely lower-middle-class, but their sameness stopped there, as academics have recently discovered. There have been several recent studies of baseball that include general examination of fans' social roots, and two deep studies of Brooklyn's neighborhoods (Canarsie and Brownsville). These collectively make clear, as George Will affirms, that baseball in part crystallizes Americans' "yearning for community."

Gerald Sorin's study of Brownsville youth confirms locally that widely held belief. A significant part of Jewish street culture in Brownsville revolved around the Dodgers, and the team figured largely in the consciousness of the Brownsville Boys Club. In fact, its founder and patron saint, Abe Stark, made a political career out of his combined identification with the Dodgers and the Boys Club.

Ball clubs, Ray Robinson has written, "invariably duplicate the temperament of the cities in which they play," and he characterized Dodger fans as "underdog, recidivist ... from a land of people with hard-to-pronounce names." That Brooklyn was ethnic was a fact widely perceived in the nation as one of the sources of its strangeness. No team "had more fans with foreign accents" than the Brooklyn Dodgers, said Wilfred Sheed, a Dodger fan who had one himself. Inasmuch as foreign origin and lower-class assignment by the majority native culture usually went hand-in-hand, Brooklyn was an especially obvious example of this American social judgment.

Brooklyn's experience with the Dodgers was not unique. Chicago and its Cubs and Boston and its Red Sox offer up analogous examples. The ballclubs, in these instances, seemed often to take on the character of their communities even as they provided deep unifying forces within those cities. Is it possible to see this phenomenon as sport-related social symbiosis at work? If so, then Brooklyn was one city that needed any unifying force a baseball team could provide.

The borough was ethnically atomized. Almost all its neighborhoods were ghettos, immigrant and racial enclaves of largely homogenous groups. The neighborhood was as much the base point of residents' loyalty as the borough. Where local identity was concerned, greater New York City was not even in the contest. Yet in an isolated environment, Brooklynites shared common bonds: Brooklyn's children and their first-and-second generation parents spoke a common and unique street language; all felt detached from the greater city of which they were a political part; most felt ill-judged by outsiders who looked down on them (a pretty good defining component of class awareness, if not of class difference, all by itself); and locals were defensive about the misconceptions the rest of the world seemed to hold about them.

Linguists in particular in the generation after World War II seemed mesmerized by the hidden meanings of Brooklyn's language and culture, especially the latter's relationship to the Dodgers. "To the world," philologist B. A. Botkin concluded in 1954, "'Dem Bums' spells out not only the Dodgers but much-maligned Brooklyn." Francis Griffiths, in a 1972 essay, said that "these linguistic confusions in Brooklyn were the reflections of deeper confusions. They mirrored the inverted psychology of natives who called their heroes 'Bums.'" Borough dwellers in general, Griffiths concluded, possessed a very poor self-image. Academic insights like these, linguist Goeffrey Needler concluded, together formed "fearful evidence of Brooklyn's dark, sidereal pathology." As if to bear all this out, the borough never seemed more star-crossed than it did when it responded so explosively to sportswriter Jimmy Cannon's infamous *New York Post* column satirizing its Dodger-centered provincialism. Led by their cheerleaders at the *Brooklyn Eagle*, many Brooklynites responded in much the same way as hornets do when their hive is threatened.

Writing a tongue-in-cheek column in pseudo–Brooklynese describing the implications of recent Dodger success, Cannon deftly pushed all of Brooklyn's buttons. "The way they holler about the Dodgers," Cannon wrote in the summer of 1952, "you think they had a choice.... Over in Brooklyn you got to root for the Dodgers or root for the Bushwicks." This essay mauled the borough by parading the stereotypes by which it was known. "All they got in Brooklyn is to go to a ball game or stay at home and get loaded. If you don't, you got to come to New York any time you want to have a little fun." And still, Cannon continued, Dodger fans have delusions of grandeur. "Brooklyn, Brooklyn, Brooklyn, I'm sick of hearing it. The way they talk you think it was a whole country with an army and a king or something. All they got is a ball club."

The "borough of churches" took a pasting, and the word "bum" was sprinkled liberally through the narrative: "Lots of Brooklyn bums I know would never go inside a church unless they could rob the poor box. But Churches, churches, churches is all you hear from them. Let's face it, Brooklyn is out of town." The cemeteries also came in for a few caresses: "It groums me because I got to get buried in that lousy place," Cannon wrote, but what choice did he have? If you lived in Manhattan, you either got buried in the boroughs or, God forbid, Jersey.

The *Brooklyn Eagle* was furious. An editorial called Cannon's satire "coarse, even obscene," a "filthy attack upon [our] hometown ... upon its churches ... upon its cemeteries where our loved ones are buried." The *Eagle* deliberately fanned the embers of local outrage into a red-hot blaze. Columnist Robert Grannis, calling Cannon "Mr. Screwball," used the event to lash out at Manhattan's perpetual seizure of the lion's share of the city's resources, long a Brooklyn complaint. "The only mistake we ever made, sweetheart, was when we merged with the other boroughs."

It was, all in all, a vituperative and very defensive response, one that put an exclamation point to an almost institutionalized self-consciousness that personified Brooklyn's frustration with its inferior political and social station in greater New York City. Judging from the popular response, the borough felt itself almost pathologically isolated from the world around it.

Predictably, the *Eagle*'s aggressive retort uncorked a ton of letters. A few pointed out that Cannon's essay was genuinely funny, in both dialect and content, and no big deal. But the vast majority were pained outpourings of individuals who gave voice to long pent-up chagrin over the perceived disrespect accorded Brooklyn. Cannon touched a nerve. Residents by the hundreds expressed outrage at yet again suffering disrespect. The *Post* sportswriter's reference to "a bum from Brooklyn" who "never said a prayer in his life" in particular drew angry responses. James Kelly, Deputy County Clerk for Brooklyn and a well-connected local pol, in one of the more pompous rejoiners reminded Cannon that if he "had taken time out to see the thousands of God-fearing, God-loving people turning out to attend divine services … his filthy pen might have been stayed."

A gold-star mother, on the other hand, wrote poignantly that her son was "a bum from Brooklyn who now lies in a Brooklyn cemetery, a 'bum' who dared to die for the likes of James Cannon."

The allusions to Cannon's references to "bum" rang the bell in Brooklyn. Many tied their responses to perceptions of elitist Giants fans from Manhattan and the suburbs. Mary Nockowitz and others wrote that they wished the response to the *Eagle* could have been printed in the *New York Post*, "where those Giant fans could have read it and hang their heads in shame." Still smarting from the 1951 Giant "miracle" and its associated history of a long, deeply personalized rivalry, one large group of responses to Cannon was linked to newly reopened wounds caused by the eternal Giant-Dodger enmity. Cannon only wrote the column, one Dodger partisan said, "because the Giants' fans must rationalize the fact" that the Dodgers were leading the league. The Bum, many said, would triumph in the end.

In essence, the Dodger Bum, the sense of inferiority many Brooklynites felt within the context of the greater city, and the longstanding rivalry with the Giants were all wrapped up in the widespread overreaction. "Don't worry," Grace Ward reminded her townspeople, "it's the slams that made Brooklyn famous."

So if any place needed the face a winning major league team could provide, it was Brooklyn. The Dodgers were really part of the soul of the community, and the team's eventual departure must be understood in that light. Not until just before its move to Los Angeles, when the team became world champions at last, one writer has said, "would Brooklyn expunge its image as Sad Sack of the Globe." Roger Kahn caught well the nearly spiritual role the Dodgers played in Brooklyn in the face of this siege mentality. In a short retrospective piece he quoted this poetic excerpt: "Lives rooted in weary brownstones … /were lit up by the gods at play nearby."

Meat-handed humor was inescapable. Brooklyn was a distant place, a different place, Brooklynites a species apart. "It was rumored," *P.M.* reported, that "Professor Ernest A. Hooton, head of Howard [University's] Department of Anthropology, was in the stands for the purpose of studying the Brooklyn rooters, but this couldn't be

verified." The Dodgers provided a singular and critical source of positive, even aggressive, response, a validation of the class-grittiness that white natives embraced in the
borough. The ball club's newly reinforced image, though, did not build a bridge to
African-Americans in Brooklyn.

A 1954 *Brooklyn Eagle* serialized survey of neighborhoods identified the changing character of what was for the first time being "loosely" called Bedford-Stuyvesant.
It was an emerging ghetto increasingly inhabited by Hispanic and African Americans. Irish, Italians, and Jews were often hostile to them. Jackie Robinson's visibil-
ity mattered at one level of consciousness; but at another level, an increasing black
presence in the population sent out shock waves, a reaction seemingly divorced from
the example of Brooklyn's almost uniquely integrated ball club.

Jews, feeling the pain of discrimination themselves, were nevertheless often fear-
fully anti-black. Their exodus to New Jersey and, in particular, Westchester and Long
Island, began in earnest in the early 1950s. "Ninety-five percent of them have been
mugged and moved away." Then, as now, that was code for race prejudice. "With
blacks moving in came great fear," one Jewish observer noted. "There was block-
busting. There was panic selling ... parasites and vultures (real estate agents) who
circle any changing or transitional neighborhood." One African American angrily told
Jonathan Rieder that "people forget one thing: I didn't destroy *their* Brownsville."

Another uncomfortable truth was that Irish and Italians fully shared Jewish attitudes towards blacks and felt aggrieved in general at the threat to neighborhood
seemingly posed by African American and Hispanic encroachment. "Blacks moved
in and whites fled" was a common Italian perception, as they followed Jews to Long
Island, according to Jonathan Rieder. "Respect" is a freighted word among Italian
Americans, embracing a sociological concept involving definable conscious feelings
of honor and deference due. As African Americans moved in, one Italian worker said,
"Respect, it's been lost."

White groups were no better with each other. Alan Lelchuk, a novelist, indulged
a common stereotype applied by Jews to Italians by characterizing Carl Furillo's
"patrolling the right field pasture" as the rightful work of "an Italian gardener." Peter
Golenbock reported that as Thomson's home run carried into the left-field stands at
the Polo Grounds in 1951, an Irish grandfather "bent over, called Branca a 'dago bastard,' spit at the screen, and keeled over dead."

Eagle columnist Tommy Holmes ran a story in 1951 featuring the complaints
that fans had sent him about perceived changes at Ebbets Field. The perpetual presence of "drunks" in the park figured prominently among the laments and was an
encoded reference to the Irish regulars who attended many games. Allan Guttmann,
an academic, fell into the same trap, unconsciously stereotyping Irish fans in talking about baseball as the sport of choice for "blue collar" Irish, and relating it to the
saloons around ball parks generally run by "Irish political bosses." Even the liberal
daily *P.M.* unthinkingly bought into the characterization of Irish fans as universally
hard-drinking. The "majority" of Irish Dodger partisans, *P.M.* reported in 1947, "listen to a Dodger broadcast within the cozy confines of a bar and grill."

The Irish were no better in the aggregate than Jews and Italians in firing off prej-
udicial broadsides. One Irish correspondent wrote Tommy Holmes denouncing "the

increasing presence of foreign-language speaking families" (Puerto Ricanos) in Ebbets Field as the 1950s dawned. Roger Kahn reminded readers that in Brooklyn, "on Sundays the Irish of St. Teresa's Parish worshipped a gentle Christ. Other days some of them distributed the fascist newspaper *Social Justice*," a product of the anti–Semite priest Charles Coughlin, which "warned of a revolution being organized by Jews."

Although Brooklyn was a metropolis, with three million people, it lacked even the limited political autonomy of a city, and thus any real political control over its own destiny. Large as it was, it was only a minority component of an even more mammoth urban entity. The problem was compounded because by far the largest part of the population felt itself marginalized for ethnic, racial, or economic reasons. The difficulty was magnified in the 1950s, as many of those with the means moved out. The white immigrant minorities, especially, felt a deepening sense of ethnic and racial embattlement. Each Brooklyn immigrant group had always stereotyped the others as it competed for space, political access, and work. After World War II the social transition that took place took the form of the suburbanization of American life, and that only magnified Brooklyn's urban problems.

Few escaped the sting of a prejudice newly reinvigorated by the departures. The decamping of the Dodger franchise in its turn needs to be understood in the context of these other 1950s exoduses from Brooklyn. African Americans and Puerto Ricanos who replaced the departing whites were routinely made invisible when they were not otherwise disparaged. Jews felt the pressures imposed by a widespread feeling that they were largely left-liberal in a politically conservative borough; had they not spawned Judith Coplon (convicted of espionage) and buried the Rosenbergs in their midst? Italians, both Jonathan Rieder and Jerry Della Femina made clear, felt a generalized lack of respect from outsiders who lived alongside them. When newspapers wrote engagingly about colorful Brooklyn watering holes devoted to their Bums, the subtext was that they were Irish bars where some serious drinking took place.

Peter Levine suggests that this harsh view of ethnic division may be exaggerated. In *From Ellis Island to Ebbets Field* he makes the point that sports played such a large part in Brooklyn's Jewish life that it softened the rough edges of immigrant confrontation. This was especially true in the development of a fellow feeling between Irish and Jews in Brooklyn and elsewhere, particularly when boxing was the sport. Deborah Dash Moore, on the other hand, suggests in *At Home in America* a New York tapestry of separation of Jewish ethnics from other immigrant groups. A strong inner sense of Jewish community prevented much bonding with other immigrant groups who shared Jewish outsider status.

The other side of this story, then, deserves mention. The study of history is in part the study of social paradox, and Brooklyn formed no exception in embodying historic inconsistency. People got along in Brooklyn's insular environment because there were things that brought them together as well as things that divided them. It wasn't only the Dodgers. There was as well a shared sense of embattlement, a common and much-maligned language, a pervasive male youth culture, and a shared role as outsiders.

The Dodgers, however, proved to be a much-needed catalyst, so the team's presence was central to the sense of community. While the Dodgers did not make tensions go away, the team's universality in the borough, both real and psychic, helped ease social stress. It provided the single largest common center of local identification in a complex urban society, and rounded off the roughest edges of social pressure by periodically bringing Brooklyn together. As I said before, this is not a unique baseball phenomenon. It happened the same way, I suspect, in other immigrant-laden communities, Boston and Chicago providing possibly the most visible examples.

"The city's soul" is the phrase that Alan Lelchuk used in *Brooklyn Boy* to describe the depths of loss the Dodgers' departure inflicted on Brooklyn. "Forget the sweatshops," Lelchuk wrote, "forget the class wars, forget the family squabbles, forget the racial antagonisms ... forget the anger and quiet despair." The Dodgers offered many inhabitants a national face and more: "All the subtle art of baseball was put on display by the Dodgers." The Dodger presence was very close to the spiritual core of the community in an otherwise racially, religiously, and ethnically divided city. Neil Sullivan, in *The Dodgers Move West*, has amplified the immediate meaning of the loss of the Dodgers to the borough. He wrote of the anguish, pain, and loss of focus for the retired, the working-class parents and their kids. The erosion of community in Brooklyn in the years following 1957 cannot fully be laid at the door of the Dodgers, for that erosion was part of a larger urban malaise present in most American cities. But the Dodgers' departure contributed.

III. Middle Innings

...the magnolia-scented voice of Red Barber coming in over the
radio from Ebbets Field softly suffusing the night, giving the feel
of a front porch. Preacher on the mound, Pee Wee patrolling short,
Robbie just beside him, and Hilda Chester of Flatbush swinging
a cow bell between pitches.
Dem Bums— That team, in that neighborhood, seemed exactly
what a national game is supposed to be.

—Jackie Robinson and the Integration of Baseball
by Scott Simon

Scott Simon in his book Jackie Robinson and the Integration of Baseball *sets the stage for Jackie's entrance to the big leagues when he aptly describes Brooklyn in 1947. If you were there, you would yearn for a chocolate egg cream.*

BROOKLYN, 1947

Scott Simon

At the end of World War II, Brooklyn was often regarded as Manhattan's sister among the New York boroughs. Comically plump, a little plain, perhaps—but with an appealing personality. In the way in which siblings find themselves assigned roles in families, Brooklyn was the sidekick to Manhattan's star, a one-word setup to a punch line: "I'm from Brooklyn. And in Brooklyn, we…"

Manhattan was the borough of office towers and neon lights, while Brooklyn proclaimed itself the borough of well-attended churches, neatly tended trees, and trolleys. Manhattan was Carnegie Hall, Gershwin, Toscanini, and Duke Ellington's Harlem. Brooklyn was Coney Island, stickball, half-sour dills, and doo-wop.

Manhattan was "the city," where fathers worked, mothers shopped, and children were taken a few times a year to buy a new coat, see a museum or show (although Brooklyn had outstanding museums, stage shows, and bargain racks), and ride the subway back home. Manhattan was a destination. But Brooklyn was where the city *lived.*

Brooklyn was forlornly incorporated into greater New York in 1898. But it was never quite reconciled to being one of five boroughs of an empire city. In the 1940s, Brooklyn rolled over eighty square miles and was filled with at least thirty distinct neighborhoods and almost three million residents. Had Brooklyn been left contentedly autonomous, it would have rivaled Chicago as America's Second City.

Manhattan, of course, is an island, defined by rugged escarpments and man-made shores, each inch precious for being so scarce. Brooklyn had its own shore along Coney Island and Brighton Beach, but beyond that widened into a vast urban interior that gave much of the borough the feel of an inland city—flat, broad, almost midwestern. Great ships docked in Manhattan, but they were built in the Brooklyn Navy Yard.

Manhattan had a landscape of towers and skyscrapers that was identifiable in most places around the world. But Brooklyn had its own distinct panorama: church spires and three-story brownstones, small parishes and neighborhood shuls, trolley cables spitting sparks and children leaning out to shout over flower boxes, black-topped school yards and precinct houses, redbrick factories and red-lit corner saloons, bare-chested men in shorts and tall black socks tanning their shoulders while sitting on tarpaper apartment house roofs, and drying laundry flapping against fire escape rails.

Manhattan was New York's crown. Brooklyn was the city's heart and lungs.

The delis in Brooklyn's Williamsburg were distinctively perfumed by kosher dills bobbling in brine, and the scent of honey cake and challah. There were old red-checkered tablecloth Italian *jernts* in Red Hook serving spaghetti with garlicky red clam sauce and speckled bricks of spumoni. There were yeasty-scented Irish pubs in Flatbush, glowering and giddy, and spotless Scandinavian bakeries in Bay Ridge, sober and bright. Street stands in Canarsie sold long skinny salted pretzels and tech-nicolored Italian ices, while men with handkerchief-hats fluffed over their bald heads clacked bocce balls and families sat on stoops below their open windows, Caruso, Sinatra, and Louis Prima crackling over record players out into the streets, as kids bickered over stoopball rules, played for stakes of lime rickeys, malted milks, and egg creams.

Manhattan boasted that the world came to its doorstep. But Brooklyn was at the Statue of Liberty's side door, and much of the world moved in. There were Italian, Irish, Poles, and Swedes, Germans in Bensonhurst, and blacks who had moved up from the South into Stuyvesant Heights. There were Russians in Greenpoint, some of New York's first Syrians and West Indians, and, most exotic of all, a community of Newfoundlanders, fishing families, who had come to settle in Prospect Park West.

More than a third of the borough's population was Jewish. In the mid–1940s, Brooklyn was probably the world's largest Jewish territory. Williamsburg, Benson-hurst, and Crown Heights abounded with Jews of every variation, from Orthodox to Reform, secular to Hasidic and Lubavitcher; from stoop-backed Talmudic schol-ars wrapped in shimmering sharkskin suits. Brooklyn Jews were considered LaGuar-dia and Roosevelt lovers (both Franklin and Eleanor), *New York Post* and *PM* readers, and champions of Henry Wallace, the Hollywood Ten, Leon Trotsky, kibbutzniks, and fellow travelers. From Pistol Pete Reiser to Paul Robeson, Brooklyn loved lefties.

This figured in the thinking of Branch Rickey, who left the St. Louis Cardinals to become general manager of Brooklyn's baseball team in 1942. He had run the St. Louis Cardinals for nine years. Missouri was an old border state in which segrega-tion was still observed, but Brooklyn was a different territory. White Brooklynites were not any more liberal than most white Alabamians when it came to welcoming blacks next door. But Branch Rickey believed that he might persuade Brooklyn Dodger fans to accept an accomplished black athlete in the Brooklyn Dodger infield.

All characterizations of a place as vast and varied as Brooklyn were, of course, incomplete. In 1947, Brooklyn also had some avenues so elegant (still does) as to make Central Park West covetous. It had outposts of high culture, a dense and intense society, a cosmopolitan outlook, and — a last mark of a vital society — its own utterly distinct accent. Manhattan was "Rhapsody in Blue," bright lights, and DiMagg. Brooklyn was *dese, dose,* and *dem* — Dem Bums.

Only a team greatly loved could become known by so many nicknames. *Dodgers* itself was shortened from *Trolley Dodgers,* the sobriquet Manhattanites hung on all citizens of the borough across the East River. *Dem Bums* was the moniker meted out by a frustrated fan who sat in the grandstand seats just below the press box. Other fans and reporters picked up his bleats whenever Dodgers booted ground balls, threw to the wrong base, or — as they did at least once in a game against the Boston Braves in 1926 — contrived to have three base runners arrive at third base at the same time. Who's on first? *Evvverybody!* The team was also called *the Flock,* from the days when they were managed by Wilbert Robinson, and his players were known as *the Robins.* Manhattan sports sections tended to boldface them as *the Brooks.*

The Dodgers, by any and all of their names, grew out of the Brooklyn baseball team that was created for the old American Association in 1884. They were determinedly un–Yankee-like from the first. The Dodgers cultivated working-class fans by playing their games on Sundays, the only full day off for many laborers. Ticket prices were cheap, so as to leave sufficient budget for beer, from which the team made its real money.

Brooklynites spoke of the team with an affection that was deepened by familiarity, identification, and accumulating frustration. Fans followed and admired the Yankees; they cheered for the Giants; they lived and died with the Dodgers. Ebbets Field was as flesh-and-blood familiar to most Brooklynites as their own block, their church, or their synagogue. The Dodgers were community property in a port of entry for immigrants and new arrivals. In a borough that often felt stunted and overshadowed by the towers of Manhattan, the Dodgers were an emblem of big-city status. As much as the Brooklyn Bridge, Ebbets Field was a gateway to an enchanted territory.

Yankee Stadium was as large and sumptuous as a great cathedral. But Ebbets Field, at 55 Sullivan Place flat smack in the middle of Flatbush, was small and close, *haimish,* as was said in the delis and shuls of Williamsburg. With just 32,000 seats, it held some of the same disordered warmth and jumble of an overstuffed family apartment. The first and third base foul lines were no farther from fans' seats than the length of an apartment house hallway. Yankee fans might be able to see Phil Rizzuto smile, but Dodger fans could see when Pee Wee Reese broke into a sweat. Clothier Abe Stark put up a signboard in right-center field:

HIT SIGN, WIN SUIT

Few did. (The fence in right center field, happily enough for Abe Stark, was the farthest from home plate at 403 feet; the left field foul post was fixed just 357 feet away — where a sign could have cost Mr. Stark a lot of haberdashery.) But the implication was also important: while Yankee sluggers got tailored on Fifth Avenue, journeymen Dodgers slugged for Abe Starks's sign. There was a gap at the bottom of the metal gate in right center field, which was thoughtfully left unbreached, so Brooklyn kids could put their sweaters and chins carefully against the sidewalk and see the backsides of Carl Furillo and Eddie Stanky chase plays around the field. A brewery installed a neon sign atop the right-center scoreboard:

SCHAEFER

The H blinked to signify a hit; the E lit up when the scorer ruled an error. The Dodger Symphony, a five-piece band from Greenpoint, kept a chorus going in the left field bleachers through most home games, playing "Three Blind Mice" when the umpires took the field. The close quarters and familial kidding, the birth-day cakes fans dropped off at the locker room for their favorite players, the players hanging on a passenger strap in a Brighton Beach train car on its way to Ebbets Field, riding the subway like any workman — all made the Dodgers part of Brooklyn's heart-beat.

The Dodgers reached the World Series in 1916 and 1920; they lost. They finished fifth and sixth through the rest of the 1920s, then sank into last place during the 1930s. Those were the decades in which the team's character was instilled: winsome losers, adorable incompetents, perennial basement-dwellers buoyed by steadfast fans with pungent accents. Westbrook Pegler, the best-read columnist of the time, dubbed them "The Daffiness Boys."

Baseball clubs seeking tax breaks from their communities like to point out that sports teams are also cultural institutions. By the 1940s, the Brooklyn Dodgers were more of a cultural institution than a competitive baseball team.

The team was revitalized in 1939 when an operator named Larry MacPhail came to town from Cincinnati to run the club. They played the first of their World Series against the New York Yankees in 1941, and were about to win the fourth game to tie the Yankees at two apiece when Hugh Casey threw a strikeout curve to Tommy Hen-rich. But the spin of the curve was so strong — or, as some Brooklyn fans might have it, the fates were so fixed — that the ball slipped through the web of the glove of catcher Mickey Owen and dribbled toward the backstop, guided by a force no more visible than that which steers a candy wrapper across a street. Owen, a shrewd and experienced catcher, began to turn as soon as he felt the ball was missing from his mitt. But his path to the ball was blocked, by blue-suited New York cops with their backs turned to keep Dodger fans from rushing the field in celebration. Henrich took first base. The Yankees scored four runs to win that game, and then won the next one, to win the World series. Brooklyn had just begun to mend its crushed heart two months later, when Pearl Harbor was bombed.

Half a century after they left Flatbush for Los Angeles, the Brooklyn Dodgers are still among the best-known sports franchises in history. The name of a team so profitably departed is probably still better known than that of most teams that have come into baseball by expansion over the past generation. The players, arrayed in loose-fitting flannels with a cursive *Brooklyn* rolling over their chests like the inter-lacing lines of diverse clans and villages; and the ways in which the fans found them-selves reflected in the players, the field, and even the feeling that their striving often went overlooked and unrewarded, all amounted to absolute empathy.

We can still treat ourselves to a reverie of Brooklyn on a summer's night: front room windows lifted open up and down the broad avenues, Atlantic, Neptune, and Flatlands; bikes at rest against candy stores, women in flowered housedresses watch-ing kids clamor over brownstone stoops on small, tight streets; the rumble of the BMT against your toes; the overhead iron clangor of the elevated train prickling your ears; the aroma of the Taystee Bread bakery perfuming the walk over from Prospect Park Station; and the magnolia-scented voice of Red Barber coming in over the radio from Ebbets Field (in Brooklyn, after all, Mississippians were just another group of immigrants) softly suffusing the night, giving the streets the feel of a front porch. Preacher on the mound, Pee Wee patrolling short, Robbie just beside him, and Hilda Chester of Flatbush swinging a cowbell between pitches. *Dem Bums.* That team, in that neighborhood, seemed exactly what a national game is *supposed to be.*

The day finally came. Jackie Robinson was the first African American to appear on a major league ball field in the twentieth century. In addition to the abuse and the bigotry he'd had to face, there was now a right-hander named Johnny Sain to contend with.

Jackie Robinson's First Major League Baseball Game

Jimmy Cannon

[April 15, 1947:] Someone such as Norman Corwin should sit down at a typewriter and intelligently explain to the people beyond the Hudson what happened at Ebbets Field yesterday as the Dodgers opened their season by beating the Braves, 5–3. It would be small compensation for the abuse the people of Brooklyn have taken from the incompetent and unfunny liars who describe them as Metropolitan hillbillys. There were 25,623 of them in the joint and they behaved with dignity and compassion. Their wit was clean and good-humored as they pulled for Jackie Robinson as he struggled through a hitless day. They had opportunities to chastise him and no one could have quarreled with their peevishness because he hit into a double play and seemed tight and unnatural as he played first base. They convinced him they were going to be square with him and that cooled off some of the heat that burns around him constantly because he is the first Negro ever to come up in what even in the reign of Happy Chandler is still our national sport.

After the ball game Robinson sat off from the other players with Eddie Tolan, the old Olympic sprinter, and the misery of his impotence at the plate dissipated as soon as he spoke about what has happened to him since coming to Brooklyn.

"The help I've had on the ball club," he said. "It's really something."

Someone asked him how he liked playing first base because he had come up a shortstop, was switched to second and now is trying to learn the mechanics of another strange position.

"It's a tough play for me," he said. "A man on first and a left-handed hitter. I don't know when to jump off the bag. It will backfire in a tough spot if I don't learn."

I asked him what impressed him most on his first day as a big-leaguer. He made a gesture as though he were throwing a ball, letting his wrist flop limply as he completed the motion.

"The way Johnny Sain threw the fast ball and the curve in the same motion," Robinson answered.

"Is Sain the best pitcher you ever hit against?" Tolan asked.

"I hit against Bob Feller on the exhibition tour," Robinson said.

"Sain is a hell of a pitcher," a guy said.

"If Sain doesn't give me more trouble than any other pitcher I'm going to face," Robinson said, and then paused to laugh, "it's going to be a very tough season."

The sports journalist said the crowd didn't get on him and they wanted to see him stick.

"I know the crowd was pulling for me," Jackie said. "I could hear them at first base. They're sure with me. I hope I can keep them with me by playing some baseball for them."

"You will," a guy said. "After a while the pressure will lift."

"When the game starts I don't give that a thought," Robinson said. "My only hope is I can be of some service to the Dodgers."

"How do you feel, Jackie?" said a sports writer who had just walked in.

"Great," he said. "You always feel great when you win."

Baseball has been an inspiration for fiction for a very long time. In his novel, Mr. Renino has chosen an interesting perspective, the Brooklyn Dodgers of 1947 as seen through the eyes of their bat boy. Ralph Branca won 21 games for the Dodgers that year. In this excerpt, he pitched a gem.

JULY 18, 1947

Christopher Renino

Late the next afternoon, I hung the Dodgers' newly cleaned uniforms in their lockers and tried to picture the LaVistas driving to the shore. The shore I imagined was gray and silent, interrupted now and then by a dry complaint from Mrs. Alcott about Mr. LaVista's driving, but for all I knew, they were talking and laughing happily, freed from Brooklyn and the strain of the past month. I felt relieved when the clubhouse started to fill, and I followed Furillo and Reiser up to the field and ran off some of my mood by shagging batting practice in the outfield. But when I went back down to the clubhouse to finish my pregame chores, Sam's fleeting smile and Alma's tearful face followed me and wouldn't leave. I felt empty and drained.

All week long the *Eagle* had run stories about how this series with the Cardinals was the biggest series of the year. If Durocher had still been manager he'd have kicked a few chairs into sticks and given the Dodgers an earful: "Fuckin' this" and "Fuckin' that" and "Those guys swept you in St. Louis last month. You don't wake up now, they'll leave town with your peckers in their pockets." But there wasn't any of that from Shotton — there never was. Team meetings were between him and his players. With a cagey smile, he quietly shut the clubhouse door, leaving the rest of us standing in the corridor, trying to guess what words he'd choose to go with his dull, flat tone. I pictured the guys fidgeting, anxious for him to finish, and wondered what good a talk like that would do. He needed to fire them up, not put them to sleep. The door finally opened and the Dodgers made their way down the tunnel toward the dugout, toward the field, toward the noise from the keyed-up crowd that moved white-shirted through the stands, scraps of light beneath the early moon and seeping darkness. Shotton came up soon after, spruce in perfectly creased pants and a short-sleeved shirt. He glanced around the ballpark and said to himself, sounding almost surprised, "Full house." Then, uncharacteristically, he turned to me, his smile faint but sly, and said, "You think the boys are excited about playing for this crowd, Stidgie?" and I realized that he'd set the guys up. He bored the team into readiness. It made me see him in a new way.

At the All-Star break, Shotton had arranged the rotation so that Branca would start this game against Red Munger, who'd only lost twice all year. Ralph brought it to the Cardinals good right from the first pitch, and after he set them down in order in the first, Stanky led off our half of the inning with a skipping, skimming ground shot that hugged the foul line all the way into the right field corner. By the time the relay came back to the infield, Eddie was on third and the crowd was loving him. After that, it was all Eddie and Jackie, Eddie scoring on Jackie's fielder's choice, doubling in the third and scoring on Jackie's single, then doubling again in the fourth to drive in two. Jackie capped the scoring with a hooking line-drive home run off the left field foul pole.

In dropping four of our last five games, we'd struggled for runs, and this sudden seven-run outburst had everyone so keyed up that the real story—Branca—snuck up on us. Ralph had the Cards lunging, swinging late, connecting weakly when they connected at all. It was all slaps on the back and "Way to go, Ralph" for the first four innings, but once he retired the side in the fifth—fifteen outs in a row without a base runner—he found himself alone on the small section of the bench between the stairs to the runway and the far dugout wall. No one would sit there with him, and of course, no one would talk to him, let alone say what we all knew we weren't saying—that he was working on a perfect game. The old superstition is that talking about perfection ruins it. Even the fans knew that. When a guy in the first row near the on-deck circle said, "What do you think about Branca, Max?" his friend said, "I don't think anything except you should keep you mouth shut before you open it again, and I'm only gonna say it once." The Cards trotted out their big guns—Moore, Musial, Northey, Kurowski—and Ralph set them down one after another. It was like watching someone dodge cars in heavy traffic. The pauses between pitches seemed to take forever, but it was thrilling. St. Louis went down in the sixth and again in the seventh without reaching base.

It seemed strange to feel bad for a guy who was pitching a perfect game, but that's how I felt when I glanced at Ralph as we batted in the bottom of the seventh. Taking his hat off, wiping away the sweat, putting his hat back on too carefully, shifting in his seat, staring with dark, heavy eyes at a spot in the center field seats where the shirts blurred anonymously: he looked lonely. The rest of us on the bench talked and laughed too loudly, pretending we weren't pretending that nothing was going on. Then, as Ralph walked to the mound in the top of the eighth, Gionfriddo leaned toward me and said, softly, "Don't look now, but there's a guy who could use a friendly word." I didn't answer, hoping that was all he would say about it, but he added, "You think he can do it?"

"Jeez, Al," I said, looking around to see if anyone else had heard.

Shoulders slouching toward the plate, right hand tucked behind him, Ralph took the sign from Edwards and started his windup, hands meeting at his side, front leg kicking upward, kicking outward, hips twisting open, arm whipping over the top, body falling away toward first base. The pitch zipped toward the plate and Enos Slaughter met it squarely, lining the ball toward left. Even before I had a chance to wish it into Reiser's glove, it fell for a hit. Three things, then: Ralph kicking the dirt of the pitcher's mound, scattering a cloud of dust; Slaughter shouting something at him across the infield; me glancing at Al and Al saying, "Don't look at me like that." So that even though Ralph shut St. Louis down on one hit for his fifteenth win and fourth shutout of the year, the thing that followed me into the clubhouse after the game was the sound of Al saying, "You think he can do it?" just before Slaughter's drive fell for a hit.

As the guys were undressing and showering, Al pulled me aside and said, "You think I jinxed Ralph, don't you?"

"I don't know," I answered.

"Listen, nothing I say is gonna change the way he pitches. Besides, it's not like he heard me. I don't buy that superstition stuff like you do."

"I don't buy it either. I just think as long as the guy's going good, you shouldn't rock the boat."

"Come on, Stidge, it's crazy. 'Stay away from Branca. Don't talk to him. Don't say perfect game to anyone.' What is that?" He was annoyed.

"I just think if you're on a good streak, you don't mess it up. If you're on a bad streak, then you try to change things."

His face soured. "Is that a message for me?"

"What do you mean?"

But I knew what he meant, even though I hadn't intended it that way. He hadn't started a game since June. His only appearances that month were as a pinch hitter, and he was 0 for 5. I knew it was bugging him.

"Never mind," he said. "What the hell, we beat the sons of bitches, didn't we?" He said it dismissively but I could see he was still bothered.

It was one in the morning by the time I finished my clubhouse chores. I considered making the trip home, but the thought of riding the empty train through the sleeping stations before finally stumbling into bed was discouraging. Besides, we had a day game tomorrow. I pulled out the old sheets and ratty pillow I kept in my locker, threw them over a bench in the trainer's room, and tiredly blotted the light. I dropped off instantly to the sound of the wind flinging raindrops against the windows, but I slept badly, waking disoriented and sweat-soaked in the strange darkness, still feeling dreams I couldn't recall, yet knowing they had something to do with Sam. Maybe if I'd been in my own bed or if there'd been no rain, I'd have fallen back to sleep right away. But places have their sounds, and become, without them, otherworldly. Crowd-less, playerless, dark Ebbets Field was a cave of elusive whispers that sharpened my senses. Everyday things seemed more than real: the canvas of the trainer's table, rough beneath the threadbare sheet; a whiff of ammonia reaching through my nose to the wells behind my eyes. I lay there thinking about Sam, and for the first time all summer, I let myself doubt him. Not wonder, not question — doubt. It seemed like all the steps and moves toward reclaiming our friendship had come from me, and that he'd been fighting them deliberately since the night we'd taken our drive together. It made me mad, so mad I couldn't lie still, and I got up and wandered through the clubhouse in the powdery streetlight that sifted through the windows.

And then I saw his smile, the old, bright smile he'd flashed just before he'd bowled his winning ball the other night, and I felt sad. It had only flickered for an instant before unhappiness had wiped it from his face. It was that smile I wanted back, and the things it stood for, things I'd never touched or held, but which I knew had been real: days together, long ago, me calling his name, his face turning toward me, open, clear. We'd made discoveries together: friendship, the back streets of Brooklyn, carefree ways of filling what would otherwise have been empty days. I suddenly felt disloyal. If I missed those things so much, how must he be feeling if he couldn't find them now? He'd been to war and had come back changed. Was that his fault? I stared across the room. Empty and limp in the whispery silence, the ghostly uniforms stared back from the lockers.

Once before this, I'd thought I'd lost him in the dark. During the summer of '40, when we'd been in our early teens, he'd made a trip to the Adirondacks with my mother and me, and we'd spent a week in a cabin rented by my aunt Lizzie and uncle Tony. There were caves up there, and we went exploring one afternoon, the small dark mouth of the polished tunnel sucking us into the cool silence that ran deep beneath the mountain. Sam led and I followed, lighting my way and backlighting his with the only flashlight. First on hands and knees, then on our stomachs, we squeezed and twisted our way through the narrow, descending passage toward the distant sound of gurgling water. "I bet it's an underground waterfall!" Sam cried, moving ahead quickly, disappearing around one of the turns. Scrambling to keep up with him, I lost my grip on the light and heard it clatter down the rock. It went out with a crash.

Flat on my stomach in the blind dark, the cool stone pressing against my cheek, I called to him again and again, but the only answer was my echoing voice and the gurgling water. Frightened, I lay without moving until I heard Sam groan below me, and I knew he must have fallen. I started forward, inches at a time, arms outstretched, fingers groping the blackness. I found the turn but couldn't feel anything beyond my hands. A drop. The opening was wide enough for me to turn around, grip the rock, and lower myself to Sam's side. He was breathing, but it was thirty seconds before he spoke.

"Can you move?" I asked.

"Yeah. But my head."

"Hold on to me."

We'd never have gotten out if the drop had been deep. I don't remember much about the black return through the cold rock, just the relief of finally spotting light at the mouth of the cave and seeing Sam's face.

I cracked a window now. The wind had died, but rain still fell: I heard the drops and felt the soggy air. The concrete ledge's gritty dust clung dryly to my hands and filled my nose with an old, tired smell. Suddenly, the summer was too short. July was half over. September was closer than April. The last couple of weeks must have had their lazy mornings and long, hot afternoons, but they felt now like a string of blurred nights that had slipped emptily away.

I woke early the next morning, stiff and achy, heavy around the eyes. I showered, had breakfast at Toomey's and went for a long walk. The sky was thick and drab. The light from the early shops squinted weakly, too yellow. Parked cars squatted along the curbs of the dark, shiny streets, fallen rain beading their roofs and fenders like blobs of oil. The traffic was as sluggish as I was. For the first time all year, I hoped we'd be rained out — I wanted to go home and sleep — but we played on a soggy field, and the Cardinals scored twice in the seventh to break a 4-4 tie and scratch back to within four and a half games of us. All afternoon, I'd been bothered by my conversation with Al. Thinking it over, it did seem like I'd blamed him for Ralph's losing the perfect game. Maybe that was part of the reason I'd slept so badly last night. On my way home I stopped into Gowan's Pawnshop and bought an old horseshoe. I'd give it to him tomorrow, hoping he'd understand.

In 1947 the Dodgers won the pennant for the first time since 1941 and again lost to the Yankees, this time in seven games. But this time Brooklyn fans had something to cheer about. In game four, the Yanks' Bill Bevens was pitching a no-hit game with two out in the ninth — and then...

LOOKIE, LOOKIE, HERE COMES COOKIE!

Dick Young

[OCTOBER 3, 1947:] OUT OF THE MOCKERY and ridicule of "the worst World Series in history," the greatest baseball game ever played was born yesterday. They'll talk about it forever, those 33,443 fans who saw it. They'll say: "I was there. I saw Bill Bevens come within one out of the only series no-hitter; I saw the winning run purposely put on base by the Yankees; I saw Cookie Lavagetto send that winning run across a moment later with a pinch-hit double off the right-field wall — the only hit, but big enough to give the Brooks the 3–2 victory that put them even-up at two games apiece."

And maybe they'll talk about the mad minute that followed — the most frenzied scene ever erupted in this legendary spot called Ebbets Field: How some of the faithful hugged each other in the stands; how others ran out to the center of the diamond and buried Lavagetto in their caresses; how Cookie's mates pushed the public off because they themselves wanted the right to swarm all over him; how Cookie, the man who had to plead for his job this spring, finally fought his way down the dugout steps — laughing and crying at the same time in the first stages of joyous hysteria.

Elsewhere in the park, another man was so emotionally shaken he sought solitude. That was Branch Rickey, the supposedly cold, calloused businessman, the man who has seen thousands and thousands of ball games and should therefore be expected to take anything in stride. But Rickey had to be alone. He left his family, sat down in a quiet little room just off the press box, and posted a guard outside the door.

After ten minutes of nerve-soothing ceiling-staring, Rickey was asked if he'd see a writer. He would. Now he was calm and wanted to talk. He wanted to talk about the ninth-inning finish — but he started a little earlier than that.

He flashed back to the top half of the frame, when Hughie Casey had come in with the bases loaded and one out, and got Tommy Henrich to hit a DP ball right back at him on the first serve. "Just one pitch, and he's the winning pitcher of a World Series game," Branch chuckled. "That's wonderful."

Rickey then turned to his favorite subject. "It was speed that won it," he said. This tickled Rickey because it had been the speed of Al Gionfriddo which saved the game. They had laughed at Gionfriddo when he came to the Brooks back in June in that $300,000 deal with the Pirates. They had said: "What did Rickey get that little squirt for; to carry the money in a satchel from Pittsburgh?" And they had added, "He'll be in Montreal in a couple of weeks."

But here it was World Series time, and "little Gi" was still around. Suddenly he was useful. Furillo was on first with two out. Carl had got there just as eight Brooks before him had — by walking. For a prospective no-hit pitcher, Bevens had been under constant pressure because of control trouble. A couple of these passes had led to the Brooks' run in the fifth, and had cut New York's lead down to 2–1.

That's the way it still was when Gionfriddo went in to run for Furillo, and Pete Reiser was sent up to swing for Casey. Only now Bevens was just one out away from having his bronze image placed among the all-time greats in Cooperstown. Already, at the conclusion of the eighth frame, the chubby Yank righty had pitched the longest string of no-hit ball in series history — topping Red Ruffing's 7⅔ innings against the Cards in '42.

Now Bill was out for the jackpot. He got the first out in the ninth on a gasp provider, a long drive by Edwards which forced Lindell up against the left field wall for the stretching grab. Furillo walked and Jorgensen fouled meekly to McQuinn, who was white as a sheet as he made the catch.

One out to go— and then came the first of several switches that were destined to make a genius of Burt Shotton and an eternal second-guess target of Bucky Harris.

"Reiser batting for Casey," boomed the loudspeaker, "and Gionfriddo running for Furillo."

Soon the count was 2–1 on Pete. Down came the next pitch — and up went a feverish screech. Gionfriddo had broken for second. Berra's peg flew down to second — high, just high enough to enable Gi to slide head first under Rizzuto's descending tag. For the briefest moment, all mouths snapped shut and all eyes stared at umpire Babe Pinelli. Down went the umpire's palms, signaling that the Brooks' had stolen base No. 7 on the weak-winged Yankee backstop corps.

The pitch on which Gionfriddo went down had been high, making the count on Reiser 3-and-1. Then came the maneuver that makes Bucky Harris the most second-guessed man in baseball. The Yankee pilot signaled Berra to step out and take an intentional fourth ball from Bevens.

The cardinal principle of baseball had been disdained by Harris. The "winning run" had been put on — and Miksis replaced the sore-ankled Reiser on first.

It was possible for Reiser to hurt more than Stanky in such a situation — and the Brooks had run out of lefty pinch hitters. But a good right-side swinger, a clutch money player like Lavagetto, who batted for Muggsy, didn't get to be a fourteen-year man by being able to hit only one kind of chucking.

On the first pitch, Harris' guess still looked like a good one. Cookie swung at a fast ball and missed. Then another fast one, slightly high and toward the outside. Again Lavagetto swung. The ball soared toward the right corner — a territory seldom patronized by Cookie.

Because of that, Tommy Henrich had been swung over toward right-center. Frantically, Tommy took off after the drive, racing toward the line. He got there and leaped, but it was a hopeless leap. The ball flew some six feet over his glove and banged against the wooden wall. Gionfriddo was tearing around third and over with the tying run.

The ball caromed under Henrich's legs as Tommy struggled to put the brakes on his dash. On the second grab, Henrich clutched it and, still off balance, hurried a peg to McQuinn at the edge of the infield. The first-sacker whirled desperately and heaved home — but even as he loosed the ball, speedy young Miksis was plowing over the plate with a sitting slide. A big grin on his puss, Eddie, just turned 21 last week, sat right on home plate like an elated kid. He was home with the winning run, and he didn't want to get up. For what seemed like much more than the actual three or four seconds, Miksis just sat there, looked up at his mates gathered around the plate and laughed insanely.

That's when God's Little Green Acre became a bedlam. The clock read 3:51, Brooklyn Standard Time — the most emotional minute in the lives of thousands of Faithful. There was Lavagetto being mobbed — and off to the side, there was Bevens, head bowed low, walking dejectedly through the swarming crowd, and completely ignored by it. Just a few seconds earlier, he was the one everybody was planning to pat on the back. He was the one who would have been carried off the field — the only pitcher ever to toss a no-hitter in a series.

Now he was just another loser. It didn't matter that his one-hitter had matched the other classic performances of two Cub pitchers — Ed Reulbach against the Chisox in '06 and Passeau against Detroit in '45. The third one-hitter in series annals — but Bevens was still just a loser.

Bev felt bluer than Harry Taylor had at the start of this memorable struggle. In the first five minutes, Taylor had been a momentous failure. Unable to get his sore-elbowed arm to do what his mind demanded of it, the rookie righty had thrown his team into a seemingly hopeless hole before a Yankee had been retired.

Stirnweiss had singled. So had Henrich. And then Reese had dropped Robinson's peg of Berra's bouncer, loading the bases. Then Harry walked DiMaggio on four straight serves, forcing in a run. Still nobody out, still bases full. Taylor was through; he had been a losing gamble. In one inning, the Yanks were about to blow the game wide open and clamp a 3–0 lock on the series.

But, just as has happened so often this year, the shabby Brook pitching staff delivered a clutch performer. This time it was Hal Gregg, who had looked so mediocre in relief against the Yanks two days before. Gregg got McQuinn to pop up and then made Johnson bang a DP ball right at Reese.

Only one run out of all that mess. The Faithful regained hope. This optimism grew as DiMag was cut down at the plate attempting to score from first when Edwards threw McQuinn's dumpy third-frame single into short right. But, in the next stanza, as the Yanks did their only teeing off on Gregg, the Brook hopes drooped. Johnson poled a tremendous triple to the center-field gate and Lindell followed with a booming two-bagger high off the scoreboard in right.

There was some hope, based on Bevens' own wildness. The Brooks couldn't buy a hit, but they had men on board in almost every inning, sometimes two. Altogether, Bev was to go on to issue ten passes, just topping the undesirable series record set by Jack Coombs of the A's in the 1910 grapple with the Cubs.

Finally, in the fifth, Bill's wildness cost him a run. He walked Jorgensen and Gregg to open the stanza. Stanky bunted them along, and Jorgy scored while Gregg was being nailed at third on Reese's grounder to Rizzuto. Pee Wee then stole second for his third swipe of the series, and continued on to third as Berra's peg flew into center. But Robinson left him there with a whiff.

Thus, before they had a hit, the Brooks had a run. And right about now, the crowd was starting to grow no-hit conscious. A fine catch by DiMaggio, on which Joe twisted his left ankle slightly, had deprived Hermanski of a long hit in the fourth, and Henrich's leaping stab of another Hermanski cloat in front of the scoreboard for the final out in the eighth again saved Bill's blossoming epic.

Then the Yanks threatened to sew up the decision in the ninth.

Berhman had taken over the chucking an inning earlier as a result of Gregg's being lifted for a pinch swinger and Hank got into a bases-bulging jam that wasn't exactly his responsibility. Lindell's lead-off hit through the left side was legit enough, but after Rizzuto forced Johnny, Bevens' bunt was heaved tardily to second by Bruce Edwards. Stirnweiss then looped a fist-hit into right center. Hugh Casey was rushed in.

Hugh threw one pitch, his million-dollar serve which had forced DiMag to hit into a key DP the day before. This time the low-and-away curve was jammed into the dirt by Henrich. Casey's glove flew out for a quick stab … the throw home … the relay to first … and Hughie was set up to become the first pitcher credited with World Series victories on successive days.

Tough luck cost Hughie two series defeats against these same Yanks in '41. Things are evened up a bit now.

And just two days later, Dodger fans could cheer again.

Maybe Rickey Is a Genius After All

Tommy Holmes

[OCTOBER 6, 1947:] WHY?— You know, the longer you live around these Dodgers of ours the more you're likely to concede the possibility that Branch Rickey is an authentic, licensed genius, after all.

I am thinking now of the evening of May 1 when the announcement came that the Dodgers had traded five Dodgers, including Kirbe Higbe, to the Pittsburgh Pirates for $300,000 and Al Gionfriddo.

Anyone and everyone could understand Rickey grabbing the $300,000 but no one knew why in the world he wanted Gionfriddo.

All we knew about that young man is that he isn't much larger than a matchbox, that he looks like Dolph Camilli in miniature, being five feet, six inches and even smaller than Vic Lombardi, the welterweight pitcher, and that he once set a record in the Eastern League for three-base hits.

Well, the National League season ended without an answer to that one. The Dodgers won the pennant but Gionfriddo had nothing to do with that. It was extremely rare for him to break into a ball game and when he did it was only in an obscure spear-carrier's role.

THE ANSWER— Meanwhile, he was merely an extra mouth to feed and presumably he didn't eat very much although this is by no means certain because some of these jockey-sized characters you see around and about are duly qualified two-steak men.

The World Series started and for several days, little Al Gionfriddo continued to be another one of those fellows who shagged fly balls in the outfield while the Dodgers were taking batting practice.

Only a couple of days ago did the truth begin to dawn. And until yesterday afternoon at Yankee Stadium, most of us were a bit slow on the pick-up of a conclusion that today seems as clear as crystal.

Why did Rickey take Gionfriddo?

Originally published in the *Brooklyn Eagle*, October 6, 1947. Reprinted with permission of Historical Briefs, Inc.

To win the World Series, that's all.

HE'S ROLLING — Consider what this left-handed half-man has done in the last three games. Friday, he ran for Carl Furillo in the ninth. He stole second base with two out. That was the maneuver that opened the way to ultimate victory, for Bucky Harris ordered Pete Reiser purposely passed and Harry Lavagetto followed with the bases-clearing double that was the only hit the Dodgers got off Bill Bevens all day.

Saturday was a dull day for Gionfriddo. He batted for Joe Hatten, drew a base on balls, ultimately scored. And that was the only run the Dodgers registered in their losing battle with Frank Shea.

And yesterday — well, by this time you surely must have heard of the catch he made off the great Joe DiMaggio before 74,065 fans, largest crowd ever to see a World Series game. Incidentally, before I die, I fully expect that at least one million people will tell me they were there.

This was another one of those ball games that induce stomach ulcers and heart palpitation. The Dodgers, grimly gunning for the victory they needed to stay in the series, were off to a four run jump. The Yankees caught them with a crashing rally in the third, scoring a run in the fourth to take the lead. In the sixth the Dodgers came roaring back with four more. Now they were three runs ahead but what good is a three-run lead with the kind of pitching the Dodgers have been getting?

A COUNTRY MILE — Their advantage was in immediate jeopardy. The Yanks had two on with two out in the last of the sixth and the mighty DiMaggio cow-tailed one.

This was a longer ball than either of the two that Joe had hit into the upper deck at Ebbets Field. The thing was hit a country mile.

Out in left field, Gionfriddo turned tail and ran. Half way to the low fence that bounds the bullpen, he whirled, looked up, started running again. Just as he was within a step of that low fence, he looked over his shoulder and stuck out his glove.

In the pressbox, there was a bewildered silence. You couldn't see what had happened because Gionfriddo's body was between you and his own glove.

"I can't see the ball," complained someone and we were are hoping to see the ball bounce out from the fence, feeling sure that if it didn't it would be in the bullpen for a home run.

Shucks, at that distance, you could hardly see Gionfriddo.

It must have been five seconds before what must be the truth managed to penetrate at least one mind.

"I'll be darned," he yelled, "if that little sonuvagun didn't catch it!" And he had.

SUDDEN DEATH — That didn't end the ball game. This sixth contest was another that went right down to the last pitch and the phlegmatic Casey was in there at the end. All of the last four series games have gone down to the last pitch and the chances are better than even that the seventh and sudden death struggle for the championship today will do the same.

But there wasn't anything afterwards as explosively dramatic as Gionfriddo's catch, which must rank way up there as one of the truly great plays in World Series history.

I'm willing to concede Rickey's genius in getting this little guy last May just to have somebody extra to bedevil the hostiles in a World Series.

Gene Hermanski had played left field for four innings. Eddie Miksis was out there in the fifth. Hermanski wouldn't have had the speed to reach that ball and Miksis hasn't the outfield savvy for such a play.

Come the sixth and Gionfriddo is sent to left field and — zing! It happens.

If Rickey had that figured out last Spring, he's more than a genius — he's Merlin reincarnated.

Red Barber watched the outfielder instead of the ball so as not to make the mistake of mis-judging where the ball might land. This technique is aptly demonstrated in his classic call in the 1947 World Series.

RED BARBER'S CALL OF THE GIONFRIDDO CATCH, OCTOBER 5, 1947

Radio Broadcast

RED BARBER: Joe DiMaggio up, holding that club down at the end. Big fellow sets. Hatten pitches. A curveball, high outside, for ball one. So the Dodgers are ahead 8–5. And the crowd well knows that with one swing of the bat this fellow is capable of making it a brand-new game again. Joe leans in. He is one for three today. Six hits so far in the series. Outfield deep around toward left. The infield overshifted. Here's the pitch. Swung on. Belted. It's a long one! Deep into left-center. Back goes Gionfriddo, back, back, back, back, back, back. He makes a one-handed catch against the bullpen. Oh, doctor!

Leo Durocher had been suspended for the entire 1947 season by "Happy" Chandler, commissioner of baseball. He came back for the '48 season, but in July of that year the unimaginable happened: Leo crossed over to manage the hated Giants.

1948—LEO CROSSES THE BRIDGE

Gerald Eskenazi

Campanella remembered Durocher quickly got into a foul mood early in the season. The Dodgers had been picked to repeat—after all, if they could finish first under Shotton, why not again under Leo? But the Brooks lost four of their first seven games, and not one Dodger pitcher went the distance. Leo started to get on Robinson and Reiser over their weight. Jackie complained that his arm was sore, but Leo wouldn't hear of it. "I'll get him in shape or else," vowed Durocher.

The next day, Durocher commanded Sukeforth to hit grounders at Robinson. For one hour, Sukeforth pounded one after the other to Robinson. Robinson struggled, in pain, but said nothing.

Jackie was out of the lineup then; Gene Mauch took over at second. Leo was so miffed at Robinson that he was even thinking of moving Billy Cox, maybe the best-fielding third baseman of his time, to second, and putting the injured Spider Jorgensen at third. Cox got so upset that he jumped the club and went home to Harrisburg, Pennsylvania. There was more than a sensitive infielder at play with Cox. He had taken an emotional beating during World War II. Some of his teammates described him as being shell-shocked.

The team lost four in a row, and Durocher turned to Campanella. "You're catching tomorrow," he said.

Campy caught for the erratic Rex Barney, one of those wild, promising fastball hurlers that clubs hate to give up on (like Sandy Koufax and Nolan Ryan), and he caught him for a complete game. But the next day, Campy was relegated to the bullpen. If Campy did too well, it would mess up Rickey's plan.

Campanella recalled that because of this, "the feeling between the two men became strained. Looking back, I think that started the rift between Durocher and Mr. Rickey that finally ended with Leo being fired."

Pages 221–30 from *The Lip: A Biography of Leo Durocher* by Gerald Eskenazi. ©1993 by Gerald Eskenazi. Reprinted by permission of HarperCollins Publishers, Inc.

Finally, on May 15 — cut-down day — Leo got his orders and had to tell Campanella he was being sent down. But not before Durocher marched into Rickey's office and demanded Campanella get a raise and a big league salary.

At the end of June, the sixth-place Dodgers recalled Campanella from St. Paul, where he was batting .325. Leo was ecstatic, and when Campy showed up, Leo said, "Hah, fat as ever!" He returned against the Giants in Ebbets Field. The Dodgers had lost five straight. They lost again and fell into last place. During the Dodgers' fall into the second division, Leo tried everything. He started fights. He picked pitchers on hunches. He damned Rex Barney, saying he'd never pitch for him again.

One sports fan was Harry Markson, a raconteur, fight promoter, and all-around good guy. In the summer of 1948, he was the assistant to Mike Jacobs, the famed Madison Square Garden matchmaker. During a long drive home to Flatbush from Pompton Lakes, New Jersey, where Joe Louis was in training, Markson heard dire reports on the radio about Israel's future. The Arab nations were massing on the borders of the new country.

When Markson got out of his car, he spied his rabbi, who lived in the same apartment house. "It's terrible, what's going on," said the rabbi. "It's just one bad thing after another."

"Frightful," agreed Markson, thinking they were talking about the Arab-Israeli situation.

"And do you know," the rabbi added, "I think it's all Durocher's fault. He's moving the players around too much."

With last place a sad reality, O'Malley and Smith wanted Rickey to move on Durocher. But they waited a day too long to dump Leo. For the Dodgers recovered and went on to win 16 of 19. Leo kept pushing back. He had to know he was a goner. He certainly knew Rickey was about to be unloaded himself.

On July 4, the Dodgers met the Giants in Brooklyn. Leo was thrown out of the game and was in the clubhouse when Parrott came down with a message: "Mr. Rickey wants you to resign." Leo stormed around and demanded Rickey call on him himself.

Campy pulled the game out with a bottom-of-the-ninth homer, and the club embarked on a winning road trip. Recharged, Leo let it be known to his friend, Bill Corum, the *Journal American* columnist, that there was front-office turmoil on the Dodgers. Leo got all his gripes against Rickey and O'Malley off his chest, but Corum wrote the piece as if it was all coming not from Leo, but from the writer.

Meanwhile, Giant president Horace Stenham had come to a reluctant decision: Manager Mel Ott had to go. This was a wrenching moment for Stoneham, for Ott was one of the three Giant managers that defined the team in the twentieth century, following John McGraw and Bill Terry. It was a terrific legacy, and Ott had been a terrific player, the National League career home run leader, the final symbol of the great days of the Giants. But they weren't so great anymore. In 1947, even with a record 221 home runs, the Giants had finished fourth, making the first division for the second time since 1939. They had become perpetual losers.

Stoneham approached Rickey. The pair met in Ford Frick's office in New York. Down through the years the story has been that Stoneham actually wanted to talk to

Rickey about Shotton. "No," Rickey answered, "I may need him at any moment myself."

Stoneham, who had always admired Durocher, asked, incredulous, "Does that mean Durocher will be available?"

"You may talk to him," replied Rickey.

This is what actually may have happened — Stoneham went fishing for Shotton and wound up with Durocher. Rickey, though, told it with a slightly different angle. And so did Leo.

The way Rickey remembered breaking the news to Leo was this way: Durocher, accompanied by Lorraine, walked into Rickey's office and asked what his status was in Brooklyn if he refused the Giants job. "Your future," Rickey replied, "lies over the river, Leo."

Finally, there is Leo's version. This much is certain. The Dodgers were in St. Louis after the All-Star break. Leo was told by Rickey to go on a scouting expedition to Montreal. Leo saw that as an excuse to get rid of him and announce a coaching change. Rickey, according to Leo, said he could still be the manager in Brooklyn, although he had been offered the Giants job. "I wouldn't work for you another day after all that's happened," Leo said in his book.

It seemed inconceivable that Leo could become a Giant. It was like oil and water. There was Manhattan and there was Brooklyn. There were the Dodgers and the Giants. But what there never could be was a manager of the Dodgers managing the Giants.

"That was a little hard to believe," recalls Reese. "The skirmishes we had with the Giants — a lot of times it was war. If you could play well against the Giants, and you had a good year against the Giants, you were successful, whatever the ball club did. They'll never be another rivalry like the Giants and the Dodgers."

Back in late January 1934, Bill Terry, then manager of the champion Giants, had returned to New York for a hot-stove league conversation with the writers. When asked which teams would give the Giants the most trouble, he said, "Pittsburgh, St. Louis, and Chicago would be the teams to beat."

"Do you fear Brooklyn?" he was asked, a facetious question since the Giants had finished 26½ games ahead of the Bums.

"Is Brooklyn still in the league?" he replied, in the same spirit.

With whatever distinction there was between Manhattan and Brooklyn, that remark, which came back to haunt Terry, widened the gulf between them.

Did they hate each other? Passionately is a mild word. The fans couldn't stand each other either. There was that July in the 1930s, when a Dodger fan was drinking at Pat Diamond's bar on Ninth Street, not far from Flatbush. The bartender began to taunt the fan, calling the Dodgers bums. Another patron got on the guy, too, but all in fun.

The Dodger fan was unhappy. He ran out of the saloon. He went to the post office, where he was a trusted employee, unlocked the gun cabinet and took out two revolvers. He returned to the bar and shot both his tormenters. When the police picked him up fifteen minutes later, he told them he had been taking a razzing about his team far too long.

Branca was also shocked because he believed the Dodgers were on their way. "We had started to turn it around. It wasn't because of our record. I just think Mr. Rickey had enough of Leo. He couldn't handle him. I'm not talking off the field. Rickey wanted it his way. He wanted Leo to play the lineup he wanted. He was always interfering."

And so Leo was gone, replacing the "nice guy" whom he had referred to with disdain.

Leo, as usual, claimed that he really didn't mean that nice guys finish last. It's just that nice guys... Well, how this most famous of sports quotes worked its way into the lexicon began at the batting cage one afternoon before a Dodgers-Giants game.

It was July 5, 1946. Red Barber was needling Leo about the home runs the Giants had hit the day before. Some of Leo's writer friends were around him, including Frank Graham, the respected columnist.

Barber's barbs irritated Leo. Durocher looked over at the ponderous Giant hitters and their amiable manager, who had a virtual lifetime mandate from the hero-worshipping Stoneham, who had inherited the team from his father eight years earlier. "Home runs?" snorted Leo, as if anyone could think the mere act of hitting the ball out of a park was enough to make you a finished ballplayer.

"But Ott's a nice guy," continued Barber.

"A nice guy!" barked Leo. "I've been in baseball a long time. Do you know a nicer guy in the world than Mel Ott? He's a nice guy. In last place. Where am I? In first place. I'm in first place. The nice guys are over there in last place, not in this dugout."

And so, the back-page headlines the next day screamed: "NICE GUYS FINISH LAST — LEO." A new expression was born. Leo contended that only Graham got it right, but it was too late. Evermore, Leo was to be connected with that phrase which, unfortunately, had a ring of truth to it. And what if Ott had said it? It would have been forgotten. But coming from Leo, the guy who *could* have said it, and did in fact say something very close to it — well then, it took on an added dimension, even truth.

Recalling Leo's "nice guy" statement, Branca concluded, "It's not true. Nice guys finish first. You couldn't be a bad guy and get your team to play for you well enough consistently to finish first." To Branca, Leo *was* a nice guy, at least not a bad guy. A guy the Dodgers would have won repeated championships for if he hadn't moved to the Giants. Instead, the Dodgers failed to repeat in 1948, won in 1949, but not again until 1952. And that was the team of Duke and Jackie and Campy and Skoonj and Newk and Preacher and Oisk and Gillie and Pee Wee. But not of Leo.

In 1950, Shotton was still managing the Dodgers. The next year — the Bobby Thomson–Ralph Branca playoff year — Dressen managed the Dodgers. "When Leo moved over to the Giants, and Charlie became our manager and we played the Giants, I think Charlie managed against Durocher, not the Giants. I think it was like the pupil trying to outdo the professor," said Branca.

Stoneham and Carl Hubbell, the director of the Giants' farm system, went to Leo's Manhattan apartment to meet with him. Leo wasn't home yet, and they barged in on Lorraine. She was listening to the Dodgers game on the radio. "I don't know whether Leo has had a chance to tell you, Mrs. Durocher," said Stoneham, "but he is going to start managing the Giants in Pittsburgh tomorrow."

"Then why," she asked, "am I listening to the Dodgers?" And she turned off the radio.

"Durocher is out, Shotton is in," Rickey told the press. This was something more than page-one headlines. This was a social revolution. And for at least two new immigrants to America, the change was profound. George Freeman, the senior legal counsel for the *New York Times*, explains:

"In 1948 my parents came over from Hungary. They had just got off Ellis Island and they were proud that they knew all about American politics. They had studied hard. They knew about Washington and Jefferson and the election coming up with Truman and Dewey. And then they see on the newsstands every paper has this story on page one — 'Durocher Quits', and here's a name they never heard of. Durocher. They were so upset because they had never heard of him and they had never studied about him. And they thought they were Americans."

The Dodgers were 37–38 under Leo. Many of them still had confidence he would have gotten them in the chase. Others, though, implied they were happy he was gone. All of them seemed as stunned as the Freemans.

As Jackie Robinson waited in the visitors locker room in Cincinnati for Shotton to rejoin the club and replace Leo, he said, "I sure do like to play for that man. I can hardly wait."

Pee Wee was honest: "I'm a Durocher man myself. But Leo was on the spot. He had to win or quit, and he never would have quit. But I'll play my head off for Shotton."

Furillo, volatile, and no friend of Leo's, added, "May the best man win always has been my motto."

The Dodgers' powerful right-handed hitting slugger unloaded on an August day in 1950. He was at the time only the second major leaguer to hit four home runs in a nine-inning game in the twentieth century. The other was Lou Gehrig.

HODGES ERUPTS

Dick Young

Gil Blasts 4 Homers
As Dodgers Blitz Braves, 19–3

[AUGUST 31, 1950:] IT BEING NO PARTICULAR distinction to hit three homers in one game, Gil Hodges hit four last night. The muscular Brook first sacker, who was begging for a regular job only two years ago, is the only National Leaguer to accomplish the tremendous feat in a regulation nine-inning game and take his place alongside immortal Lou Gehrig, the lone AL slugger to achieve that multiple seat-smashing total since the turn of the century.

Gil's blasts formed the chrome trimming to Brooklyn's bizarre 19–3 schalumping of the Braves before 14,226 of the gasping Faithful.

Unlike Gehrig's, Hodges' homers were not consecutive, although Gil owns the strange distinction of hammering each of his four off a different hurler. He hit the first off Warren Spahn in the second stanza, his second off Norman Roy in the third, and, after grounding out in the fourth, slugged one into the same lower deck off Bob Hall in the sixth.

Next stanza, Gil poked a measly little infield single, and everybody thought he was through for the night. But because of the magnitude of Brooklyn's 21-hit hurricane, Hodges was given another swing in the eighth against Johnny Antonelli, and he put a flourishing finish on his historic act by belting this one upstairs.

In all, there have been six players who hit four homers in a single game. Two of them, Bobby Lowe and Ed Delahanty, did it in what was considered the pre-historic era of the game — Lowe in 1894 and Delahanty two years later.

The other two, Chuck Klein and Pat Seerey, required extra-inning contests in order to make the grade. Klein, swinging for the Phils in 1936, hit his fourth in the 10th inning. Seerey, a Chisoxer in '48, did it in the 11th.

Then, of course, there's Gehrig, who did it in '32, and now Hodges.

Hodges' fourth of the night, and 23rd of the year, was something of a memorable shot for all Brooklyn, at that. It was the Dodgers' 153rd circuit smash, topping last year's output by one. Thus, as of this moment, the 1950 Dodgers are the homer-hittingest club ever to represent Flatbush — and have 35 more games in which to pile it up real high.

It is customary to observe in such debacles as this 21-hit affair that all Dodger batters, or at least those in the starting lineup, hit safely. Therefore, consider it so observed. Observe, too, that Duke Snider crashed his 24th homer in the shadow of Hodges and that pitcher Carl Erskine poked four straight hits of his own.

Carl had four hits before the Braves did. They didn't get their fourth hit until the seventh and then, with Erskine presumably easing up slightly behind his 17–1 lead, they collected four more in the last two stanzas.

Three of the Boston blows were by Sid Gordon, who caught the homer spirit by clouting his 24th. Sid, in fact, set the style. His sock in the second stanza actually put Boston ahead by one run. Then, in the home half, Hodges blasted his first homer with one on, and the Brooks were off on their torrid tear.

Warren Spahn, who rarely lasted long enough at Ebbets Field to make a close study of our special type of fan, suffered his quickest kayo in six starts against the Brooks. He was battered out in the next stanza, as the Brooks batted around for seven runs.

Norman Roy succeeded Spahn and found himself facing Hodges. The first pitch to Gil landed in the lower deck. The next pitch was stroked into left for a single by Campanella. At this point Boston pilot Billy Southworth called catcher Walker Cooper to the mound, and there ensued a little confab, at which, it is assumed, this famous piece of baseball dialogue took place:

Southworth to Cooper: "What's the matter; doesn't he have anything?"

Cooper to Southworth: "I don't know. I haven't caught one of his pitches yet."

Whereupon the meeting broke up, and Roy continued pitching. But not for long. Two batters later, he was replaced by knuckler Mickey Haefner, and before the frame ended, the displaced hurler felt the sting of Snider's sock over the clock atop the scoreboard.

Haefner went out for a pinch-swinger, eventually, and Bob Hall, an Adonis whose stuff isn't nearly as beautiful as his physique, took the sixth stanza shelling wherein the Brooks batted around for the second time.

Hall was tagged for Hodges' third shot, and immediately all the boys in the press box started figuring that Gil was the third Dodger to hit three in one game this year — the others being Campanella and Snider — and the sixth player overall to accomplish it this season.

But Gil wasn't content to hang around in such unselect company. He wanted a less crowded spot. He found one — one that he can share with a guy named Gehrig, and he thinks the company is just wonderful.

Robin Roberts won 286 major league baseball games and was elected to the Hall of Fame in 1976. In his autobiography, My Life in Baseball, *he describes the Phillies' final game of the 1950 season against the Brooklyn Dodgers.*

MY LIFE IN BASEBALL

Robin Roberts and C. Paul Rogers, III

If we lost again on Sunday we faced an immediate three-game playoff, with the first game at Ebbets Field and Games 2 and, if necessary, 3 in Shibe Park. A playoff, given the state of our pitching staff and Andy's (Seminick) injury, was not something we felt very confident about. Our best shot was to win on Sunday.

With our depleted pitching staff, it was far from clear to me who Eddie Sawyer would name to start the final game. I had started games the previous Saturday, Wednesday and Thursday. But I had two days' rest so I thought I could pitch. The small visitors' clubhouse at Ebbets Field was very quiet and tense before the game because we all knew that we had just about blown the pennant. I was sitting in front of my locker about an hour before the game when Eddie walked over, handed me a new ball, and wished me luck. That was how I found out that I would be starting.

It turned out that the Dodgers started Don Newcombe in what would be our fifth head-to-head meeting of the year. Both Newk and I were trying for our first 20-win seasons, although 20 wins never entered my mind. When I began to warm up I really did not feel particularly good. I was having trouble getting loose and was not sure I could crank up my arm like I needed to. I was nervous and tense because so much was riding on the game. But for some reason I glanced over at Newk warming up for the Dodgers and I thought to myself, "Hell, he is just as tired as I am." I knew Newk had pitched almost as much as I had and probably was just as tired, nervous, and anxious as I was. Once I realized that, I never gave another thought to how tired or nervous I was supposed to be.

Ebbets Field was packed with a standing-room-only crowd of 35,073 on a mild, sunny afternoon. Thousands more were turned away, but a few fans from Philadelphia managed to secure tickets and get into the ballpark. Newk and I both pitched well early. I did not give up a hit until Pee Wee Reese's no out double in the fourth. I got out of it by retiring Duke Snider, Jackie Robinson and Carl Furillo in order to leave Pee Wee stranded. Through the first five innings we managed only three scattered singles and a walk off Newcombe, so the game remained scoreless in the sixth inning.

We broke through for the first run in the top half on consecutive two-out singles by Dick Sisler, Del Ennis, and Puddin' Head Jones. I got the first two batters in the bottom half of the inning to bring Reese to the plate again. Pee Wee hit a fly ball near the right-field foul line, which was only 297 feet from home plate. The ball hit the screen and dropped down to a six-inch ledge where it stayed. Although the ball was in the field of play, it was beyond our reach and Reese, instead of a double or maybe only a single, had a freak inside-the-park home run. Andy Seminick was so frustrated that he yelled at Del Ennis in right field to throw his glove at the ball. The ball sat on the ledge the rest of the afternoon, a constant reminder of why the score was tied.

The score remained that way through eight and a half innings. We had a base runner against Newk in the seventh, eight, and ninth innings but were unable to score. I had given up only three hits, including an eighth inning single to Roy Campanella, while we had managed eight hits against Newcombe.

As I trudged out to face Brooklyn in the bottom of the ninth, I knew that if the Dodgers scored we would very likely lose not only the ballgame but the pennant. Mary and I had planned on taking a vacation to Florida after the season with some of my World Series money, and I remember for a brief moment thinking, "If we don't win this one, we're not going to Florida."

Cal Abrams led off the inning, and I went to a 3–2 count on him. I threw a fastball on the inside corner, but umpire Larry Goetz called it ball four. Goetz was an outstanding umpire, probably along with Al Barlick the best in the league. But I really thought the 3–2 pitch was a strike, but Goetz didn't and so Abrams led off with a walk.

Reese was next and tried to bunt Abrams over. I threw high and hard, trying to make it tougher to bunt and Pee Wee fouled two off. With two strikes, I thought he might try to go to right field so I tried to jam him inside. Either I didn't get it far enough in or Pee Wee guessed with me, because he hit a rope to left field, his third hit of the game, to put runners on first and second with no one out. Now I was in a real pickle; a base hit would win the game for Brooklyn. Eddie had Jim Konstanty warming up in the bullpen but left me in. Duke Snider was the next batter. Although Duke was a dangerous hitter (he had 31 homers, 107 RBI's, and a .321 batting average for 1950), I assumed that with the game on the line and no one out Duke would try to bunt the runners over. So I threw the first pitch right in there, thinking of nothing but breaking to cover the third-base line to try to force Abrams at third if Snider bunted in that direction.

Well, Snider was not bunting. He ripped that first pitch right over my left shoulder into center field. The ball was a low line drive, and as I turned to watch it I could see Abrams at second hesitate a moment to make sure Mike Goliat, our second baseman, could not reach it. Richie Ashburn in center was not known to have a strong throwing arm, and the Dodgers often ran on him. Milt Stock, Brooklyn's third base coach, decided to test Whitey and waved Abrams home, even with his late start. Richie caught the ball on the first hop and threw a beautiful one-hop strike to Stan

Lopata, who was catching after Andy Seminick had been lifted for a pinch runner. Stan caught the ball and tagged Abrams out by 15 feet.

Some people believe that I missed a sign to try to pick Abrams off at second and that Richie came in shallow to back up my throw. If there was a pick-off play, it would have been the first one all year. I never even threw over to first base, much less second.

Ashburn's throw was the biggest in Phillies history, but we were still on the brink of disaster. Reese and Snider had each moved with the throw to the plate, giving the Dodgers runners on second and third with only one out. Eddie Sawyer came to the mound to tell me to walk Jackie Robinson intentionally to set up a force at any base. That meant Carl Furillo would bat with the bases loaded. He was an excellent right-handed slugger who already had 106 RBI's to go with a .305 batting average.

When Eddie came out he also reminded me to keep the ball down on Furillo, who was a high fastball hitter. Well, my first pitch to Carl was about eye high, but it must have had something on it because he swung and popped it up to Waitkus in foul territory by first base. Another Dodgers slugger, Gil Hodges, was next. Hodges was a dangerous clutch hitter who had already driven in 113 runs. He took a strike and a ball and then lifted a soft fly ball in front of the scoreboard in right field, which was a short porch in Ebbets Field. It should have been a can of corn, but right field was the sun field in the late afternoon, especially in the fall. Del Ennis drifted back, battling the sun all the way. He stayed with it and actually caught the ball against his chest to complete my escape from the jam. After the game, Del actually had the seams of the ball imprinted on his chest, so hard did Hodges' fly ball hit him in right field.

I did not have much time to reflect on the inning because I was the leadoff hitter in the top of the tenth. Eddie told me to go ahead and hit, which was fine by me. He often let me bat in late innings of close ballgames when I was pitching. At this point, I was too charged up to feel tired, even though I'd already pitched nine innings. Getting out of that jam revitalized me, and I did not want to come out of the game.

At bat, I was often overanxious and lunged at the ball, trying to hit it hard. But in this situation I just tried to put the ball in play. Newk was also still in the game, and his first pitch was a ball. I swung at the next pitch and hit a bouncer up the middle through the infield for a base hit.

Eddie Waitkus, our leadoff hitter, followed me. Sawyer had him bunting, but after Waitkus fouled one down the third-base line and dodged a high inside fastball, Eddie let him hit away. Waitkus responded by looping a Texas Leaguer in front of Snider in center, sending me easily into second because I could see that the ball was going to fall in safely.

We now had runners on first and second with no one out and Ashburn coming to the plate. Whitey bunted the first pitch along the third-base line, and I busted my tail to get to third, sliding headlong into the bag. But Newk made a fine play, getting to the ball quickly and firing to Brooklyn third sacker Billy Cox to just nip me. Now we had men on first and second with one out.

Dick Sisler was next. Dick was a left-handed batter with power. He had a good year at the plate, with close to a .300 batting average, 12 homers, and 80 RBIs. He seemed pretty much fully recovered from the sore wrist that had plagued him late in the season. He had generally swung the bat well the past few days and had already touched Newcombe for three hits in the game.

Newcombe immediately got ahead in the count two strikes, as Sisler foul tipped the first pitch and fouled the second back to the screen. It was clear that Newk was really going after Dick, hoping to strike him out. After taking a ball high and outside, Dick hit another foul back into the press box behind home plate.

Newcombe's next pitch was another fastball out over the plate. Dick swung and really connected, driving a low line drive into deep left field. Sitting in the dugout, I knew that the ball was hit hard, but I was not sure that it was going out because a low line drive hit to the opposite field doesn't normally carry all the way out of the park. But Dick's blow did carry, landing in about the third row of the left-field stands, 350 feet from home plate. My teammates charged from the dugout to mob Dick at the plate and celebrate our 4–1 lead.

That lead felt like a real cushion, given the tension of the game and the suspense of the bottom of the ninth. The next two Phillies made outs, and before I knew it I was walking to the mound to pitch the bottom of the tenth inning, three outs from winning the pennant.

There was no real conversation as I left the dugout. Sawyer put Jack Mayo, a fleet rookie outfielder, into left field for defensive purposes, replacing Sisler. I felt good and loose and had too much adrenaline to be tired. Roy Campanella, another dangerous Brooklyn slugger with 31 homers, was up first. With the count 1–1, he drove a line drive to left that Mayo quickly moved over to nab. Dick would probably have made the play as well, but Jack had no trouble getting to it with his excellent speed.

Brooklyn manager Burt Shotton then sent Jim "Rip" Russell up to pinch hit for Billy Cox. Rip was a veteran switch-hitting outfielder with good power also; he had hit 10 home runs in little more than 200 at-bats. But I was pumped and struck him out swinging on four pitches. It was only my second strikeout of the game and my first since the third inning.

Next Shotton inserted Tommy Brown to pinch hit for Newcombe. Tommy, who would become a teammate the following year after he was traded to the Phillies, was a young utility player who hit .291 and had seven pinch-hits for the Dodgers in 1950. After fouling one back to the screen, he popped the next pitch to Waitkus at first. Eddie caught the ball, and the Whiz Kids had finally won the first pennant for the Phillies since 1915 and only the second in Phillies history.

The clubhouse was pure bedlam after our white-knuckle victory over the Dodgers. My teammates carried me off the field, and when I got to the clubhouse, I just sat by my locker while the celebration went on all around me. Eddie Sawyer came over and kissed me on the cheek, certainly the only time he ever did that. Amid the hubbub, Jackie Robinson quietly came into our clubhouse and went around shaking our hands and congratulating us in a remarkable display of sportsmanship from a fierce competitor.

As we boarded the bus to the train station outside Ebbets Field, a woman kept calling Richie Ashburn by name. When finally he turned around to look at her, she spat right in his face. I had to grab Whitey and push him into the bus to keep him from going after her. Some Brooklyn fans had taken that loss personally.

In the October 1951 issue of Sport *magazine, Milton Gross wrote this article heralding Jackie Robinson's finally getting the opportunity to be himself.*

THE EMANCIPATION OF JACKIE ROBINSON

Milton Gross

When he entered organized baseball as the first and only Negro pioneer, he was shackled by more restraints than any ballplayer had ever known. Now, five years later, Brooklyn's second-base star is at last expressing his real personality.

Jack Roosevelt Robinson of the Brooklyn Dodgers made his precedent-shattering invasion of organized baseball wearing an armor of humility. It was, for him, an unnatural garment that chafed continually and on certain occasions dug ruthlessly into both his flesh and his spirit. Hiding his true combativeness behind the armor carefully selected for him by Branch Rickey, allowed to vent his boundless competitive instincts only with his bat, glove and flying feet, Jackie was the unresponsive target for barbs of humiliation that no man but Robinson could fully appreciate.

The humility he practiced so conscientiously — rigidly might be an even better word — did not come naturally to the gifted Negro. No meek and humble man could possibly play baseball with the fire and dash Robinson exhibits. But there was reserve in Jackie, far more reserve than any white ballplayer ever had shown. He had to have it, and just as he pounds the ball between the outfielders when a base-hit has to be obtained, so he managed to restrain his emotions when it had to be done to assure his success. But it had been five years since Jackie broke into the National League, years chock full of astonishing feats, of endless honors, and each year the great second-baseman of the Dodgers has been inclined to placate fewer and fewer people. It is a noteworthy milestone in the history of baseball that Robinson is today, at long last, his own man.

Jackie has thrown off the shackles gradually but purposefully. In 1949, he wrangled with the umpires and was forced by Commissioner A. B. Chandler to tender an apology to umpire Cal Hubbard during the World Series. In 1950, he took the brakes off his feud with Leo Durocher and it burst forth into the open. He accused certain

National League umpires of having formed a heckling cabal against him and charged they were attempting to provoke him. He invited an investigation by National League President Ford Frick. This past spring in an exhibition game at Asheville, North Carolina, he stood on the diamond chin to chin and argued heatedly with umpire Frank Dascoli for several minutes.

He resented bean balls being thrown at his head and the heads of his teammates in their interboro scraps with the Giants. In one game, he laid down a bunt to force pitcher Sal Maglie to field the ball on the first-base line where he could bump him.

"I did it deliberately," Jackie admitted, "to force the league to step in and stop this beanballing before somebody gets hurt. I'll take the fine, the suspension or anything else that goes with it, but this throwing at a man's head has got to be stopped. If the umpires haven't the courage to stop it, then Mr. Frick should step in himself."

"Last Sunday," Robinson said, "Larry Jansen hit me with a pitch. The mark's still there. Maglie had already thrown one too close to me. I made up my mind to do something to protect myself and the other fellows. I set out to create enough of a disturbance to bring this thing to a head."

That night, watching the game from her usual seat at Ebbets Field, Jackie's charming wife, Rachel, who has made priceless contributions to her husband's pioneering job in baseball, was particularly aware of the tension. As she has from the very beginning, she kept her ears attuned to the comments about her husband. A man seated near her said, as Jackie bumped Maglie, "There's a guy getting big-headed." It was a remark Rachel repeated to her husband later that evening as they drove back to their home in St. Albans, Long Island. It is a comment that has been made many times within recent months in one way or another as Robinson has demonstrated that he recognizes no longer any limitations upon him which do not circumscribe other players.

I have heard it in dressing rooms, dugouts, bars, on planes and trains, where baseball people gather or among plain fans. I have watched Jackie from the beginning and have seen his aggressiveness become more pronounced.

Once, the Phillies turned their dugout into a vile cesspool, denouncing him in what passes for "jockeying." They carried black cats on the field and shouted, "Hey, Jackie, here's one of your relatives."

Some of Robinson's teammates came to him and said, "You can't give it back to them, but we'll do it for you." Robby answered, "No, I can take it as long as they can give it. If I've got what it takes to be a big-leaguer, I'll make the grade on my own."

There was a manager in the International League, when Jackie was at Montreal, who admitted, "We have tried everything against him. We have thrown at him, knocked him down, called him names, but we just can't get a rise out of him."

But those days are gone. Never again will Jackie wear the armor of humility.

This, then, is the real Jackie Robinson — with the wraps off. Is he really big-headed, or getting a "god complex" as one reader wrote me following the Maglie incident, or has Robinson merely passed from stage to natural stage in the evolution of his great experiment in baseball?

Countless words have been written about the cold, calculated fury of Eddie Stanky, the emotional combativeness of Enos Slaughter, the profane, goading insolence of Leo Durocher. For the most part, they have been words of praise because the personalities of these men are the reflections of that aggressive quality which lifts them above others of equal or greater ability.

To appreciate what has happened to Robinson, undoubtedly one of the all-time greats of baseball, although he was forced to operate under the most harrowing circumstances and conditions, one must understand how it must have been for him to play baseball, as Bill Roeder so expressively put it in his book on Jackie, "in a mask." Jackie expected crank notes, abuse, roughhousing, segregation in certain hotels, animosity from the opposition and even from some of the players on his own team. But what happens to a man within whom emotion rages, yet who is not allowed to let the searing feelings escape him?

Bench-jockeying is a part of baseball and the man who gives it expects to get it back. But at the start, Jackie could not give, only receive. In tight flag races, in slumps, in spurts, on bad plays and close decisions by umpires, in the thousand little disturbing moments that mark the 154 games of every baseball season, there are times a man must let off steam or burst. But for Robinson there was no safety valve, no outlet.

Consider these circumstances before judging the man. Remember what Robinson has accomplished, pacing the Dodgers to their flags in 1947 and 1949 and winning the most valuable player award in the latter year as he had won the rookie of the year honor in '47. Despite his obvious success on the field, far surpassing what Rickey had hoped for at any time, Jackie could not be satisfied with things as they were. Within him welled a resentment at being stifled, bound by restrictive do's and don't's that chafed not only physically, but threatened his own mental stability.

Perhaps the first to know about it was Mel Jones, Jackie's general manager at Montreal. Once, Robinson came into his office and said, "Nobody knows what I am going through this season."

It wasn't until a few months ago that Mrs. Robinson, a registered nurse who understands the limits to which a man can expose his body and mind to self-discipline, disclosed what torment she and her husband went through in the seasons Jackie wore his armor of humility.

"At the end of his first season in baseball," she said, "I became extremely worried about Jack. I knew nobody could go along day after day, week after week, and month after month bottling up his emotion. I knew what Mr. Rickey had advised and, like Jack, I agreed. Yet I expected my husband to break loose at home, even if he couldn't do it on the field. Understanding his problem, which was mine as well, I would have welcomed an outburst at home. I asked him to speak his peace when we were alone together. Every man needs to talk himself out when he has a problem, but instead Jack became less talkative.

"He couldn't eat," Mrs. Robinson said, "and at night he'd toss constantly in his sleep. Finally, I insisted that Jack consult a doctor, who warned him if he didn't stay away from the ball park he would surely suffer a nervous breakdown. But Jack wouldn't give it up. In two days, he was back, playing as well as he ever did before and carrying the same problems around within him."

There have been stages in Jackie's life as he advanced from being a hungry little boy in a fatherless family of five children to the dominating personality he is today. There was the kid who sold papers, did odd jobs, searched for lost golf balls and junk and peddled them in and around Pasadena, California, to bring money into the house and help put food on the table.

There was the young college student pushing a broom to stay in school, while he also played football, baseball, basketball and starred for the track team. There was the Army lieutenant, in uniform as millions of other Americans were, railroaded into a court martial, charged with serious military infractions because he refused to abide by Jim Crow laws while riding a bus on an Army reservation in the South. There was the ballplayer, the first of his kind but one who had to subordinate his natural inclinations and personality because he knew he would not be allowed to disassociate himself from the color of his skin.

A point in each stage must be examined before the full significance of what Mrs. Robinson had said can be realized. For only by examining the boy and the circumstances under which he lived can one come to know the man.

Jackie's grandmother was a Georgia slave and his mother was a half-cropper on a big plantation. As she later was to tell her five children and a cousin who came to live with them after their father deserted them, "It was all right. If you tend to your own business, nobody bothers you."

But Jackie never got to know about that. When he was barely over a year old. Mallie Robinson moved her family to Pasadena, California. A woman who would work, doing domestic chores for others, could raise a family there. They were the only Negroes on their street, but the Robinson's got along. He played with white boys, Japanese and Mexicans and even a little white girl, who, at ten, was Jackie's own age when they had their first argument.

The two kids had the same chore. Each morning, they were assigned to sweep the sidewalk in front of the house in which they lived. Jackie doesn't remember who started the name-calling, but as all kids do he said, "You're a this," and she accepted the challenge by shouting, "You're a that." It was strictly kid stuff, the kind of spats that are all but forgotten ten minutes later. "But when the girl shouted, "You little black nigger," Jackie grabbed a stone and threw it at her. The girl, in tears, called for her father, and as he came from his house, she shouted what had happened. The adult called Jackie the same name and tossed a stone at him.

Tears streaming down his face, Jackie threw some debris at the father. It started a rock fight that lasted well over an hour. The neighbors, locked behind their doors, watched the pitched battle. Mallie Robinson tried to stop it, but each time she would open her door, a stone would force her to bang it shut. Jackie's brothers, Edgar, Frank and Mack, loved it. They formed an ammunition train for their youngest brother, running from tree to tree carrying armfuls of stones.

The shame of the spectacle finally forced the man's wife to dare the barrage and drag her husband off the street and into their home. The last words Jackie heard as he and his brothers stood triumphant in the street was the woman shouting to her husband, "You ought to be ashamed of yourself out there fighting with that little boy."

It must have been out there that Jackie first learned he could not run and hide from the basic hatreds which surrounded him, or perhaps it was in high school and college where he found he could give free rein to his competitive spirit and an aggressiveness which was to make him one of UCLA's all-time great athletes.

In Muir Tech, Jackie scaled only 143 pounds, but light as he was, he could not be convinced to stay away from varsity tryouts. He made the football team, as well as basketball, baseball and track, but his first public notice came on the gridiron. He was most spectacular in that sport. Pasadena Junior College wanted him, and after two years there, it was the big time with Robinson running beside Kenny Washington at UCLA.

In the years to come, as Rickey and his "bird dogs" narrowed their search for the Negro player they sought down to Robinson, there was to be more considered than what sort of an athlete Jackie had been in his college days and how good a baseball player he had become. They dipped deeply into his athletic record, of course, but they went beyond Jackie's 12-yard ball carrying average in 1939. Rickey is a man with friends and contacts in every big city and little hamlet in the nation and it was from them that he obtained information about Robinson which never appeared in the headlines or found its place in the box-scores.

He learned, for example, that in high school and college, Robinson had not been the kind other students, players, officials and coaches embraced and took to their bosoms. They cheered his performances on the athletic field if they were on his side and tried to knock him out if they were against him, but most of them disliked him. The sum-up came in one remark that as an athlete Jackie had been "over-assertive."

As Rickey searched in the remote corners of Jackie's personal life, he came across one interlude which should have made it crystal clear that Robby was not the kind of man who would knuckle under to intolerance, or, if he did, it would build a backwash of emotion in him which would have to burst its dam one way or another.

In April, 1942, Robinson entered the Army as a cavalry private. By 1943, he had won a commission. An old football injury had left bone chips in one ankle, however, and Army medics soon discovered these and placed him on limited service. For the next few months, Robinson shuttled between the hospital in Waco, Texas, and Camp Hood while he underwent re-examination. On one such night, Robby decided to visit the officers' club. To reach the club from the hospital sometimes took the better part of an hour. It was several miles from Waco to the post, a change of busses and another ride on Army property. To his keen disappointment, when Jackie reached his destination he learned the friends he wished to see were out on maneuvers.

Jackie started back to the hospital almost immediately, accompanied by the wife of one of his fellow officers, who was going into Waco. She was a light-skinned Negro, whose fair color was emphasized by Jackie's dark skin. As the pair took seats midway in the bus, other occupants stared at the two. But Jackie didn't notice. He was exasperated by the Army's indecision over his status and was explaining it to his companion.

In the midst of his explanation, Jackie became aware that his companion was no longer listening. She was looking to the front of the bus and as Robinson followed her gaze he heard, for the first time, the bus driver shouting at him.

"You hear me?" he called. "I said go back and sit in the rear of the bus."

The driver rose from his seat and came toward Robinson. Standing above Jackie in the aisle, his face set in rage, he snarled, "Get in the back where you belong or there'll be trouble."

For a moment, Robinson said nothing. The driver was a civilian, but he must have known there was no segregation on the post. Jackie restrained his companion as she started to rise. "I'm not moving any place," he answered. "You better drive this bus and leave me alone."

He couldn't cow the lieutenant, the driver knew. He turned to his seat, but still did not throw the vehicle into gear.

"When this bus gets to the front gate you better be in the rear or there's going to be trouble," he warned.

Robinson was resolute. "The directive said there's no segregation. Now just drive the bus and let me alone."

The bus moved toward the gate. When it got there, the driver jumped off before his passengers. As Robinson and his companion stepped down, the driver was there. He thrust a finger at Jackie. "This is the nigger's been giving me a hard time," he said, talking to a dispatcher.

Jackie wanted no trouble. He had broken no rules. He led the girl across the street where the bus to Waco would come in. As they waited, a jeep stopped at the curb. An M.P. sergeant said to Jackie, "Excuse me, sir, but the bus driver and dispatcher have complained to me there's been some trouble. They've put in a complaint about you."

Robinson explained what had happened. The M.P. said, "Would it be all right with you to come over to the Provost Marshall and get this thing cleared up? I've got to carry it through because of the complaint." Jackie entered the M.P. jeep and told his companion it shouldn't take long for the matter to be straightened. She wanted to come with him, but he assured her he would not need her testimony.

As Robinson recalls the incident now, there is understandable bitterness in his recollection and voice. To this day, he has never taken a drink of whiskey, but before that day was over, Jackie was charged with drunkenness, conduct unbecoming an officer, willful disobedience of an order and disrespect to a commanding officer.

His fellow Negro officers at Camp Hood were dismayed by what had happened. They protested the action and appealed for assistance to the National Association for the Advancement of Colored People. Before the unpleasantness was done, Jackie was forced to stand a court martial. It was under reduced charges and Robinson was completely exonerated.

I have gone back into Jackie's early life because it is the only way to understand what he has become and why he has become it. The restrictions that were placed upon him when he started made for an unnatural baseball life, which would have been strange enough as it was because of the color of his skin. A complete code of conduct was preordained for Robinson before he ever stepped on a field. Wherever he was due to appear as baseball's pioneering Negro, Rickey sent his advance man and advance plans to control the natural — and sometimes bestial — forces.

Committees were set up through churches and social organizations and civic leaders were formed into "how to handle Robinson" clubs. Each prepared its own list of do's and don't's for Jackie. His conduct on and off the field was to be decided for him and supervised from day to day. His deportment received more attention before he ever swung a bat or fielded a ball than is lavished on Princess Elizabeth.

He could not endorse breakfast foods or lend his name to magazine articles or newspaper stories, which go to swell a player's income and reputation. He came to the ball park secretly and left the same way. Adulation had to be avoided as much as criticism from the stands and the fans. It was feared Jackie would represent a symbol more than a ballplayer attempting to make good.

How long could a man be expected to take this? Indefinitely, if what was once said by Rickey can be accepted as the real meaning of his plans. It was a bitter, wintry night on February 5, 1947. Robinson had made good at Montreal the year before. The fact was indicated by the announcement that the Dodgers had shifted their base of spring training operations from Florida, where they were threatened with locked ball parks because of Robinson, to Havana and Panama. Herbert T. Miller, executive secretary of the Carlton YMCA had assembled 30 distinguished Brooklyn Negroes as Rickey's guest at a dinner. They expected that Branch would announce Robinson's historic promotion to the Dodgers.

The only white people in the room, as Rickey rose to speak, were Judge Edward Lazansky, Rickey's friend, and a stenographer, who had been brought along to inscribe the minutes of the meeting. An accomplished speaker, Rickey seemed to have difficulty beginning his talk. Few in the audience realized that the Brooklyn Mahatma had written three speeches for this occasion and had discarded them all.

When he did talk, Rickey talked extemporaneously. "You good people who have come here on a bitter night such as this," he said slowly and with great pause, "sort of embarrass me. The pleasant smiles on your faces are not entirely due to the fine chicken dinner. Well, I'm not going to tell you what you expect, what you want to hear."

With these words the atmosphere of the room changed suddenly. There was a tenseness, a chill, as though a cold draft of wind had somehow come through the windows into the warm room. "I was told by someone close to me that I couldn't tell you what I wanted to say. That I didn't have the courage to give it and that you people won't be able to take it.

"Well, I don't believe that," Rickey said. "I think all of us here tonight have courage enough to give or take anything. I have a ballplayer named Jackie Robinson. He is on the Montreal team. He may stay there. He may be brought up to Brooklyn. I don't know at this point exactly when or if at all. But I want to say that if it happens, if Jackie Robinson does come up to the Dodgers as a major-leaguer, the biggest threat to his success—the one enemy most likely to ruin that success—is the Negro people themselves."

Rickey had anticipated the effect of his words on his audience. Through the room there were exclamations of shock, amazement, even anger. "I mean it and I'll repeat it as cruelly as I can, to make you all realize and appreciate the weight of responsibility that is not only on me and my associates but on Negroes everywhere. Every step of racial progress you have made has been won by suffering and often bloodshed. This step is being taken for you by a single person whose wounds you cannot see or share. You haven't fought a single lick for this victory, if it is one.

"And yet, on the day that Robinson enters the big league, if he does, every one of you will go out and form parades and welcoming committees. You'll hold Jackie Robinson Days and Jackie Robinson Nights. You'll get drunk. You'll fight. You'll wine and dine the player until he is fat and futile. You'll symbolize his importance into a national tragedy — yes, tragedy. For let me tell you this." Rickey shouted, his voice brimming with the full measure of emotion within him. "If any individual group or segment of Negro society uses the advancement of Jackie Robinson in baseball as a symbol of a social 'ism' or schism, I will curse the day I ever signed him to a contract, and I will personally see that baseball is never so abused and misrepresented again."

As a result of this extraordinary meeting and speech, further committees were formed dedicated to one purpose: "Don't spoil Jackie's chances." From the Negro pulpits throughout the territory in which baseball is played, sermons were preached on the subject. In cafes and saloons patronized by Negroes, waiters and bartenders advised their patrons against doing anything which would jeopardize Jackie's standing.

On the whole, it was an admirable campaign and for the most part it served a tremendous purpose. Yet here there was an attempt to stifle unnaturally the enthusiasm of the millions who saw in self-identification with Robinson their own step toward 100 percent citizenship.

Rickey's detractors still say that when he opened the door for Negroes in baseball, his eye was on the ticket gate rather than on any humanitarian possibilities. Rickey himself has insisted, and those who were close to him all during the period leading up to the great experiment agree, that the motivating force behind the challenging action was pennants for the Dodgers.

This may be correct, but surely of considerably more enduring significance were the sociological aspects of Robinson's pioneering.

To those who have not traveled the road with the Dodgers, it may be difficult to comprehend fully, but those who have seen Robinson enter or leave the ball parks around the circuit know what a tremendous influence he has been on a whole race of people.

The objective bystander inside and outside Wrigley Field, Chicago, for example, is struck by the full meaning of Jackie Robinson for his people. They regard him with nothing less than adoration, which, in its strictest sense, is a word that can be applied only to the deity. This is not meant, in any sense, to be sacrilegious. It is a recognition of things as they are — of what Robinson has come to mean to the Negro people.

The Dodgers travel to and from their downtown hotel to Wrigley Field in a private bus, which is parked on a side street. Literally thousands are waiting to see them when the bus arrives at the ball park, but after the game the crush is so thick it is almost impossible to traverse the few hundred feet from the players' exit to the waiting vehicle.

Every Dodger is a hero of sorts, of course, for any who come in contact with Robinson have assumed, in the mind of his worshippers, certain of Jackie's attributes. Roy Campanella and Don Newcombe, Jackie's Negro teammates, come in for their share of attention, naturally, but the true adoration is reserved for Robinson. There is an ecstasy that borders on religious relief as the crowd sees Jackie and crushes itself into an immobile mass on either side of him.

They call his name in a way no other player's name is called. They plead to shake his hand or ask for his autograph. They touch his clothes as he walks by, unhurrying, pleasant, friendly, cooperative, because Jackie has never once lost sight of what the game has meant to him and what he has meant, means now, and will always mean to his people.

Despite his pioneering, Robinson never wanted a role of reformer. All he ever asked, once he had proved himself to Rickey, who believed in him from the beginning, was to be accepted as a player among other players. He didn't once whimper when the restrictions were placed upon him and the opposition began to test his courage and temper. He took anything anybody had to give. He began his career in organized baseball under a manager reared in the anti–Negro tradition of Mississippi and was faced in his first season with the Dodgers with threat of two strikes against him, both literally and figuratively.

Robinson may never have heard what Clay Hopper, his Montreal manager, said about him, but Jackie surely knew how the pilot felt. This was during his first spring training at Daytona Beach in 1946 when Robinson played in an intra-squad game. Robinson was splendid in the field and Rickey, who sat next to Hopper, raved about Robinson's performances. Robby ranged far toward second base, scooped a hard-hit ground ball from the dirt, wheeled and threw to first base for a spectacular out.

"No other human being could have made that play," Rickey exclaimed to Hopper.

The Mississippi man, who had remained completely uncommunicative in the previous days which must have constituted the most tumultuous period of his life, turned to Rickey. "Mr. Rickey," he said, "do you really think he *is* a human being?"

Before Robinson, whose performances that year sparked Montreal into a playoff victory, and Hopper parted company as Jackie moved up to the Dodgers, the man from Mississippi came to Rickey and said: "You don't have to worry about that boy. He's the greatest competitor I ever saw. And what's more, he's a gentleman."

This was what Rickey wanted to hear, but it took more than Hopper's okay to convince some of the men with whom and against whom Jackie was destined to play in 1947.

The seeds of dissent were sown months before the announcement of Jackie's actual promotion to the Dodgers. Rickey knew Robbie would be moved up, but many considerations prompted a delay until the propitious moment. The suspension of Leo Durocher just before the 1947 season opened hastened the matter and ruptured Rickey's timetable, but by that time, at least, a hurdle Rickey had not anticipated had been cleared.

The Dodgers had definite weaknesses at first base and third base. Robby's arm was not fit for the long throw from third. The shift of Robinson to the position at which he had never played before seemed indicated. Rickey also had in mind the series of exhibition games between the Dodgers and Royals in which he felt sure Robinson would impress himself on the minds of the Brooklyn players as the man who could help them win the flag. There was even a dramatic meeting planned at which Durocher was to shout he didn't care about the color of a man's skin. He wanted Robinson advanced from Montreal to Brooklyn because he was the kind of player who could do a winning job. He would point to Robby's great performances in the intra-organization exhibitions as proof that Robby belonged. He would demand Robinson.

The first step in this complicated plan was put into effect while the Dodgers were off for three weeks of side trips to Venezuela and Panama. Left behind was the Montreal club, with Robby ostensibly still a third-baseman. One morning, Mel Jones, the Royals' general manager, handed Robinson a first-baseman's glove.

"What's this all about?" Jackie asked.

"It's Mr. Rickey's idea," Jones explained. "He wants to give you a chance to make his club. He says there's no other place for you to play. He thinks you can learn to play first base in no time."

Robinson was definitely against the switch. He had been a shortstop with the Kansas City Monarchs and had spent a full year mastering second base. Now he was being asked to break in at a new position.

Hopper, the Montreal manager, was equally enraged. He was beginning to get the idea that Rickey was using Montreal merely as the proving ground for Robinson. By so doing, Branch was keeping Howie Schultz and Ed Stevens from competing for the Royals' first-base job.

Rickey was adamant. Robinson began to work at his unfamiliar job and the strange sight, when the Dodgers returned to Havana, erased any doubts in their minds about Jackie's status.

At first, the plan seemed to be proceeding in the fashion Rickey had hoped. Branch soon learned that all was not well. Certain players were surreptitiously stirring up sentiment against Jackie's promotion. The grapevine reported a petition was being prepared. Harold Parrott, the Dodgers' traveling secretary, was the first member of the front-office staff to learn of the underground dissension. Two men, reared in the tradition of the South, gradually emerged as particularly obstinate. One was Bobby Bragan, the other was Dixie Walker, who, in his years of playing with Brooklyn, had become the most popular performer at Ebbets Field.

Rickey's interview with Bragan was one of the most heated, but Bobby, a third-string catcher, remained firm in his conviction against Robinson.

"Would you like your contract transferred to another club?" Rickey asked.

"Yes, sir, I would," Bragan said. "But I don't want to be made the goat of a mess I didn't create."

"Then I may accommodate you, sir!" Rickey replied. "Good night."

On March 26, 1947, Rickey received a letter from Walker, which Dixie later sought to have returned to him. In it, Walker spoke feelingly of his years in Brooklyn but said it would be best for all concerned if a trade to another team could be arranged for him. Branch quickly attempted to effect such a deal.

"Pittsburgh agrees to accept Walker for $40,000 cash, Gionfriddo and Kalin," Roy Hamey, general manager of Pittsburgh, wrote in agreement. But the deal did not go through.

So it was that Bragan and Walker played through a season with Robinson. The trouble they had anticipated from within did not arise, but as Jackie's teammates, they had front row seats in observing how he reacted to the hostility from the opposition, if not from his own teammates.

When the season was over, Bragan came to Rickey and said while his attitude toward Negroes in general had not changed, he felt it only fair to say he had begun to like Robinson and playing on the same team with him. Rickey could not have asked Bobby to say more. When a managerial opening developed at Fort Worth, Rickey gave the job to Bragan. Walker, of course, was eventually sent to Pittsburgh, but not until he had spurned an offer from Rickey to manage the Dodgers' St. Paul farm.

In their one season together on the team, Robinson and Dixie were particularly circumspect in their relations with each other. Robby knew and appreciated the torment that the season must have been for Dixie and when it was done and Robinson was asked about their relationship, he said: "I think Dixie has accepted me on the ball club so far as the playing end of it went. Socially, no. But that was perfectly all right with me. I understood and it wasn't embarrassing except once or twice when he hit a home run while I was on base.

"Normally, you wait at the plate to shake hands with the man who hits the home run. With Dixie, I wasn't sure what he expected me to do but I thought it would be the smart thing to get out of there. I would just go to the dugout without waiting for him to reach the plate."

In the sum total of incidents which have surrounded Jackie's days in baseball, this now becomes a minor one. Difficulty was avoided by walking around the corner, so to speak. But there were others that would have to be met bluntly, with a head-on attack, if necessary.

A short while after the Phillies, under Ben Chapman's direction, worked Jackie over profanely, Robby appeared in the Dodger offices. It was thought at the time that he had come to ask for some sort of assistance against the vilification. One Dodger official asked Jackie if he wanted an emissary to go to Chapman or Robert Carpenter, the Philly boss.

"I do not," Jackie said bluntly. "They'll either stop it by themselves or they won't stop it at all. Either I can take it or I can't. I didn't come for that anyway."

Jackie took a letter from his pocket. "This came in the mail for me today. It may be nothing but a crank. It may be serious."

The contents of the letter was, indeed, reason to act because it was the first of many such threatening notes Jackie was to receive. Even to this day, when Negroes are secure in the big league and Robinson has proved he is the kind of a player any club would hasten to obtain, Jackie still receives such letters. One was sent to him early this year in Cincinnati, but Robby, reporting the note to the authorities, also disclosed of what kind of stuff he is made when he said, "Anybody who was going to shoot me wouldn't advertise it in a letter."

But back in 1947 no one could be sure. The letter, threatening physical harm to Jackie and his family, was turned over to New York's police commissioner. The authorities learned the name signed to it was fictitious and so was the address.

Hardly had this crisis been discovered to be a very minor affair when one arose which had repercussions all through the nation. Stanley Woodward, sports editor of the New York *Herald Tribune,* uncovered a plan by the St. Louis Cardinals to strike in protest against Robinson on May 16. The disclosure was all that was needed to prevent what could have become the seamiest incident in the history of baseball. To this day, Jackie himself expresses uncertainty that any strike was contemplated. Yet despite denials by the Cardinal players, president Sam Breadon, their owner, as well as Branch Rickey and Ford Frick, president of the National League, admitted that such a movement had gained headway in the Red Bird locker room. Quick action had rendered it stillborn.

Frick sent an ultimatum to the Cardinals. In it he said, "If you do this, you will be suspended from the league. You will find that the friends you have in the press-box will not support you, that you will be outcasts. I do not care if half the league strikes. Those who do will encounter quick retribution."

There was no strike and as the season progressed the opposition, which had contended that the idea of playing a Negro in the majors could not possibly work and would only breed trouble, noted soon enough that Robinson's presence on the diamond was good for baseball instead of being bad for it.

Wherever the Dodgers played, great crowds came to see Jackie. Not just Negroes, although Jackie's presence on the field increased their numbers in the stands immeasurably, but there were more whites, too, and like all others, they soon discovered Robinson was a big-leaguer in every way.

Not since the heyday of Babe Ruth has a player come along to have so profound an effect on baseball. Like Ruth, Jackie was both a player and a side show. The player helped make the game more exciting and helped the Dodgers win pennants. The side show was beneficial to the boxoffice.

It was only natural for Jackie to come to appreciate his own worth at the gate and want to tear away from the unnatural bonds that restricted him. You could pick any point during this past season when Jackie completed his own emancipation and you would be both right and wrong. The Maglie incident at Ebbets Field, perhaps, would be as close as any in estimating when the last shackle was torn loose.

To one who remembered the restricted Robinson playing with a fence about him, so to speak, that incident characterized the new Jackie. There had been telltale evidences of his new approach to the business in which he earns his living before he ran up the Giant pitcher's back, and there were to be more after he did so, but this one wrapped up the new Jackie into a neat little package for all to see.

Robinson was a pioneer, but identification in the role of a reformer was something he never sought and did not relish when it came to him. But he felt that hectic night at Ebbets Field last April that he had to see it through even at the risk of his reputation, his body, his wealth and against the advice of his wife. Such was the explanation he made to me when he told why he had decided to make himself the avenging aggressor for the beanballing feud which had become the motif of the Dodger-Giant series.

I told Jackie that Maglie had denied throwing at him.

"I suppose I'm at fault," he said. "Everytime something happens, I pick up a paper and read I'm at fault. If Maglie didn't throw at me, then his catcher thought differently. After the bunt, I came back to the plate and picked up my bat and Westrum said, 'Sal wasn't throwing at you. You've been wearing us out. He was just brushing you back.'

"That's too fine a difference for me," Robinson said. "This morning I read where Durocher said it was a bush-league trick. If I'm bush, Durocher made me that way. He taught it to me. Right here in this clubhouse, he used to tell us every day, 'If they throw one at your head, don't say anything. Push one down and run right up his neck.' Leo's an expert at it. He was right. The next two times at bat, not a pitch came close to me."

Following the game that night, Jackie and Mrs. Robinson drove back to their Long Island home and Jackie explained his point of view to her. She, in turn, talked of the larger picture. Some time later, she repeated their conversation to me and said, "I've been trying to make Jack see it from the fans' point of view because they can't understand what's in Jack's mind. They don't appreciate that he's willing to run the risk of injury to stop what he believes is wrong. To them it appeared he was maliciously trying to injure Maglie. How can they know what is in his mind?

"Maybe today Jack feels differently about what happened," she said. "I think I understand his problem better than most. When he's at bat, he doesn't have much time to stop and think. Maybe a few hours later, he thinks and does differently."

As much as I admire Mrs. Robinson and her incomparable contribution in her partnership with Jackie, I knew as she spoke that she was wrong because Jackie had indicated as much to me.

"I don't want to have to do something like that again, but if I have to I will," he said.

The fact is Jackie today feels under no restraint whatsoever. Perhaps even less than any other player because, in effect, he has accomplished more. Other players hesitate to air their opinions, but Jackie, who had allowed so much to be shut inside him for so many seasons, speaks his piece whenever there is something on his mind. Much of it is of an incendiary nature, but Jackie doesn't mind explosive quotes. He despises Durocher and he says so. He thought he was ticketed for trade before the start of this season and he felt free to tell me about it.

When I printed in my column in the New York *Post* his conviction that he had played his last season with the Dodgers, the piece created considerable stir in newspaper and baseball circles. Jackie had a great big "out" when the Brooklyn front office and manager Burt Shotton denied the story and reporters came to Jackie to confirm the denial.

"I told that to Gross," Jackie said straightforwardly. "I didn't think he would print it, but what he wrote he got from me."

It was much the same way on July 4 this season when the Dodgers knocked off the Giants in a doubleheader and began to show real light between themselves and the rest of the league. Before the twin bill began, the Dodger bench was empty except for Robinson. His pigeon toes stretched before him, he tossed a new baseball petulantly from hand to hand. His lips moved, making muttering sounds, as he glowered across the infield.

"You talking to yourself?" a visitor asked. "No," Robinson answered sharply. "I was just getting warm and they pulled me off the field for pictures."

"It's always that way," he was told. "Why should it bother you more now?"

"This one is different," Jack replied. "We've been playing lousy ball. In Boston we pointed for this one and we got beat. Looking ahead, we handed a game away. This is the one we want to win. This one always sets us off."

He looked across the field where Durocher's second-place Giants were warming up. The reporter looked, too, and asked, "Do you mean that team or do you mean that man?"

"You mean Leo?" Jackie asked, and then he said, "The man, the team. It's the same. We want to beat them."

"You really dislike him, don't you?"

It was the first time Robinson smiled. "I say the hell with that…. Yes, I dislike him. He feels the same way about me. He doesn't keep it a secret. Neither do I. That makes us even."

Even … it's the way Jackie wants it and has it now. Starting from scratch with all the rest and letting the best get there first. Rickey wanted him to play Alphonse and Gaston, but Jackie discarded the role. Once this season Russ Meyer of the Phils had the Dodgers beaten. Jackie's voice joined the others in riding the hot-tempered pitcher, who, himself, is one of the league's sharpest jockeys.

Finally, in a late inning, Robby got on base. He drove Meyer crazy with his antics, stealing second and going to third on an error. He came dashing for the plate and Meyer was there with the ball to meet him, but Jackie charged him, knocking it from the pitcher's glove to score.

Russ went livid with anger. Philly manager Eddie Sawyer, sensing the pitcher could not be effective any longer in such a state, took him from the game. Sitting on the bench, Meyer shouted across the field to Jackie. The television cameras, trained on the dugouts, picked up Russ' arm-waving and shouting and finally his unmistakable challenge for Robby to meet him and fight under the stands in the alleyway that connects the rival dugouts.

Meyer rushed down the steps to the battleground. Jackie dashed after him and both dugouts emptied into the narrow passageway. The umpires came off the field and fortunately put an end to the business before a blow could be struck, but it is significant that Jackie felt free to take up the challenge and that his teammates raced behind him to back him up.

This is the unencumbered Robinson and his relation with his teammates. The only difference between Jackie and the others is that he, Don Newcombe and Roy Campanella cannot stay in the same hotel in St. Louis because of the city's segregation customs.

But there the variance ends. Where he once could not make endorsements, Jackie now considers there are no strings upon him in the matter of cashing in off the field on his talent on the field. If he wants to make a public appearance, for free or for money, he does so without first taking the matter to the Brooklyn higher-ups. He admits no reason why he should follow a course of conduct any different from that pursued by the Joe DiMaggios, the Bob Fellers, or the Ted Williamses. He asks no license but accepts no special restrictions.

On the field his bat speaks louder than the others and in the clubhouse there is

no deference in his voice and his actions because of his delicate position. Not physically, morally or spiritually does Robby consider himself delicate any longer. He
proved to Rickey he could take it. He kept his mouth shut and his emotions bottled
for a reasonable period of time, but that time has come to an end. And there's none
who cares to challenge him or has a right to say he is wrong.

Two of the unsung heroes of the post–World War II Brooklyn Dodgers were right fielder Carl Furillo and third baseman Billy Cox. In his novel Brooklyn Boy, *Alan Lelchuk sees them through the eyes of Aaron Schlossberg, the young protagonist of the story. It is fitting that these artists of the game be regaled so poetically.*

THE ARM

Alan Lelchuk

He had a long Roman nose, hardly ever smiled, and always used two hands to catch the ball. An Italian gardener, say, whose domain was right field, with the high fence looming behind him. Actually, there were three parts to that fence: the black scoreboard high up in right center, the 150-foot-high hurricane fence above and to the right, and the low ten-to-twelve-foot base of the wall lined with advertisements that ran the length of right field all the way to the stands. No one ever doubted, for a moment, that Furillo would catch any fly ball or line drive that came his way — in ten years of watching him, the boy never saw him muff one — and that he would manage those tricky bounces and odd ricochets off the walls with consistent skill. In his fielding Carl was always there, always consistent.

The element of elegance entered after he had caught a ball, by means of his golden arm. You see, when it came to throwing a baseball from the outfield with strength and accuracy, Furillo was no longer a gardener, but a prince. Style was added to competence. In fact, when the kids sat out there in the lower right-field grandstand, they rooted for the moment in the game — especially if it were a late inning in a tight game — when an opposing player would hit a shot off the fence and try for a double; or when a player already on the bases tried to make third or home on that shot. When the dare was there, Carl was ready, along with Aaron and pals. Turning and firing on baseball instinct, Furillo threw overhand on a line directly over his shoulder, flinging the small white hardball nearly three hundred feet in the air to a precise point: an infielder's or catcher's glove. Robin Hood was not more accurate with his bow and arrow. And that throw, or peg — a "clothesline," according to Red Barber — was a flight of beauty, a line of poetry amidst prose of ordinary hits and outs.

It affected its audience, the knowledgeable crowd, like a sudden poetic revelation. For example, take a game against the feared Cards, when the great Musial was up, with two men on base. Now Musial owned the right-field fence; he was prob-

From *Brooklyn Boy* by Alan Lelchuk. ©1990 by Alan Lelchuk. Reprinted by permission of Georges Borchardt, Inc., for the author.

153

ably the best Ebbets Field hitter who ever played there. Two on, two out, in the sixth inning, and the Bums leading by 4–2. The middle-age couple in front of the boy had been arguing the whole damn game, with the straw-hatted pock-faced man repeating how sorry he was to have taken her to the game. "Shit, never again, what a damn waste!" Aaron was tempted to lean over and tell him to knock it off, except it wasn't his eleven-year-old business, and besides, he'd probably get his block knocked off. Anyway, old Stan the Man did his usual thing, lashing out from his corkscrew batting stance and walloping the ball on an upward arc out to the scoreboard, Repulski and Schoendienst on the move, and Carl on the move too. Running to an exact point to play the ricochet, Carl grabs the ball on the fly off the scoreboard, turns, and, in one motion decides where and how to throw. He lets loose his clothesline, a high peg beyond the cutoff man and on a fly to Campy at home. For three long seconds the boys are filled with silent hope and wonder while watching the little white ball traveling on its low arc in the race to beat the Card runner home. Campy has to move maybe a half-step up the third-base line (the right direction) to catch the exacting peg, and confront the runner Schoendienst barreling down at him. An explosion of bodies and a whirl of dust. For a fraction of a second there is quiet, while the ump checks the ball in Campy's grip, and the fans replay the peg, the brazen decision to try to cut down the fleet Red. When he's called out, the crowd lets loose its appreciation, cheering like crazy, while Carl trots in, deadpanned, oblivious, dutiful.

"Would you believe that, Alice? Cutting down Schoendienst! The ogre in the next row chants, "Would you believe that?" and he grabs his slender wife and hugs her! And would you believe that from then on the ogre turns into a pussycat for the rest of the game, doing a complete turnabout and treating his wife like a dear soul, never once cussing again?

The prince's arm, and magical peg, could do those sorts of things: turn the nasty into the chivalric, the petty into the poetic. "Attaway, Carl, attaway to go!" Aaron screamed as he half-ran off the field, but Carl treated it like just another play, just another workday.

But just imagine if we could take that peg, and put it right up there on a stage for all the world to see? You know, like a kid's version of a Shakespeare monologue or something. Only I guess it belonged right where it was, on Ebbets Field turf.

The Glove

Toward the hot corner, third base, the balls were slammed the hardest and swiftest, it seemed, and our man out there was the smoothest fielder. His name was Billy Cox, and, playing with the old four-fingered mitt, he made it all look easy. It didn't matter if the ball was a fine bunt, a hard grounder, a line drive, a foul pop down the line. It was all butter-smooth easy. Fielding was *his* way, his habitation, and, like DiMaggio in center, he didn't have to throw his body on the ground and dirty up his uniform to make the plays. He knew the batters, knew what they could and couldn't do, and what the inning and the score meant. He was positioned always perfectly, that's all.

The hands were fast, so fast, faster than the fan's eye. Like some gunslinger out West who could outdraw anyone, Cox could get his hands down on the ground or suddenly out into the air swifter than any mortal infielder. If the ball was sometimes slammed up the line in a perfect blur, his glove would somehow be there, scooping the ball easily, the crowd gasping at his skill. If the ball hit a pebble and took a sudden crazy bounce, no problem, Billy's glove was right there, fielding it. A couple of times I saw him catch the ball with his bare hand, out of dire necessity, and his right hand handled it just fine. Frequently he got to the ball so fast that he'd wait a second or two, sometimes even inspecting the ball, before throwing over to first to get the batter by a step. Curious, how often he made the hot corner a position of some leisure, enjoying the cat and mouse game.

Bunts, the cruel bane of so many third basemen, he treated with ease, and a touch of disdain. As though you could try to trick him or cheat the pitcher by trying to get on first base, with a meager fifteen-or-twenty-foot tap. No chance. He'd pounce down on the ball, pick it up in that sure right hand, and already, in that same one motion, be tossing the ball sidearm to first. Thus the strategic bunting game was nearly taken away completely from other teams, just as, for right-handed hitters, a whole normal region of safe hitting ground was suddenly an easy out. And you might judge the full unfairness of Billy when certain hitters, robbed of sure hits by those special hands (and his positioning), couldn't help cursing the "sonofabitch" as they crossed the field back to the visitor's dugout. He had no interest in answering them, however, since he was already hunting for stray pebbles amidst the soft dirt that might intrude on the next play. Working all the time, he patrolled his turf efficiently, keeping it clean and tidy.

He had the eye and the fast hands, and the butter glove, to make him the god of third base. In his great years, such as '52 or '53, he made fewer than ten errors during a whole season — neatly immaculate reception for a third baseman — and stole how many hits away? Those hands probably could have made a polished pool-shooter, a feared gunfighter, even a superb surgeon. As it was, he was all smoothness at the toughest infield position. He made fielding into an art, an art for the keen fan, and was cheered for it as richly as any slugger. Brooklyn fans knew the subtleties of the game.

In the wake of Bobby Thomson's "shot heard 'round the world" in the 1951 play-offs, it is often forgotten that Brooklyn had to beat the Phillies on the final day of the season just to get to the play-offs against the New York Giants.

Robby's HR, Grab Force '51 Playoff

Dick Young

Dodgers 9, Phillies 8
14 innings

[SEPTEMBER 30, 1951:] PHILADELPHIA — Folks will always say that the Brooks of 1951 blew the biggest lead in pennant history — a lead that was a huge 13½ lengths as recently as Aug. 12 and which dissolved entirely under the inexorable stretch drive of the Giants. But they will never be able to say the Brooks of 1951 lacked clutch guts.

Not after the way they salvaged a pennant tie here today to create the second NL flag playoff on record. Not after the way they rose from an early five-run deficit against the Phils and — in the face of the realization that the Giants had already won their vital game in Boston — went on to snarl the score and struggle through 14 innings before Jackie Robinson's circuit smash off Robin Roberts preserved the pennant tie via a stomach-bubbling 9–8 triumph.

Game-Saving Grab

Before he could win the game with his No. 18 seat-smasher, Robby had to save it. He did it with as self-punishing and spectacular a money play as the 31,755 attending fans, thousands of whom had poured down from Brooklyn, will ever see.

It was the 12th inning. Don Newcombe, who had become the sixth Dodger hurler in the eighth, was tiring — and no wonder. Newk had hurled nine innings of shutout ball the night before and now he was dealing more zips with his long arm and strong heart. He had given up a hit to the first man to face him in the eighth and was to give up no more through almost five innings of blank ball.

But the ordeal was telling on Newk's control. He'd walked a man in one inning, hit a man in another. He started the 12th by walking Roberts. When the Phils later had first and third with only one down, an intentional pass to Puddinhead Jones was dictated by the situation.

That soaked the sacks and brought up Del Ennis, who fanned. Then Ed Waitkus shot a low, slightly looped loner to the right of second. It seemed ticketed for the outfield, labeled hit ... game ... pennant to Giants. But Robby, diving face-first, speared the ball an instant before he hit the ground.

Many failed to realize he had held the ball until, in his pain, Robby rolled on his side and flipped the pill clear.

Gil Hodges was a slugging first baseman for the Brooklyn Dodgers during the ballclub's most prolific era. He hit 370 home runs and had 1,270 RBIs. He drove in more than 100 runs for seven consecutive seasons and hit more than 20 home runs for 11 consecutive seasons. He was arguably the best defensive first basemen of his time and one of the best in baseball's history. And yet, with all this, it was the character of the man that set him apart.

CHARACTER, DIGNITY, COURAGE

Marino Amoruso

In the 1952 World Series Gil Hodges came to the plate 26 times. He walked five times but went hitless in his other 21 attempts. A powerful weapon in the awesome Brooklyn Dodger attack, Hodges was humbled by Yankee pitching. Although he went hitless through seven games and the Yankees beat the Dodgers for the fourth straight time in Series play, not once did Gil hear a boo or a catcall from the crowd. Instead, they cheered him louder and louder each time he came to bat.

The slump continued through the early part of the 1953 season. By the middle of May Gil was hitting an anemic .187. Still he heard nothing but cheers from the Ebbets Field faithful. Each week he received hundreds of letters and telegrams wishing him luck and offering advice. His locker was filled with good luck charms sent by concerned fans everywhere. Concern welled up from the streets to support Hodges through his prolonged slump.

"The fans started sending me letters telling me they were praying for me," recalled Gil of this period of his career. "Some of them said they were making novenas for me. Others said they were saying the Rosary for me during the game. Some kids wrote that they were going to Mass for me every morning before they went to school. I even got a letter from two nuns in Pittsburgh who told me not to give up; they're saying prayers for my special intention in their convent every day."

On a hot Sunday in late May of 1953, Father Herbert Redmond addressed his congregation at the St. Francis Xavier Roman Catholic Church in Brooklyn. "It's too hot for a sermon today," he told them. "Go home, keep the commandments, and say a prayer for Gil Hodges." Father Redmond's words reflected the feelings of all Brooklyn Dodger fans. They loved the slugger and suffered with him as he struggled at the plate.

From *Gil Hodges: The Quiet Man* by Marino Amoruso. ©1991. Reprinted with permission of the author.

Even Ty Cobb, who has been described as "mean, vindictive, selfish, vain, [and] cruel," got into the act. Writing Hodges that he had "been in deep water myself and no one to help me," Cobb offered to correspond with Hodges about fundamentals, stipulating only that there be "no publicity crediting me."

The slump became so bad that Dodger manager Charlie Dressen finally benched Hodges. "Maybe you're just trying too hard," Dressen told Gil. The big first baseman rode the bench for five games. Then Dressen sent him in to pinch hit in a game against the Giants at the Polo Grounds. Gil lined a solid single to left field off Dave Koslo. As Gil rounded first the Giants fans gave him a rousing ovation.

Gil was back in the starting lineup the next day, but went hitless in his first two games. Then, in the following two games against Philadelphia, Hodges got five hits. The slump was over. He finished the year with a .302 average, 31 homers and 122 RBI's. In the 1953 World Series he led the Dodgers in hitting with a .356 mark, and in 1954 he had the best year of his career, hitting .304 with 42 home runs and 130 RBI's. The next season, 1955, the Brooklyn Dodgers won their first and only World championship, with Gil delivering the game-winning hit in the seventh contest. Across 18 major league seasons Gil Hodges hit a solid .273 and blasted 370 home runs. He hit over 20 home runs in 11 seasons, topping the 30 mark six times and the 40 mark twice. He walloped 14 grand slams, placing him third on the all-time list, and is one of only nine players to launch four round-trippers in a single game. He was also a clutch hitter, knocking in more than 100 runs in seven consecutive seasons from 1949 to 1955; and he was durable, playing in over 100 games for 14 straight seasons between 1948 and 1961. One of the greatest defensive first basemen in the game's history, he was elected to the National League All-Star team eight times.

As a big league manager, Hodges led the 1969 New York Mets to what was perhaps the most exciting and remarkable World Championship our national game has ever known. It was a World Championship that lifted the spirits of an entire nation, and it came at a time when America sorely needed its spirits lifted.

But for all his heroics on the ball field, perhaps Gil's finest hours in baseball came during his slump of the 1952 World Series and early 1953 season. It was a time of frustration and misery for Hodges, but the fans stuck by him and proved how much they loved him.

Baseball fans loved Hodges for more than his formidable abilities on a baseball diamond. They knew that although he was a large and powerful man, it was inner strength that motivated the big first baseman. He was a man of high ideals, of great character, dignity and courage. In moments of success and triumph he was modest and reserved. In times of trouble and failure he was a calming and reassuring force. He held a special place in the hearts of fans and players alike. In many ways he typified the American hero of a bygone era — a man of action and few words. In the excitement, chaos and emotional roller coaster that was Ebbets Field in the Fifties, Gil Hodges was a sea of calm, at least on the surface.

Strong, reserved, soft-spoken and always a true gentleman, Gil was also a stoic man. Whatever pain, frustration, anger, aggravation or pressure he felt he bore silently and battled against within himself. He rarely vented stress through emotional outburst. It wasn't Gil's way. He believed a man dealt with his own problems and fought his own battles. A man lived up to the responsibilities he had taken on. He took care of his family and friends. He understood what the priorities in life were, the important things. He paid for his mistakes by himself, and shared his successes with others. A man was modest about his triumphs, knowing that failure is far more frequent in his life than is success. A man took everything in stride, with humility, grace, modesty and dignity.

This was the credo Gil Hodges lived by every day of his life. It wasn't always easy, but he never faltered in his beliefs. In the pressure cooker that is big league baseball, especially big league baseball in New York City, it is doubly difficult to live by these standards. But Gil always stood by what he believed in. The stress and pressure of eighteen years as a big league ballplayer and nine as a manager stayed locked within him. It is ironic that many of the qualities for which Hodges was admired and loved were also personality characteristics that in some measure contributed to his early heart disease.

"He was a quiet strength on the field, and in the clubhouse," remembers pitcher Carl Erskine, Gil's Dodger teammate for 12 years. "His presence was always felt even though he wasn't a holler guy. I can remember that he'd walk to the mound in a tight situation, and he didn't have a whole lot to say, but whatever he did say was right to the heart of the matter. Just his being out there gave you strength. It gave you confidence."

"A silent leader" is how Brooklyn relief ace Clem Labine remembers Gil. "He was the quiet man, a great silent strength. I always felt Gilly was someone I could turn to and rely on. He was sort of a father figure on the club."

"When I think of Gil Hodges, I think of a perfect gentleman," says Preacher Roe, Gil's fellow Dodger for seven seasons. "I liked Gil so much. He was such a fine man. He was kind, good-natured, very mild and very intelligent. I just couldn't believe it when he passed away," Roe continues, shaking his head sadly. "I always thought that there was a man who was going to live forever. He was so strong, so healthy. And then back in '72 when I read that his heart gave out on him ... Jeez, I just couldn't believe it ... He was only 47 years old."

"The irony of life, and in this case, of our team," says Carl Erskine, "is that the two strongest men on the field, Gil Hodges and Jackie Robinson, were the first to have these serious health problems that resulted in their death.... You know, I went to Gil's father's funeral in Petersburg some years ago, and his father died exactly the way Gil did; his heart gave out on him. Then Gil died, and after his death his older brother Bob died from a massive heart attack as well. Afterwards, whenever I happened to be going down Highway 57 here in Indiana, I always stopped by to see Gil's mom out in Petersburg. She lost all three of her boys in the same way."

"Baseball lost one of its greatest men when Gil died," says Hall of Fame pitcher Don Drysdale, who roomed with Gil on the road for six years. "You know, it's a funny thing. I talk baseball with hundreds of people—players, coaches, managers, fans, executives—and whenever Gil's name comes up in conversation everybody becomes quiet and listens closely. It's really interesting to see. The absolute respect everybody has for this man. And when people talk about Gil, people who knew him, they speak with a respect, reverence and emotion that's different from the way they talk about anybody else. It always makes me smile when I see that. I was very lucky to have known Gil, to have been his roommate when I was a young player. He taught me how to be a big leaguer. I guess everybody who knew him was lucky. He was just a great human being. My life is greater because of him, having known him."

The Brooklyn Dodger team that Hodges played for from 1947 to 1957, when the franchise moved to Los Angeles, was not only one of the greatest clubs ever assembled, but also one of the most popular and best-loved teams in baseball history.

Indeed the Dodger-Yankee post-season confrontations represented the classic American rivalry: the underdog Dodgers, team of the masses, against the mighty, affluent New York Yankees. And the Damn Yankees always won.

Of course the Dodgers' several defeats at the hands of the Yankees in World Series play were not the only heartaches Brooklyn fans had to endure during those years. Not by a long shot. On three separate occasions between 1946 and 1951 the club managed to lose the National League pennant on the last day of the season.

"You may glory in a team triumphant," wrote Roger Kahn, "but you fall in love with a team in defeat." This was without question true of the Brooklyn Dodgers. In all of baseball there was no more loyal, fanatical and loving fans than the Ebbets Field faithful. The entire borough of Brooklyn lived and died by the fortunes of their beloved Dodgers. Indeed, it was this loyalty and love for the team that helped in some measure when Jackie Robinson broke the big-league color line in 1947. If Branch Rickey knew he had the right man in Jackie Robinson, he also knew he had the right city in Brooklyn.

The city of Brooklyn supported their team through the good times and the bad. Yet, for all the support they gave the Dodgers, fans were disappointed year after year as their team either lost the pennant in a tight race or, if they won the title, lost to the Yankees in the World Series. And every year, after another Dodger defeat, the fans kept the spirit alive with their rallying cry of "Wait 'Til Next Year!"

"Next Year" finally came for the Dodgers in 1955 when they beat the hated Yankees in seven games to win their one and only World Championship in Brooklyn. It is well known that Sandy Amoros' running catch of Yogi Berra's slicing line drive down the left-field line in the seventh inning of the seventh game probably saved the Dodgers from yet another defeat. What is not so well known is that Gil Hodges drove in both runs in the Bums' 2–0 victory with a single and a sacrifice fly.

During Brooklyn's glory years of the late Forties and early-to-mid Fifties, the team had many heroes, among them Pete Reiser, Jackie Robinson, Duke Snider, Roy Campanella, Carl Furillo, Billy Cox, Carl Erskine, Clem Labine, Preacher Roe and Pee Wee Reese; but Gil Hodges was a special favorite of the fans. He was the only player the fanatic but fickle Brooklyn fans didn't boo at one time or another. At Ebbets Field this was sort of miraculous. "If I had ever sold or traded Hodges," said owner Walter O'Malley, "the Brooklyn fans would hang me, burn me, and tear me to pieces."

"Not getting booed at Ebbets Field was an amazing thing," says Clem Labine. "Those fans knew their baseball and Gil was the only player I can remember whom the fans never, I mean never booed. That tells you a lot about the way they felt about him and the kind of man he was."

As much as the people of Brooklyn loved Gil Hodges, that's how much he loved the city of Brooklyn. In the spring of 1948, at a party given by his landlady, Gil met a pretty young Brooklyn girl from Bay Ridge named Joan Lombardi. He liked Joan at first sight and asked her for a date. Before the year was out, the bells were ringing for their wedding at St. Gregory's Church in Brooklyn. They bought a home on Bedford Avenue and settled down to raise a family.

"The city of Brooklyn has always been one of warmth and friendship and Gil loved that," recalls Hodges friend and attorney Sid Loberfeld. "He wouldn't think of living anywhere else. He found a home in Brooklyn. Anybody that knew Gil loved and respected him, and if you didn't know him personally but you followed him, you came to love him because of the kind of man he was. If baseball had more men like him it would be a great asset to the game. He was genuinely honest, decent and respectful; and he was probably the greatest man of character the game has ever produced."

In this 1953 column the Brooklyn Eagle *expressed the pride of the entire borough in their ballclub. This was following their second consecutive pennant under manager Charley Dressen.*

WHAT WINNING THE PENNANT MEANS TO BROOKLYN

Brooklyn Eagle

[SEPTEMBER 20, 1953:] Few communities have as much home-town pride as Brooklyn. The fact that the City of Brooklyn united with the old city across the East River in 1898 to form the present City of New York never changed the allegiance of real Brooklynites.

They are proud of the Brooklyn Bridge, our most famous landmark; of Coney Island, our internationally-known playground of the people; of our unexcelled water-front, of our great industries, many of whose products are sold all over the world.

Brooklyn has been known as the City of Churches and the City of Homes. The number and beauty of our churches and synagogues are unsurpassed. Here there are many attractive residential sections in the midst of this greatest metropolis in the world. For Brooklyn has long since outstripped old Manhattan and has become by far the most populous of the five boroughs.

But no institution in our midst has done more to spread the fame of Brooklyn to the uttermost parts of the earth than the Brooklyn Dodgers baseball club.

The pennant just won under the leadership of Manager Chuck Dressen is thoroughly deserved. While the team excels in batting and fielding and all the arts of the game, it has been the personalities of the players, their fighting qualities and, above all, their colorful characteristics in action that have made them so popular.

So the feat of the Dodgers in winning the National League championship for the second year in a row is not just another great sports victory. It has a meaning for this borough which we feel that many Brooklynites do not fully comprehend.

It secures constructive publicity for our town wherever baseball is followed. In every city and hamlet in this country will be found Dodger rooters. Everywhere the word "Brooklyn" is on the people's lips. Wherever the Dodgers play on the road they draw good crowds and there will often be as many people in the stands cheering for the Brooklyn players as for the home team.

Originally published in the *Brooklyn Eagle*, September 20, 1953. Reprinted with permission of Historical Briefs, Inc.

Thus the Dodgers have created a warm place in the hearts of great numbers of people all over the nation for the Brooklyn which they represent.

It is not easy to track down the results of such popularity in terms of commerce and of dollars and cents but we have no doubt that many products have greater acceptance when the consumers learn that they come from Brooklyn.

So Pee Wee Reese and Roy Campanella and Carl Erskine and Duke Snider and Carl Furillo and Jackie Robinson and all their teammates may be far more than great baseball stars on a championship team. They may be — without their knowing or even thinking about it — ambassadors extraordinary for Brooklyn. This community is certainly fortunate to be represented by such a team.

In the World Series of 1953, the Dodgers once again were defeated by the Yankees, this time in six games. In game three, Carl Erskine dazzled the mighty Yanks with a record-setting 14 strike-outs, including Mickey Mantle four times in four appearances.

DODGERS DEFEAT YANKS; ERSKINE FANS 14

Red Smith

[OCTOBER 3, 1953:] THE LATE LAMENTED stirred fitfully yesterday, twitched, moaned softly and got shakily to their knees, helped up by a plump old gentleman with a busted paw and a young accident case of two days earlier. Yesterday the Dodgers was dead. Today they is weak and gasping for breath, but the breath is still in them.

Two days after he tripped, fell and was mangled by the Yankee juggernaut in one cruel inning, Brooklyn's Carl Erskine pitched a six-hit ball game in which he broke the famous World Series strikeout record established twenty-four years ago. Two days after a pitched ball smashed a knuckle on his right hand and rendered him apparently useless as a batter, ample old Roy Campanella wrapped his aching fist around a bat and slugged a home run that won for Erskine and the Dodgers, 3–2.

After one of the most grandly exciting games since rounders became a national religion, the Dodgers still must win three of four games to achieve their first world championship. Trailing the Yankees, two victories to one, they aren't in what you'd call boisterous health, but at least they aren't three games behind.

That they would surely be if it weren't for Erskine, Campanella and Jackie Robinson, aided by a curious balk committed by the Yankees' fine pitcher, Vic Raschi.

It was a brute of a ball game. It was stiff with tension from the first pitch until the last one was batted gently back into Erskine's glove by Joe Collins, with the issue even then undecided. A peddler of pills for the pale and nervous could have found 35,270 buyers in Ebbets Field.

Erskine, of course, is the story. Brooklyn's only twenty-game winner started the first game on Wednesday and was ruined in a four-run first inning. Yesterday he had a no-hitter for four innings, yielded a one-run lead in the fifth which the Dodgers immediately erased, lost a one-run lead in the eighth, and never had another pitch batted out of the infield.

Of all World Series records, possibly the one which has been talked about most often was established on Oct. 8, 1929, when Connie Mack flabbergasted even his own Philadelphia players by starting beat-up old Howard Ehmke, in the first game against the Cubs, whereupon Ehmke struck out thirteen batters.

Yesterday Erskine fanned Joe Collins four times, Mickey Mantle four times, and had twelve strikeouts when Don Bollweg opened the ninth inning as a pinch-hitter. Down went the rookie swinging and the record was tied. Up came John Mize, whose pinch-hits mutilated the Dodgers last year.

Mize took two called strikes, fouled off the third pitch, swung at the fourth and missed. The old record was dead but the Yankees were still alive. Irv Noren, a third pinch-hitter, walked.

Now Collins could tie the record that a Yankee pitcher, George Pipgras, made in 1932 by striking out five times, or he could win the game with a two-run homer. He tapped gently to Erskine who brandished the ball in a triumphant fist and tossed it to Gil Hodges at first base for the last easy play.

It was pretty nearly the only easy play of the afternoon. Among those that will be remembered longest, the most curious occurred in the home fifth after Jackie Robinson doubled with one out. Raschi, conscious of Robinson on base behind him, hesitated in his pitching motion and Robinson called the balk himself, the umpires concurring.

Robinson trotted to third, whence he got home on Billy Cox's squeeze bunt, tying the score. Possibly Cox might have batted him home from second or maybe Erskine, who singled after the squeeze, would have knocked the run in. Maybe not, too.

Now melodrama thickened. With none out and runners on first and second, Campanella tried to bunt in the sixth because it seemed certain he couldn't hit. He popped out to Raschi.

This was the fourth time since he was hurt that Campanella had come up with big runs on the bases, and he hadn't gotten a ball out of the infield. He did not look like a man who would deliver the winning hit.

Before the sixth inning ended, Robinson singled home a run which put Brooklyn ahead, but in the eighth the Yankees made trouble again. Hank Bauer singled with one out and for the second time Erskine hit Yogi Berra with a pitch, bringing applause from fans who boo when a pitch crowds Brooklyn's batters.

Up came Mantle, three times a strikeout victim. He stood still for two strikes. Casey Stengel burst from the dugout, furious. He swung an imaginary bat in a gesture of rage: "Swing, dammit!" Then, leaning against a post at the dugout's mouth, he stood glowering. His posture has already been described:

> With neck out-thrust, you fancy how,
> Legs wide, arms locked behind
> As if to balance the prone brow
> Oppressive with its mind.

Obediently, Mantle swung and missed. The manager turned his back as the young man returned to the dugout regarding his own toes as though he'd never seen them before.

Gene Woodling's single then tied the score again, but that was all except for Campanella — a considerable exception. Incidentally, Robinson and Campanella had led the Dodgers in a special batting practice session at 10 a.m. They have been practicing batting all their lives.

Maybe those few extra minutes were just what they needed.

When the Dodgers lost an afternoon game it was often said in Brooklyn that there would be a lot of "cold suppers" that night. Mr. Heuman eloquently captures the mood in this marvelous short story set in 1954.

BROOKLYNS LOSE

William Heuman

It's one of those long, drawn-out games at Ebbets Field, and it's not over till nearly six o'clock. We come out hot and tired, and with a little headache — you know how it is after a game — and the kid says he wants a hot dog.

"I like the long ones, Pop," he says.

You know the kind they sell outside the park at those little hot-dog stands, long and skinny and rubbery.

"Never mind," I tell him.

We're hurrying for the trolley car, and the big crowd is pouring out of the exit gates. It's almost six o'clock and Madge has the supper on the table, and I can see her fuming, and the kid's talking about hot dogs.

"Forget it," I tell him.

Who thinks about food when the Dodgers lose? You sit there for nearly three and a half hours and you try to root for the home team. You're with them every minute, every play, and you have it in the bag, and then it's gone over the wall.

"That was some home run," the kid says.

"Shut up," I tell him. "Keep quiet."

"Well, it was good, Pop. Way out toward center field."

A home run in the last inning which wins the ball game and sends the Brooklyns down to defeat is never a *good* home run. What the kid means is that it was well hit. I admit that. I'm a Brooklyn fan, but I admit that. The ball travels maybe four hundred feet before it clears the fence in right center, so it's a good hit. All right, but don't rub it in. Three and a half hours I sit there in the bleachers on a hot day and we lose anyway. So what's good about it?

A guy on the trolley says to me, "They shoulda passed him, that Kluszewski."

"Alston didn't wanna put the winning run on base," I tell him. "That's baseball. You play the averages."

"He didn't put Kluszewski on, neither," this guy says, grinning. "Klu hit it an' kept goin'."

Originally published in *Sports Illustrated*, 1954.

This guy jokes, yet. This is a time for jokes when you have a ball game sewed up eight-to-seven in the ninth, and you lose it with a home-run ball.

I look out the window and the guy says, "So tomorrow's another day."

I don't even look at him. That kind of guy I don't look at.

You don't mind losing a ball game now and then, but when you lose to Cincinnati it hurts, especially when you got it sewed up, and especially in September and you're way out of first place and that old lost column can murder you.

The kid's getting wise here. He's eleven now, and I've had him down to a lot of ball games, and he argues baseball with the other kids on the block.

He says now, "They shoulda took Oiskin out."

"Never mind," I tell him. "Forget about it."

Why can't they let it drop? It's over and we lose it, so it goes down in the records, and you never change the records, not even if the Russians come over and take this country. It's down in the books.

So maybe Alston should have taken Erskine out, and maybe put in Johnny Podres, and Podres walks three-four guys and it's over anyway, and Alston's a dope again. He should have left Erskine in.

I don't like to second-guess the manager. The guy is out there with his job to do, and he knows more about it than anybody else. Just like me in the shop. In the shop I know my job and I do it. I don't like a guy coming around and telling me it might work out better some other way.

I'm just saying, though, that if it was me in Alston's shoes I'd have had Shuba pinch-hit for Erskine the end of the eighth, and maybe bring us another run or two, so when this big clown belts one over the wall in the ninth we still got the lead. With Erskine out for a pinch hitter I'd have stuck Roe in there for one inning with that slow stuff. It might have been a different ball game.

Like I say, though, you can't second-guess, and it's silly to work yourself up into a stew because we dropped one. Just forget about it; let it drop.

I hear a guy in the seat behind me say, "They shoulda pulled a squeeze in the seventh with Reese on third. When Dressen was runnin' this club we worked a lot of squeeze plays. We'd of had that extra run, and when Kluszewski hits that homer, it's only tied up an'—"

You see how they try to dope it out? It's dead; it's in the record books. So who's up when Reese is on third and one away? Gil Hodges is up, and Gil is a long-ball hitter. Since when do you ask your long-ball hitter to bunt? That guy behind me is crazy. Any kind of a fly ball would have brought Reese in. So Hodges struck out; so Alston knew he was gonna strike out?

If it was me I'd have had Reese try to steal home when it was two out. This Cincinnati guy was taking a long windup. I'm not telling Alston how to run his ball club, but you can see how it goes around and around inside your head. I've heard of guys going off their trolley arguing points like this.

Madge says when we come into the house at about six-thirty:

"What were you doing — standing outside the field asking for their autographs?"

She has that look on her face. The pots are still on the stove, all covered up, and they've been there for some time, I can see.

"It was along game," I tell her.

"It's always a long game down there, she says, and the way she says "there" you'd think she was talking of some gin mill somewhere.

She should be married to a heavy drinker or a guy who plays the horses like some of them in the shop. I don't have any bad habits; I have a glass of beer now and then; I go to Ebbets Field. That's wrong?

"Sit down and eat your supper," Madge says.

"Pop wouldn't buy me a hot dog," the kid tells her.

"I'm not surprised," Madge says. "He probably didn't even know you were with him."

"I bought him two in the park," I snap. "He wants another one on the way home. What am I — Rockefeller?"

"He'd have had a better time at Brighton Beach," Madge says as she's banging the pots around on the stove.

"My vacation," I tell her. "Monday we go to the beach. Wednesday we go to the beach. What am I — a seal?"

"Sit down," she says.

I notice that there are four places set out and I know who the other plate is for. He comes in from the parlor, snapping at his suspenders— the last guy I want to see tonight.

Uncle Nathan is my brother-in-law, a bachelor, and he lives in a rooming house around the corner from us. Every once in a while — and even once is too often — Madge invites him around for supper. I'm practically supporting this guy, and I think that, secretly, he likes the Giants.

"Lost again," Uncle Nathan grins as he sits down opposite me. "Heard it on the radio."

"Again," I tell him acidly. "Don't I know it's again?"

"The Reds," Uncle Nathan says. "The Cincinnati Reds from Cincinnati."

He's a guy who never goes to a ball game, but he can make remarks like that. He don't know first base from second.

"Kluszewski hit a home run and won the game in the ninth inning," the kid says, and I have to hear that over again.

"They should have a man like Kluszewski on first base for Brooklyn," Uncle Nathan says.

"What's wrong with Hodges?" I ask him. "What's wrong with a guy who hits over three hundred and drives in all them runs?"

"Eat your supper," Madge says.

Who feels like eating, especially with Uncle Nathan sitting across from you, smirking? Uncle Nathan is a small, pot-bellied guy with a circle of fuzzy hair around his bald head. All his life he's lived in Brooklyn, twenty minutes from the field, and never saw a game. That's a citizen!

"Who was it beat them this afternoon?" Uncle Nathan says. "I never heard of the guy."

"How many guys you ever heard of in baseball?" I ask him.

"Eat you supper, Joe," Madge says. "You'd all be a lot better off if you spent your time on something more educational."

I could make some remarks about that, too, but I don't. I got arguments up to the neck, already. Education. What's education but knowing something, and what's better to know than Brooklyn wins?

"Hear the Giants won this afternoon," Uncle Nathan says, without looking up from his plate. "Three-to-one over the Cardinals. They got it made."

"They'll fade in the stretch," I say. "They'll drop a few, and we'll catch them in the last week. We got a three-game series here, remember."

Imagine a guy talking about the Giants down here in Flatbush. A guy like that is crazy. He should be arrested.

I don't eat much tonight because I'm not hungry, and I guess I don't say much, either, because Madge says, as she's bringing out the dessert: "All afternoon you yell your head off at the game. When you come home, you shut up like a clam."

"What's to say?" I ask her. "I gotta talk every minute?"

"He'd be talkin' plenty," Uncle Nathan says, "if the Dodgers had won."

I don't even bother to answer.

The kid, sitting next to me at the table, says, "That Kluszewski sure can hit."

We have pork chops for supper, but they don't taste good; the peas don't taste good either. Imagine a guy with a name you can't even pronounce licking the Dodgers? Down at the field I hear this Kluszewski's name pronounced nine different ways. Any way you say it, though, it goes down in the books as a Brooklyn loss.

My wife says, "I spend the afternoon making a supper and he eats it like he was a bird."

"So I have to stuff myself every meal?" I say. "That's smart?"

I'm glad when I can get outside. I go down to the basement and get out the plastic hose. We live in a nice section in Flatbush here — two-family houses, with a little plat of ground out front. It's not much as far as ground goes, maybe six feet from the house to the sidewalk. Most everybody has a little shrubbery.

I get out the hose and I water the shrubbery because we haven't had any rain in a week. Next to me lives Saul Ruskin, who is my neighbor. Saul is sitting in one of those aluminum-and-plastic chairs that folds up, and you wonder how it holds his weight.

The plat out in front of Saul's house he's filled in with cement, so he has sidewalk from the house all the way to the curb, and no shrubbery, no grass or weeds to worry about.

"I should be a farmer?" Saul says. "I wanna raise crops, I move out to the suburbs."

Saul watches me as I hook up the hose. He has the stub of a cigar in his mouth, and he says around the cigar, "A tough one to lose, Joe. Them Reds allus get hot against us."

"They have to win once in a while," I tell him.

Saul is a dyed-in-the-wool Brooklyn rooter. I see he don't feel too good about this one, either, and it makes me feel a little better.

"These clubs come in here loaded," Saul says. "They save their best pitchers for Brooklyn. They do all their hittin' at Ebbets Field. It ain't right."

"That's baseball," I tell him as I start to squirt the shrubbery.

"Couple of Sundays back I see Pittsburgh," Saul says. "They score eighteen runs in two games. They don't score eighteen runs in a whole season. That's the way it goes."

"I know," I tell him sympathetically.

"That home run Klusoositz hits," Saul says. "It was a fluke, Joe?"

"He tagged it, Saul," I tell him. "He hits that long ball."

"Allus against us," Saul scowls. He pauses, then adds, "Alston maybe shoulda passed him, a guy hits like that."

"Man on second an' one out," I tell him. "Kluszewski ain't made a hit all day."

"Then he was due," Saul says. "You can't shut out a guy like that four-five times in one game. He was due."

"They took a chance. Erskine got him before."

The guy lives upstairs from me is just coming back from Sam Klein's candy store, where he has bought some cigarets, and he stops to talk. He says, "A good game, Joe?"

"Brooklyn's lose, Lennie," Saul says. "That's a good game?"

"You know what I mean," Lennie says. "That lucky Klookitz."

"Kluszewski," I tell him.

"How the hell you say it," Lennie says, "It's still a home run. That right, Joe?"

We stand there for a while, chewing the rag while I squirt the shrubbery. Saul puffs on the cigar and sits there with his arms folded across his chest. Lennie Brannick sits on the stoop and lights up a cigaret.

"You give Dressen a club hitting like this," Lennie says, "an' he'd never lose a ball game. You know what I mean? Allus liked Dressen — a noisy guy, but a great manager."

"Alston's all right," I tell him.

"That club we got this year," Saul puts in, "a two-headed zebra could manage. They oughtta win for anybody; they oughtta even win for your brother-in-law Nathan, Joe."

"Leave us not get on that subject," I tell him.

My wife calls through the screen door, "If you're going down to Klein's, stop at the delicatessen and pick up a few bottles of beer, Joe. The empties are on the back step."

I turn off the water because them shrubs have enough now. I say to Saul Ruskin under my breath, "I have to feed him beer now. It's not enough he eats my food. Luxuries he gets."

"That's relatives for you," Saul nods. "I got a cousin like that."

I get the empty bottles from the back doorstep and I head down the street towards Klein's. This is my neighborhood; this is where I was born, not on this block, but a few blocks away. This is a nice block, nice people, all good Brooklyn rooters. You feel bad, and everybody feels bad with you. That's neighbors.

Outside Klein's is the usual bunch of kids, seventeen and eighteen years old, and it's all baseball with them, too. It's arguments about baseball, and what these kids don't know about the game you can stick in your hat and forget about.

One kid who knows me says, "Hello, Mr. Armbruster."

"How's it," I say.

"You up to the game?" he asks. "You see that Klusookitz?"

"He kills that ball," I tell him.

"I see Roe strike that bum out three times," another boy says. "You give him that fast ball an' he moiders."

Inside, I talk to Sam Klein about the game.

"A hard one to lose," Sam says, "but you can't win 'em all, Joe."

"I know," I say.

"If he'd passed this Klusowsky," Sam says, "somebody else would have home-red. That's fate, Joe."

"Maybe we can still afford to lose one," I tell him.

"Sure," Sam says. "Look how it used to be years ago. You win two out of five an' you think you done somethin'."

"It's still a great club," I tell him. "The best ever."

I come out of Klein's and stop by the delicatessen for some beer. I'm feeling pretty good now, and best since Kluszewski hit that home run and robbed us of a game. You know how it is when you have good neighbors? Everybody's on your side; everybody's rooting for you and with you. You can even stand a guy like Uncle Nathan. Where do you find neighbors like this?

I come down the walk toward my house, and Saul Ruskin hasn't moved from his chair on the sidewalk. I go past Saul, and he lifts two fingers in the V-for-victory sign.

"Tomorrow," says Saul.

How can you beat neighbors like that? How can you beat Brooklyn? Uncle Nathan is standing by the screen door when I come in, and he says, "You gonna slit your throat tonight, Joe, because the Dodgers lost?"

"Jump in the lake," I tell him. "Take a long run an' jump in the lake."

Tomorrow we'll get 'em.

Following the 1953 season, Charley Dressen was let go as Dodger manager and the Walter Alston era began. Walt was a company man and generally an unknown entity to the press and the public. Equally unknown were the events that were to unfold in the future. After a dismal and disappointing 1954 season, Brooklyn would win its first World Series victory in 1955; Walter O'Malley would depart the borough for the gold of California; and Walter Alston would wind up in the Hall of Fame.

WALT ALSTON

Peter Golenbock

At the end of the 1953 season, Walter O'Malley allowed two of his employees to depart. Forever the Dodgers would seem much less colorful and exciting.

Red Barber quit as Dodger announcer. And it didn't have to happen except for O'Malley's crassness. In 1952 Barber had broadcast the World Series on TV, and they had paid him $200 a game. Gillette hadn't told the announcers what they were making until after the Series was over. Nothing was negotiated. When it was over, they just sent the check. Gillette's thinking was that the announcers would be glad to do the Series just to get the exposure. Peanuts, Barber called the money. He then decided that he would not do the 1953 Series unless he negotiated his fee in advance of the telecast. In '53 Gillette told Barber that under no circumstances would they negotiate, telling him to take the token payment or leave it. So Barber left it.

After Barber made his decision not to work the Series cheap, as a courtesy he called O'Malley, who easily could have backed him in his fight with Gillette. But O'Malley, who never forgave Barber for remaining friends with Branch Rickey, said tersely, That's your problem. Barber hung up. A few days later his regular season contract expired, and when Red Barber switched to the Yankees, it became O'Malley's problem.

Sentiment meant nothing. Business was everything. By then O'Malley knew he had Vin Scully in the wings, and Scully was making $18,000 and Barber $60,000. O'Malley was fond of expounding: Its like marbles in a pipe. You push the cheaper marble in one end, and the expensive marble falls out the other end, and that's how you make money. Vin became the new Voice of the Dodgers, and thirty years later he's still around.

The second star O'Malley allowed to depart was Charley Dressen. In three years Dressen had brought the Dodgers to a playoff in '51 and then won two straight National

From *Bums* by Peter Golenbock. Reprinted by permission of Sterling Lord Literistic, Inc. © by Peter Golenbeck.

League pennants. Dressen thought he deserved a better contract, a contract that gave him more protection than the single-year contracts he had signed in the past.

During the 1953 season, the *Sporting News* had printed a cartoon of Dressen, Leo Durocher, Charlie Grimm, and Eddie Stanky sitting around a table playing poker. The cartoon showed the Cardinals giving Stanky a three-year contract, the Braves giving Grimm a three-year contract, the Giants giving Durocher a two-year contract, and Dressen receiving a question mark. The artist was suggesting that Dressen would do better than any of the other three. The artist, though, didn't know Walter O'Malley.

Dressen wanted security. Only Casey Stengel had been more successful. Dressen wanted three years. O'Malley told Dressen it was against his policy. Dressen refused to budge. He couldn't believe that O'Malley would allow him to go. But O'Malley did.

Dressen had been successful. He had brought controversy, humor, and excitement, and he increased attendance, but O'Malley didn't care.

The owner had resented Dressen's manner, his personal publicity, and the fact that Dressen's wife, Ruth, had written a letter demanding a three-year contract. O'Malley became angry.

The O'Malleyfication of the Dodgers became complete when the new manager was named in the winter of 1953. As soon as it dawned on the New York reporters that O'Malley was merely jerking Charley Dressen around, that O'Malley had no intention of taking him back under any circumstances, the guessing game began as to who was going to replace the little bantam. Pee Wee Reese was mentioned frequently, though the Dodgers never seriously considered him. Buzzy Bavasi had called him into his office and said to him, You're not interested in the job, are you? so that even if Pee Wee had wanted it, he was savvy enough to know the answer Bavasi was eliciting. O'Malley hadn't wanted a playing manager, and Reese was still the best shortstop in the National League, and there was no way O'Malley was going to let him retire just to become manager.

Among the prominent names mentioned in the papers as candidates were Frankie Frisch, Rogers Hornsby, Joe DiMaggio, Tommy Henrich, and even Leo Durocher. Near the bottom of the list, buried with names such as Lefty O'Doul and Bill Terry, was that of a virtual unknown, "Wally" Alston, the manager of the Dodgers' farm team in Montreal.

In late November, six weeks after Dressen was axed, the Dodgers called a press conference. When Alston was introduced, most of the writers looked around in disbelief. Who was this guy? Why did O'Malley pick a guy with no experience to manage the National League champions? But these men did not understand the Dodger concept of organization. The notion of the company man had not yet been branded into the soul of America, though it would be shortly.

There are usually two reasons why an organization will hire an employee. The first is that he can do the job. Assuming many people can do the job, the search committee then looks for the next-most-important attribute: Will the man follow orders and take whatever guff we dump on him? Not all men will. Unless such individuals are exceptionally talented, like Leo Durocher or Billy Martin, they will be bypassed.

Walt Alston believed in the O'Malley organization first, everything else second. And like every loyal employee, Alston put up with whatever Bavasi and O'Malley threw at him. Every single year — long after he had established himself — he had to keep signing one-year contracts. It was said that he would show his loyalty by signing a blank contract in the fall and then wait until spring training to meet with Bavasi to discover how much money they were paying him. And always there were the rumors. Rarely did a season begin without word from some "unnamed source" high in the Dodger organization whispering that if Alston doesn't win the pennant this year he will be fired. His employers did little to make life any easier. They kept hiring assistants for him such as Leo Durocher and Charley Dressen, and each time, it was said that one or the other of his assistants was going to replace him. As a reward for his unswerving loyalty, they seemed to relish letting Alston wonder each season whether he would get the ax or not. It made for a very subservient and pliable manager. Which, of course, was exactly what Walter O'Malley wanted.

It was an untenable situation for a rookie manager. The Dodgers started poorly in '54, and never seemed to pull together. The players had difficulty getting used to Alston, and he spent the year getting to know them and the National League. He was not confident in himself, and the players realized he was depending heavily on his coaches, Billy Herman and Jake Pitler. Alston was not earning respect. All these stars and he had to learn to handle them.

The one he had the most trouble with was Jackie Robinson. Robinson had loved Charley Dressen. Every day Charley Dressen would tell Robinson what a wonderful player he was, how much he appreciated him, how special he was, and Robinson thrived on Dressen's kind words. Alston, on the other hand, saw Robinson as a threat to his authority. In '54 the two men silently fought for control of the Dodgers. Robinson bitched that Alston lost his cool under pressure, and he would rail at what he saw as "bonehead judgments" during games. Some of the others grumbled about Alston, but Robinson, whose emotions were always close to the surface, let Alston know that he didn't think much of him as a manager.

Toward the end of the 1954 season, the tension between Robinson and Alston grew. Robinson didn't like O'Malley, and he didn't like O'Malley's choice for manager. It was Alston's feeling that Robinson, now thirty-five, should be a utility player, and it didn't help Robinson's disposition any when Alston began playing Don Hoak at third base. Robinson also didn't like the fact that Alston rarely argued with umpires. Robinson loved umpire baiting, loved the wordplay and the flow of adrenaline it brought. Toward the end of the year Duke Snider hit a ball into the left-field seats that bounced back onto the field. It should have been a home run. Umpire Bill Stewart called it a double.

Robinson, furious, sprinted out of the dugout and ran to protest. He was figuring that other teammates would join him, but no one moved. And manager Alston, coaching at third, just stood there, watching, with his hands on his hips.

Robinson felt humiliated. Later, in the dugout, someone said to him, "You should have heard what Walt was saying when you were out arguing on the field." Robinson replied, "If that guy hadn't stood standing out there at third base like a wooden Indian, this club might go somewhere." By the end of the 1954 season

Robinson had had it with O'Malley and Alston both, and he was ready to leave baseball.

After the 1954 season, during which the Dodgers finished five games behind Leo Durocher's Giants, reporters were asking serious questions about Alston's capabilities, and there were rumors, as there would be for all twenty-three years of Alston's tenure, that the Dodgers would be looking for a new manager.

Before he retired Alston won seven pennants and four World Series and in 1983 was voted into the Hall of Fame. There is a theory in baseball that the best manager is the one who makes the fewest mistakes and affects his personnel the least adversely. In other words, most managers screw things up by frustrating, confusing, infuriating, misusing, or destroying the egos of their players. After his first couple of years with the Dodgers, Walter Alston never did. Once he learned his personnel, he merely wrote the proper names into the proper slots, and he left his players alone. When he had the best players, he won. When he didn't, he lost. Alston won two pennants with Brooklyn and its first world championship, and after the Dodgers moved to the coast, he finished first five times and second seven times, though by then, few in Brooklyn noticed.

Duke Snider called him "the greatest Dodger" and maybe he was. Certainly the fans of Brooklyn thought so when they gave him a night—fittingly, in 1955.

PEE WEE REESE NIGHT

Tot Holmes

33,000 Cram Into Ebbets Field
For Pee Wee Reese Night

[JULY 22, 1955:] All Brooklyn joined in the celebration of "Pee Wee Reese Night" on the Dodger shortstop's 36th birthday. Ebbets Field bulged with 33,003 paying fans (although many more were in the park) who jammed every seat and most of the standing room to honor Reese.

After a "Dixie Walker Night" some years before had nearly been a disaster—the only gift Dixie was to receive was a fishing pole, causing Branch Rickey to buy Walker a television set out of his own pocket so he would receive something of value—Brooklyn club officials determined to take charge of the celebration themselves.

The Dodgers' Irving Rudd and Dick Young, *Daily News* baseball writer, were the committee that organized the special night for Reese and they line up an amazing $10,000 list of gifts.

Fans themselves donated money for a $3,000 U.S. Savings Bond. Reese also received a 250-pound cake and he received a lifetime pass to a Catskill hotel, a trip to Europe, savings bonds, two freezers—one with 200 pounds of hot dogs, shrimp, lobster, and roast beef—a TV console, two sets of golf clubs, movie equipment, a hunting coat, 100 pounds of coffee and a silver tray which carried the autographs of all his teammates. It was presented by Carl Erskine.

Vin Scully and Happy Felton were the MC's. The ceremonies took 50 minutes. Vin and Happy read messages from President Dwight Eisenhower, who was involved in the summit meeting at Geneva, Switzerland, Vice-President Richard Nixon, Commissioner Ford Frick, Governor Averell Harriman, former Vice-President Alban Barkley from Pee Wee's home state of Kentucky and General Douglas MacArthur.

But perhaps one of the most special telegrams came from a friend of Pee Wee's in Louisville, Kentucky. It read:

From *1955—This Is Next Year* by Tot Holmes. ©1995. Reprinted by permission of Holmes Publishing Co., Tot Holmes, editor.

"Pee Wee, you did not grow into a fine personality, earning respect of all, overnight.

"You did not gain in a few moments the skill that enabled leaguer.

"You built it little by little — a word here, an act there, a today, a generous action, a firm hold on duty day by day and so on this may God bless and keep you the same old Pee Wee we all love and respect. (signed) Lou Isert."

When Reese's parents, Mr. And Mrs. C.M. Reese of Louisville, Kentucky, made their surprise appearance, Pee Wee had tears in his eyes.

The high point came when they drove a lineup of new cars onto the field — a Chrysler, Buick, DeSoto, Pontiac and Chevrolet, Ford and Plymouth. Pee Wee's 11-year-old daughter, Barbara, reached into a goldfish bowl and pulled out a set of keys and started trying them on each car. When they fit the Chevy, papers reported "The crowd breathed the biggest collective sigh of disappointment in history."

Campy said the next day the fix should have been on. He thought they should have made sure the keys fit one of the expensive jobs, like the Chrysler or Buick.

"If I had to go through this every day," Reese said with a smile, "I'd quit baseball."

"With what you're getting," kidded Bill Roeder of the *World-Telegram*, "you could afford to retire."

When he was finally called on to speak, his voice was hoarse with emotion but he carried on without a break.

"I don't know what to say," he began. "I'm still in a daze. When I came to Brooklyn in 1940, I was a scared kid." He stopped to swallow a lump in his throat, then said:

"To tell you the truth, I'm twice as scared right now."

He went on to voice his appreciation to all with his usual grace and sincerity.

While the ground crew was smoothing the infield at the end of the fifth inning, two huge cakes were wheeled onto the grass, the lights were dimmed and 33,000 fans in the stands lighted matches and sang "Happy Birthday." Headlines the next day read:

"Happy Boitday, Pee Wee. Ebbets Field is Reese Park for a Night."

Jimmy Cannon, *New York Post* wrote:

"Every game Brooklyn plays is a sort of Reese Night. Ask the players, they know him better than I do. Fortunate is the guy who has Reese for a friend. And there isn't anyone on the Dodgers who isn't close to him in some way. There have been better ballplayers, but I've never heard anyone who claimed there was a finer guy. It's too bad the guides don't print such information. It tells more than batting averages."

Roy Campanella told reporters after the game: "It's great to see a night like this for a fellow who deserves it as much as Reese. All of us in Brooklyn and around the league, everyone knows he's never been bad.

"But I know there's even more in my own heart. Branch Rickey brought the Negro into the major leagues but it was Reese who clinched our acceptance. Believe me, he had the say. He showed the world that Jackie Robinson was with the Dodgers to stay.

"When Philadelphia got on Robbie so bad, it was Reese that put his arm around him to say, 'He's my teammate and that's that.'

"He's a great guy but nobody runs over Pee Wee. He's got some of the tiger in him. All of us come to him for advice. His night should have been celebrated years ago."

Biggest Day?

When Reese was asked to name his biggest day in baseball, he said, "Every day is a big day here in Brooklyn. But the top thrill came in 1941. I became a regular that year, appearing in 152 games and hit only .238. And every one of my 47 errors hurt the club. But in spite of me, the Dodgers won the pennant and then came the big kick of playing against the Yankees in the World Series.

"Only four years previous, in my first visit to New York, I had seen the Yankees meet the Giants. I was a goggle-eyed kid of 18, never dreaming that soon I would be in the stadium battling the Bombers.

"In 1940 Jake Moody of the Cubs beaned me. A month later, sliding into second, I broke my heel and had to sweat out the rest of the season. I have read how Leo Durocher had called me into his office and said, 'Kid, I'm through. You are now the shortstop of the Dodgers.' Well, it never happened. I just moved into the job, inch by inch.

"It's my belief that Leo could have gone on playing. But he didn't want to be a player-manager. So he gave me my big chance and somehow I took advantage of it.

"One thing I want to accomplish before I hang up my spikes. I want 2,000 hits. I had 1,760 when I started this season. The way things shape up, I should get 2,000 in our pennant winning season of 1956."

Walter Alston, when asked, "What makes Pee Wee Reese tick?" listed:

"Character, natural ability, versatility, intelligence and a habit of placing his team ahead of Harold Reese at all times."

On October 5, 1955, the front page of the New York Daily News *had a question — or an exclamation — for the world to answer.*

WHO'S A BUM!

Leo O'Mealia

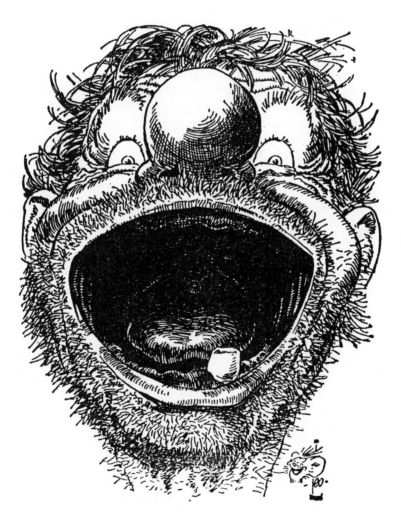

181

It was next year *in Brooklyn at long last. On October 4, 1955, the Brooklyn Dodgers were champions of the world!*

Dodgers Champs!
Podres Wins, 2–0

Joe Trimble

Johnny Brilliant in 2d WS Victory

They won't make Oct. 4 a red-letter day in Brooklyn. They'll print it in letters of gold from now on because it's only the greatest date in the history of the batty borough — the day those darling Dodgers finally won the World Series. At exactly 3:45 yesterday afternoon at the Stadium, the Brooks got the third out of a 2–0 victory over the Yankees in the seventh and deciding game.

And when they print calendars over there, they won't bother with Marilyn Monroe's picture. Not good enough. They'll have poker-faced Johnny Podres, the most heroic pitcher in Dodgertown since Dazzy Vance and the only Brooklyn thrower ever to win two games in a series. It was Podres' brilliant, crushing pitching which ruined the AL champions, sending them down to their fifth Series loss in 21.

And who do you suppose knocked in both Brooks runs? No one else but Gil Hodges, the big batting flop of the '52 Series.

There were many memorable events bright and tragic on this earth on past fourths of October, but the hallowed pages of history must display yesterday's momentous triumph above them all.

WHAT KIND OF A date has it been? Well, on Oct. 4, 1861, the Union forces massed to form the Army of the Potomac; in 1864, the Erie Railroad opened (probably not on time). In 1940 Hitler and Mussolini met at the Brenner Pass and, in 1944, the U.S. Army broke through the German West Wall. Al Smith, the beloved Governor of New York and Presidential candidate, also died on the latter date.

As far as Brooklyn is concerned, nothing could ever match the events of yesterday, when all the years of frustration and defeat were wiped out in one blazing afternoon. It was the 49th Dodger Series game in eight appearances, and the tightest, most tense and thrilling of them all.

At the finish, when Pee Wee Reese sure-handedly threw out Elston Howard, the

182

big park in the Bronx exploded with human emotion as the entire Dodger team raced out on the field and danced and drooled in delight around Podres.

While the 62,465 customers were cheering the new champs, the proud Yankees were filing slowly into the losing dressing room; a unique experience for them. Of all, only coaches Frank Crosetti and Bill Dickey and shortstop Phil Rizzuto had ever experienced a loss before. They had it but once, when the Cardinals smeared the Yanks four in a row after losing the 1942 opener.

THE DODGERS ARE in paradise, finally succeeding after numerous Brooklyn teams had tried for four decades. The 1916 Flatbushers were knocked off by the Red Sox and the 1920 crew by Cleveland. Then the drought set in and it wasn't until 1941 that a pennant waved alongside the tree that grew in Brooklyn. But that year they had to play the Yankees, and Mickey Owen muffed a third strike and everything went black in the borough.

Four times since then they won the NL flag only to find those merciless Yankees on the other side of the field — and the Brooks on the losing end of the payoff. They went down in 1947 in seven games, in 1949 it was five, in '52 seven again and six in '53.

SO THE BROOKS also went home with their heads hanging and the taunt of "Wait 'til next year!" shattering their eardrums. Now that's over. Next year came on Oct. 4 this time.

This not alone was the greatest day in Brooklyn's history. It also brought to a wondrous climax the richest World Series ever. Due to increased admission prices and the maximum number of games, the $2,337,513.64 taken in at the box office is an all-time high.

NUMEROUS RECORDS were set, but the one the Brooklyn players will remember most was their achievement in winning four of the last five games after dropping the first two. This kind of comeback had never happened in a seven-game Series before.

To do it, they had to get a second superior pitching job from the 23-year-old Podres, their little left-hander, and also they had to whip the Yankee pitcher who had given them the most trouble, 35-year-old Tommy Byrne. Although they got the three hits off the graying southpaw before an error helped cause his removal in the sixth, they put them in exactly the right places.

ROY CAMPANELLA, who had gone hitless in 12 times up in the Stadium this Series and had a lifetime average of .070 in the big park, crashed a double to left after one out in the fourth. Duke Snider, who went all the way on his bad knee, fanned just before Campy's hit. Carl Furillo followed with a slow grounder, Rizzuto making a fine play to get him at first as Campy reached third. Gil Hodges, with a count of one ball and two strikes, swung at an inside curve. He didn't get much wood on the ball but it went safely to left field and the Brooks were ahead.

The other safety was a lead-off single in the sixth by Reese, the veteran whose victory appetite was greatest because he had been on the losing side against the Yankees six times. The shortstop lined a hit to left-center and was deprived of a double when Bob Cerv made a fine retrieve. Reese eventually scored the insurance run after Bob Grim had taken the mound.

BUT BEFORE THE Brooks opened the gap, they nearly gave the Yanks a run. Yogi Berra opened the bottom of the fourth with a lazy fly to center, a bit to Snider's right. Junior Gilliam came over from left, invading the Duke's realm, and then they went into an Alphonse-Gaston Act. The ball tipped off Snider's glove as he made a last second grab after realizing Gilliam was going to let him take it. That fluke double gave Berra the distinction of being the ninth man ever to hit safely in every game of a full-length Series. The catcher made ten hits, topping the batters on both sides.

The Yankee fans screamed for blood after the break. It's an old axiom that you can't make a mistake against the Bombers. They break through the opening and kill you. But Podres wouldn't buckle. He got the next three batters, all strong righty sluggers. Hank Bauer hit a fly to Furillo, Bill Skowron grounded to Don Zimmer and Cerv popped to Reese in short left. The Dodger fans screamed: "Pee Wee! Pee Wee!" as he went out and Gilliam came in and the Dodger captain gobbled it.

THE YANKEE SUPPORTERS applauded Gilliam when he came up to bat in the fifth, one guy screaming: "He's the best man we've got!" Junior didn't get a chance to flub anything else in the outfield because he was moved to second base after the Brooks got their run in the sixth.

After Reese hit, Snider bunted deftly along the third-base line. Byrne fielded it and threw accurately to first base. Skowron stepped forward to meet the ball, taking his foot off the bag and forcing himself to make a tag play. He swiped at the Dodger runner's back and the ball flew out of his glove for an error.

WALTER ALSTON, winning a World Series in his first try, sensibly ordered Campy to sacrifice and he did. Byrne handled this bunt, too. It seemed that the pitcher had a force possibility on Reese at third, Pee Wee having not yet gone into a belly-whop slide. But Byrne thought otherwise and let Reese make it, tossing to first for the out. Casey Stengel ordered an intentional pass to Furillo and then called in Grim, his relief ace who had saved the first game but was battered as a starter in the fifth.

Grim's first batter was Hodges, a tough man with the bases filled. Gil took a strike and then drove a long sacrifice fly to center, Reese scoring. Grim walked Hoak, refilling the lanes, but got George Shuba, a pinch-hitter for Zimmer, on a third-out grounder.

AGAIN THE SIGHT of a Dodger run on the scoreboard brought a Yankee threat in the bottom of the inning. This developed into a real big one and also produced the greatest fielding play of the Series—a catch by Sandy Amoros, an outfielder who was held lightly as a prospective regular in the spring because of his shabby fielding and throwing.

Podres, who passed only two, hit a wild streak and walked Billy Martin on four straight pitches. Alston came out to give the youngster a chance to get his breath. With the Holy Grail so close, he didn't want the Kid to get hysterical. Johnny threw two bad pitches to McDougald, then got one over, which Gil bunted perfectly for a single, Martin taking second.

THEN CAME THE key play, the one which probably meant the title. Stengel, disdaining a bunt with Berra up, had Yogi swing away. Podres pitched outside and Berra stroked a long, high fly into the left-field corner. Amoros, playing him far over toward center, had to run over 100 feet. The ball stayed up a long time, being held by the wind, and Sandy just reached it, gloving the ball with his right mitt in fair territory. The stands are close to the foul line at that point, and he had to fend himself off as he hit the box seat railing.

Martin and McDougald, not believing a catch possible, were on their horses. Billy suddenly reversed himself when almost to third and Gil was past second base before he found out the ball had been held. Amoros gracefully whirled and fired to Reese, who went into short left for the throw. Pee Wee then made another perfect throw to Hodges, just getting McDougald as he slid back.

BAUER THEN HIT a hopper to short and Reese couldn't get it out of his glove for a frantic portion of a second. When he did, he had to throw a blazer and it just beat the runner, according to first base umpire Frank Dascoli. That was the 12th Brooklyn DP, a new Series record.

Grim was lifted for a pinch-hitter in the seventh, after Howard singled. There were two out, so Stengel sent up his hobbled, husky, Mickey Mantle. Podres fooled the Mick with a change-up, Mantle skying the ball to short left where Reese took it, with the Dodger fans again screaming his name. Podres had a rough time in the eighth, when the Yankees got their second runner to third base. Rizzuto led with a single to left but Martin flied to Furillo, who came in fast for the looper. McDougald then hit a sharp grounder which bad-hopped to the left arm of Don Hoak, playing third because Jackie Robinson had a sore Achilles tendon in his right foot. Rizzuto got to third as the fluke hit went into left.

THE TENSION WAS terrific, with Berra and Bauer coming up. Podres really had it, getting Berra to cut under one of his slow curves. The ball went to Furillo in short right and Carl gunned it home, holding the Scooter on third. Then the youngster faced his supreme test in Bauer, who hits left-handers very well. He took Hank to 2–2 with curves and slow-up pitches, then flung himself off the mound by putting all he could on a shoulder-high fastball which Bauer swung at and missed.

AS THE YANKS came up for the last time, with right-handed power hitters looming, the Dodger fans stayed seated and the Yankee adherents shouted for a rally. Everyone was excited.

Skowron cracked a sizzler back at Podres, the hard grounder sticking in his glove web. He was unable to get it out for a second or so, and started to run towards first base to make the putout that way. But he was able to pry it loose and make an underhand toss to Hodges. Cerv then hit a high fly which Amoros took in short left and the Dodgers were one out away from the promised land.

PODRES WENT to 2–2 on Howard and then made him swing off-stride at the change-up. Reese took one happy step towards the grounder, aimed it for Hodges and, though the toss was a bit low, Gil kept his foot on the base and the Dodgers had finally gotten to paradise.

On October 4, 1955, at 3:45 P.M. Brooklyn exploded...

—AND JOY REIGNED UNREFINED

Art Smith

Brooklyn Had a Lot of Frenzy
Saved Up; Pinches Itself
Goes Crazy

[OCTOBER 5, 1955:] Everything was crazy in Brooklyn last night... Nobody went home to supper or to bed.... Nobody talked any sense.... Everybody walked around with goofy expressions on their pans.... For the unbelievable, the incredible, the impossible had come about.... Them Dodgers had put them Yankees away under the Stadium sod and now they was champions of the whole world.

Lest anybody doubt it, the whole crazy borough was still letting the rest of the world know about it long after midnight.

The glorious nonsense continued well into the early-morning hangover hours. Two hundred strong-limbed fans marched for the thousandth time around Ebbets Field, yelling and shouting the extraordinary merits of the Dodgers.

Elsewhere, more sedate residents had registered a total of 50 complaints of disturbances and 10 false fire alarms had been sounded in the borough.

There Was a Calm — and Then the Storm

Saloonkeepers gave away booze to guys they never saw before.... Candy store owners played the big treat to neighborhood kids who'd been robbin' em for years.... Women kissed neighbors they wouldn't be caught dead talking to.... Men hollered and slugged strangers on the back and guys who hadn't been known to lift a geezer in years rolled off the wagon and barked at the crescent moon....

Never before had Brooklyn, that borough of perennial October gloom, gone so joyously screwy, so hysterically daffy, so ecstatically nuts.... Because that, at long last, was Next Year!

The trigger was pulled at 3:45 P.M. on the nose. At 3:44 such a silence as you never heard hung over Dodgertown from Borough Hall to Coney Island, from Red Hook to Brownsville. Then it happened. Pee Wee Reese threw out Elston Howard at first base and the Yankees was dead. The Dodgers win it—Two-Oh!

Well, the roof didn't blow off Borough Hall. It only sounded that way. Nor did the framework of the new Supreme Court Building across Fulton St. collapse in a heap. That terrific roar came from the riveters who turned loose their air-hammers as the last play at the Stadium came over portable radios.

Down from the skyscrapers nearby—at 16, 26, and 32 Court St.—cascaded a billion flakes of torn ticker-tape, newspapers, telephone books. From the windows of the office buildings came paper sacks of water—naughty, naughty! According to the cops. And then, as churchbells clanged all over town and whistles along the water-front boomed and shrilled, streams of delirious humans, or reasonable facsimiles, poured into Brooklyn's streets.

Nuts? Why, even a dignified jurist in Kings County Court nearly flipped. He didn't do a clog dance on his bench, but Judge George Joyce couldn't contain himself.

"I finally saw Next Year!" he cried. "Congratulations to Walter Alston and every one of his men! Now they'll stay on top for years! Congratulations, Brooklyn!"

Daffy? Along Bergen St. rolled busloads of kids from Alexander Hamilton High and Manuel Training High. Inside, each youngster staged impromptu dances, while the drivers—long-suffering gents—did nothing but grin.

Screwy? At 3:46, a minute after Pee Wee's historic putout, great banners were flying in the breeze.

"We Doo'd It!" screamed one, red letters on white.

"Say Hey, Dodgers!" another exulted.

Automobiles loaded to the guards with fanatics, whirled through Montague, Fulton, Court, Joralemon, and Remsen Sts., carrying banners proclaiming the Dodgers "Supermen of the World!"

Also at 3:46, in the window of George's restaurant at Smith and Schermerhorn Sts., across from the Central Courts Building, appeared this sign:

"TODAY: Yankee Bean Soup. SPECIAL!"

In the Edison bar, at 242 Flatbush Ave., owner John Mantol, his eyes glassy, was giving out with the drinks. The cash register didn't ring for half an hour.

"This is something Brooklyn will remember for years," and nobody knew if John meant the Series victory or the drinks on the house.

In the Concord Inn at 308 Fulton St., the boss, Gus Caminiti, also was thrown off stride by the Big Win.

"Drinks!" he yelled to bartender Bill Smith, of 341 15th St., Brooklyn, at precisely 3:45½. "Drinks for every bum in the house! Next year we win it in four!"

Along Gus' bar were ranged 100 men. One of them was Mike Munsinger, of 1314 Avenue K, an infielder formerly with a Dodger farm team and now a Kansas City chattel.

A Single Dissenter

"It was great, really great," he said. "Johnny Podres was the big difference."

And also present, but far from exultant, was a man who would identify himself as a Yankee fan. Glumly he stared into his drink. Then he raised his glass to the beaming Gus.

"Here's how," he growled. "But Wait 'Til Next Year!"

Head for Heights

It was late afternoon when offices, business houses and gin mills disgorged their thousands. And by sundown spontaneous victory marchers were winding thru the narrow crooked streets headed for the Bossert Hotel at 98 Montague St.

For it was in the Bossert's Gold Room that Dodger President Walter O'Malley was standing the biggest treat in Dodger history. He was staging the first Dodger victory party of all time.

Outside the hotel the Brooklyn fanatics gathered 2,000 strong to watch their diamond heroes enter the hotel for the big party.

There was Duke Snider and Jackie Robinson, Roy Campanella and Carl Furillo, Don Zimmer, Billy Loes, Don Hoak and Sandy Amoros. Each drew his share of applause as he entered the hotel but the crowd's thundering welcome was reserved for 23-year-old Johnny Podres, who pitched the Bums to their greatest triumph, and Gil Hodges whose bat accounted for both runs.

They Go Back

These two young men had reached the front door of the hotel when cries from the crowd caused them to pause.

"Come here," someone in the crowd yelled. "We want to shake hands."

Without hesitation both athletes dashed back into the street, shoved aside barricades and cops, and lost themselves in the hand-pumping, back-slapping throng. It was 15 minutes before the laughing pair shook off restraining hands and ducked back into the Bossert.

Inside the Gold Room, to which only invited guests were admitted, a merry mob was given its head. Podres and Snider led a crazy conga joined in by Jackie Robinson, Roy Campanella and their wives and all other Dodgers who weren't busy signing autographs and shaking hands.

Podres Interviewed

Then, while Manager Walter Alston and President Walter O'Malley beamed, slim young Podres, out of Witherbee, N.Y., was surrounded with interviewers.

A flushed and happy kid, almost frightened in the face of such unprecedented admiration, Johnny said that Witherbee's 1,500 native souls were having "one hell of a time tonight."

"How does it feel to be one of the most important guys in the United States," he was asked.

The kid shook his head. "It's a funny thing," he said, "but I just can't tell you. I really don't know how I feel. I'm numb."

Cashmore Wants 'Em to Stay Put

Brooklyn Borough president John Cashmore congratulated the Dodgers immediately after the team's triumph yesterday and asked the ball club to turn a "deaf ear" to other cities who would lure the team away from Brooklyn.

"I salute this great team and offer my sincere congratulations from the manager, Walter Alston, down to the bat boy and victory parade leader, Charlie DiGiovanni," said Cashmore.

Carl Erskine pitched in Brooklyn for ten years. He threw two no-hitters and set a major league strikeout record in the World Series. He won numerous big games for the Dodgers, and the gritty little righthander worked through a perennial sore arm. He was to the Faithful of Flatbush the epitome of their "beloved bums." He is the only "Brooklyn" Dodger to pitch two no-hitters in his career.

ERSKINE ONLY DODGER WITH PAIR OF NO-HITTERS

Tot Holmes

Carl Erskine is the only Dodger to work a pair of no-hit games. He stopped Chicago 5–0 without a hit on June 19, 1952, and New York 3–0 on May 12, 1956.

A total of 13 no-hit games were recorded by the Brooklyn club although three of them were later declared unofficial because they did not result in a nine-inning complete game. Ed Stein, 1894 (6 innings), Harry McIntyre, 1906, and Fred Frankhouse, 1937 (7.2 innings), were deleted from the no-hit category.

McIntyre worked nine hitless innings against Pittsburgh but eventually gave up a couple of hits and lost in the 12th inning.

Thomas Lovett worked the first one in 1891 before the pitching rubber was set at 60'6". Nap Rucker no-hit Boston in 1908, Tex Carlton stopped Cincinnati in April of 1940 and Ed Head bested Boston in 1946. Rex Barney controlled his wildness to blank the Giants 2–0 in 1948 and Sal Maglie nearly clinched the pennant with his no-hitter against Philadelphia in 1956.

Double Ace

Erskine won 16 and lost 12 in 1951. He had another fine year in 1952, finishing 14–6 with a 2.70 earned run average. He led the staff in starts (26), complete games (10), strikeouts (131), and shutouts (4).

His first major league shutout came on May 4, a 6–0 win over Pittsburgh, and on June 19 he drew a start in Ebbets Field against the Cubs. The afternoon was dark and threatening rain.

From *Brooklyn's Best* by Tot Holmes. ©1999. Reprinted with permission of Holmes Publishing Co., Tot Holmes, editor.

He got instant run support when Roy Campanella banged a homer in the first inning with Pee Wee Reese on base and Carl Furillo followed with another homer. Andy Pafko homered in the second. With the sky darkening, Erskine hurried to get the game past the 4½ inning mark to make it official.

"I was in a hurry because the rain was coming, and was pitching a little quicker than usual," he remembered. "I kept firing fastballs to Willard Ramsdell (the Cub pitcher) and couldn't get one of them over the plate." He walked Ramsdell and the game was delayed 44 minutes while Erskine sweated out his 4-0 lead. Erskine was playing bridge in the clubhouse during the delay and just after he made four hearts, the rain stopped and he went back out to warm up.

When the game resumed third baseman Bobby Morgan made a pair of exceptional plays. Erskine caught a shot through the box hit by Dee Fondy and Carl Furillo went a long way to catch a drive headed for the scoreboard in right.

"I was aware of the no-hitter and I began to feel a little bit of the pressure of trying to get through the rest of the game without giving up a hit," he said.

With two out in the ninth, the Cubs sent up Eddie Miksis to pinch-hit. By now Ramsdell was at Ebbets Field's television studio, about to appear on Happy Felton's postgame show. As Chicago's sole baserunner, he was the star of their game, which was worth $50. So he was now rooting against Miksis.

Ironically, it was Ramsdell who had been cut to make room for Erskine on the Brooklyn roster in 1948. "Come on, Oisk!" Ramsdell shouted to Erskine on the television screen. "You can get this bum out. You never hit for me, if you get a hit now and cost me fifty bucks, I'll kill you."

"I remember I threw him a good curveball, with which he hit a routine grounder to Reese for the final out," Erskine remembered.

Erskine's walk to Ramsdell kept him from a perfect game. It was the first no-hitter in Ebbets Field since 1946.

Erskine got a call from bridge expert Charlie Goren after the game. He had heard that Erskine was playing bridge during the break and reconstructed Carl's hand from the game and used it in one of his bridge columns later in the week.

Sore Arm Ace

Arm troubles robbed Erskine of some of the zip on his fastball in 1956. His strikeouts dropped from 187 in 1953 to 95 in 1956 but he still had a 13–11 record and helped the Dodgers to their final pennant in Brooklyn.

The day before Brooklyn opened a series with the Giants, Erskine's arm was hurting badly. He had been to the Dodger trainer so often he was embarrassed to go to him again and say it was still hurting so he called the Chicago trainer who said he would look at the knot on the back of his shoulder.

The trainer told him it was a severe muscle spasm and that the Cub doctor had treated Bob Rush for the same thing with a shot of procaine and cortisone. Erskine was reluctant but finally agreed to the treatment. He had lost two of his first three decisions when the Giants came to Ebbets Field on May 12, and Erskine read in the paper that the chief scout for the Giants said, "Erskine can't win with the garbage he's been throwing up there." When Erskine read that he remembered thinking, "The bad part is, he's right."

Erskine almost told manager Walt Alston that he couldn't pitch that day. And he could barely warm up because of the pain. Nonetheless, he retired batter after batter without surrendering a hit. Jackie Robinson made a diving catch of May's smash at third base in the fourth and Carl Furillo made a long run to catch a drive by Daryl Spencer.

"Through the first six innings, there wasn't any score. And I'm amazed every time I finish an inning. Each time I went back to the bench, I was dumbfounded that I was still pitching," Erskine said.

In the eighth inning the webbing broke on his glove. He borrowed Don Bessent's glove and worked the final two innings with it. With one out in the top of the ninth, Whitey Lockman hit a ball that cleared the right field foul pole screen several feet foul. On the next pitch Erskine threw a good overhand curveball and Lockman hit a shot right back at him on the ground.

"I went down to get the ball and was aware immediately I didn't field it. Instead I pinned the ball to the ground with the back of the glove, dead. It didn't squirt to the side or anything. And when I raised my glove, it was laying there like an Easter egg. I picked it up and threw him out. But that ball could have been a base hit easy." He then got Alvin Dark on a soft tap to the mound for the final out.

"I don't think I had overpowering stuff," Erskine said. "As a matter of fact, I didn't have overpowering stuff in either no-hitter. Just a good fastball and my control was all right."

He only used 102 pitches and 2:10 to earn his second win of the season, both coming against the Giants. He made 102 pitches in the game. During the 1952 no-hitter had made 103.

Up until that time, Christy Mathewson and Johnny Vander Meer were the only two modern National Leaguers with a pair of no-hitters.

In 1955 the Dodgers' owner Walter O'Malley began his exodus from Brooklyn by announcing that the Dodgers would play seven games in Jersey City, New Jersey, in 1956. It would be the beginning of the end for Brooklyn fans.

OVER THE RIVER

Red Smith

[APRIL 20, 1956:] JERSEY CITY — Ten years ago Jackie Robinson played here, and in 1948 Duke Snider was bombing these fences for Montreal. In this same Roosevelt Stadium, Walter Alston broke in as first baseman for Rochester. On the long, rough haul through the bushes, half a dozen other Dodgers served time in this garden spot of the marshes. Then Brooklyn beckoned, and they thought they had reached the majors. That's what they thought. Today they found out.

In gray and windy cold, a few cars crept through the Holland Tunnel, negotiated the traffic of Journal Square and groped across the flatlands past rubbish heaps and industrial plants, following the oldest established floating franchise in baseball to its home-away-from-home.

Outside the gates, newsboys hawked papers whose headlines heralded the historic event; "Jersey City's Dodgers open Major League Season."

It was the start of Walter O'Malley's ignoble experiment — baseball's return, on a part-time, piecemeal basis, to the town which the International League deserted six years ago — but Jersey City wasn't exactly beside itself. Indeed, Jersey City still wasn't beside anything but the pig farms of Secaucus. The first of Brooklyn's seven home games abroad drew 12,214 desperadoes to an abandoned auto race plant that can accommodate 25,000.

A wind howling off the Hackensack River stiffened flags on the grandstand roof, pointing them rigidly toward a muddy barren beyond right field where workman tearing up the auto track had left a bandshell uprooted. Also in the mud, fenced off from the playing field by a low temporary wall, stood a flagpole where Eddie Fisher and a Marine color guard were to soil their boots ceremoniously.

Eddie sang and an American Legion band tooled while flags went up — first the stars and stripes to tell the barnstormers what country they were in, and then a pennant hauled over from Brooklyn to remind the Dodgers that they were champions, even here.

From *Red Smith on Baseball.* ©2000 by Phyllis W. Smith. Reprinted by permission of Karen Weiss for Phyllis W. Smith.

Possibly the most appropriate touch, in view of the weather, was a big football scoreboard.

Near home plate, photographers made shot after shot of Jocko Conlon, the third-base umpire, brandishing a mask and crying, "Play ball!" It wasn't Jocko's mask, for Augie Donatelli was working behind the plate, and umpires in the majors never actually shouted, "Play ball!" But, then, major league teams never play championship games where they don't belong, either.

While bands marched and both teams were booed impartially as they straggled out for the opening ceremonies— after all, both are strangers here — a new baseball was entrusted to Mayor Bernard S. Berry. When the public address system announced the Mayor would now toss out the first ball, his honor was chatting with voters. Frantic joggling of his elbow won his attention.

"Mr. Mayor! The ball! The ball!"

"The ball?" said Mr. Berry. "I gave it to some kid."

Well, the first major league pitch in New Jersey history was a strike thrown by Carl Erskine and called against the Phillies' Richie Ashburn. The first play with real New Jersey flavor was a collaboration by Philadelphia's Willie Jones and Granny Hamner. Jones fell down backing up for a pop fly and knocked himself out of the game while Hamner stood tranquilly at his side and let the ball drop safely.

It was by no means the last play of this sort. Before the last horrid deed was done, the whole business looked like a conspiracy to stink baseball out of the state.

Del Ennis dawdled after a drive by Gil Hodges in the first inning and converted it to a three-run double. Then while Robinson played cat-and-mouse between first and second base, Hodges tried unsuccessfully to sneak home from third and killed off the Dodgers' only scoring inning against Murry Dickson.

Due chiefly to boots by Robinson and Carl Furillo and a wild pitch by Erskine, Philadelphia tied the score in the third inning. In the tenth, Philadelphia went ahead, 4–3, where upon Roy Campanella retied the score by doubling Snider home.

At long and gruesome last, Rube Walker got Zimmer home with a fly ball, and the Dodgers had their first official victory since Oct. 4.

They had waited 197 days. Jersey had waited since the dawn of civilization. It required two hours, forty-three minutes, ten innings and eight errors. As the fellow says, you can take the boy out of the bush, but — .

Far off on the gray horizon, a ray from the setting sun touched the towers of Manhattan. They were a million light years away.

By 1956 the Dodgers were old and wearing down. By rights they should have been struggling in third place. But the greatness was still there. It was as though they knew that this would be the last pennant in Brooklyn.

LAST PENNANT IN BROOKLYN

Jimmy Cannon

[SEPTEMBER 17, 1956:] DESIRE is the country of the young. Despair is the land of the aged. All the spectacular myths demand that the old be tricked by time. Big bookmakers end up old horse players. Nimble young men about midnight towns are trimmed by hustling broads when they get old. Romeo and Juliet were children. King Lear wandered through the stormy mazes of senility. The check-snatcher becomes a drink-cadger with the years. Skid Row is the last street of the year-hurt. But this season the Dodgers are making falsehoods of the legends because yesterday, after beating Cincinnati, 3–2, they are now a half a game in front of the National League.

It is an elderly team by the standards of the sport. In other times men of their ages are still shaping their careers. But in this game they should have spent, now that they have gone across the spring, used up the summer and find themselves in this muggy autumn of their sun-down year.

They are old wizards, doing wonders they learned in boyhood and have perfected for the winter of their professional lives. Their agility is genuine as if, by some mysterious process, the old folks sitting on the benches of St. Pete arose and danced a perfect ballet with a beautiful grace. Among them Junior Gilliam seems an interloper who is allowed to be part of this lodge of middle-aged athletes.

When Charlie Neal, who played second until the ninth inning, came out he might have been the bat-boy, so youthful was his appearance by comparison. They have been through this before and Pee Wee Reese has been the shortstop since 1940. It is Reese, Jackie Robinson, Roy Campanella, and Sal Maglie and this is the year they were supposed to go.

They remind me, these old ballplayers, of Alfred Lunt who by some device of his profession, temporarily can assume the elegance of youth. There is in them a bit of Jimmy Durante, too, because he can borrow back the crazy energy of his youth for the time it takes to do his turn on a night club floor. But actors depend on illusion and their wonders are effete. The Brooklyn club is sweating for what they have made of themselves in what was supposed to be their hopeless season.

The folk-tales are irrevocable. Old pugs are counted out. Old chorus girls either marry young or drift into grieving dissipation. Old reporters are assigned to file clippings in the library. Old novelists compose parodies of their earlier works. Old poets scribble their verses on the menus of Greenwich Village tea-rooms and sell them for hand-outs. Old railroad men doze their last years away in shacks where roads cross the tracks. Old bartenders become mooching rummies. Old jockeys turn touts. Old actresses open tea-rooms or try interior decorating. Old ball clubs lose but the Dodgers are a half game in front today.

It was Maglie, of course, too old for the Giants, too old for Cleveland, who came into the ninth inning with two out and a shutout. Then Wally Post hit a ground ball down the third base line. It was Robinson, moving on his football-damaged legs, getting the ball and lobbing it to first before he fell over on his shoulder and his gray-speckled head landed on the turf. It was a hit and then Smokey Burgess hit a home run and it was 3–2. There was a single and Maglie was through for the humid day. In came Don Bessent, a young stranger, and after another hit, Robinson handled the last ground ball.

It had been Robinson who doubled in the third and then Gil Hodges, who is a child no longer, who doubled him home. So Duke Snider, who isn't expected to hit left-handers, doubled Hodges home and Joe Nuxhall was the pitcher. It was Reese who scored the final run, after singling, on a bases-filled walk. He also tripled in the seventh but perished between third and home when Robinson missed a bunt. And Campanella caught with his crushed fingers.

They asked Maglie what had caused Burgess to hit his home run in the ninth. So talented is he, so suave and clever in a subtle way, he was disgusted because his deceit was exposed.

"I should have my head examined for throwing him that kind of pitch," Maglie said. "I thought it was a good spot, two out. Next time I throw it, they'll probably pop it up. It was a change-up. Make him hit your best pitch. I should have thrown him the curve ball."

Unless you have covered baseball a long while, you don't know how old they are and not one admits he's 40. But Reese, taking off his clammy uniform, pointed to Maglie.

"Number 35," he said. "That's the ball game. He really gives you a game every time he goes out. What makes Maglie is he's a hell of a competitor. He knows how to pitch."

Campanella, removing his socks with his smashed fingers, said it all for them.

"You let an old dog run loose," he said, "it's tough to get the harness back on him. It's tough to catch him. It's going to be tough to catch us."

And the old dogs are running like young ones who have never been off the leash.

In game five of the 1956 World Series, Sal Maglie, the erstwhile Giant foe, amazingly was pitching for Brooklyn. He gave up two runs and five hits and pitched a masterful game. But the fellow in pinstripes was perfect.

THE MAN WAS PERFECT

Shirley Povich

[October 8, 1956:] THE MILLION-TO-ONE shot came in. Hell froze over. A month of Sundays hit the calendar. Don Larsen today pitched a no-hit, no-run, no-man-reach-first game in a World Series.

On the mound at Yankee Stadium, the same guy who was knocked out in two innings by the Dodgers on Friday came up today with one for the record books, posting it there in solo grandeur as the only Perfect Game in World Series history.

With it, the Yankee right-hander shattered the Dodgers, 2–0, and beat Sal Maglie, while taking 64,519 suspense-limp fans into his act.

First there was mild speculation, then there was hope, then breaths were held in slackened jaws in the late innings as the big mob wondered if the big Yankee right-hander could bring off for them the most fabulous of all World Series games.

He did it, and the Yanks took the Series lead three games to two, to leave the Dodgers as thunderstruck as Larsen himself appeared to be at the finish of his feat.

Larsen whizzed a third strike past pinch hitter Dale Mitchell in the ninth. That was all. It was over. Automatically, the massive 226-pounder from San Diego started walking from the mound toward the dugout, as pitchers are supposed to do at the finish.

But this time there was a woodenness in his steps and his stride was that of a man in a daze. The spell was broken for Larsen when Yogi Berra ran onto the infield to embrace him.

It was not Larsen jumping for joy. It was the more demonstrative Berra. His battery mate leaped full tilt at the big guy. In self-defense, Larsen caught Berra in mid-air as one would catch a frolicking child, and that's how they made their way toward the Yankee bench, Larsen carrying Berra.

There wasn't a Brooklyn partisan left among the 64,519, it seemed, at the finish. Loyalties to the Dodgers evaporated in sheer enthrallment at the show big Larsen was giving them, for this was a day when fans could boast that they were there.

So at the finish, Larsen had brought it off, and erected for himself a special throne in baseball's Hall of Fame, with the first Perfect Game pitched in major-league baseball since Charlie Robertson of the White Sox against Detroit 34 years ago.

But this one was more special. This one was in a World Series. Three times, pitchers had almost come through with no-hitters, and there were three one-hitters in the World Series books, but never a no-man-reach-base classic.

The tragic victim of it all, sitting on the Dodger bench, was sad Sal Maglie, himself a five-hit pitcher today in his bid for a second Series victory over the Yankees. He was out of the game, technically, but he was staying to see it out and it must have been in disbelief that he saw himself beaten by another guy's World Series no-hitter.

Mickey Mantle hit a home run today in the fourth inning and that was all the impetus the Yankees needed, but no game-winning home run ever wound up with such emphatic second billing as Mantle's this afternoon.

It was an exciting wallop but in the fourth inning only, because after that Larsen was the story today, and the dumbfounded Dodgers could wonder how this same guy who couldn't last out two innings in the second game could master them so thoroughly today.

He did it with a tremendous assortment of pitches that seemed to have five forward speeds, including a slow one that ought to have been equipped with back-up lights.

Larsen had them in hand all day. He used only 97 pitches, not an abnormally low number because 11 pitches an inning is about normal for a good day's work. But he was the boss from the outset. Only against PeeWee Reese in the first inning did he lapse to a three-ball count, and then he struck Reese out. No other Dodger was ever favored with more than two called balls by umpire Babe Pinelli.

Behind him, his Yankee teammates made three spectacular fielding plays to put Larsen in the Hall of Fame. There was one in the second inning that calls for special description. In the fifth, Mickey Mantle ranged far back into left center to haul in Gil Hodges' long drive with a backhand shoetop grab that was a beaut. In the eighth, the same Hodges made another bid to break it up, but third baseman Andy Carey speared his line drive.

Little did Larsen, the Yankees, the Dodgers or anybody among the 64,519 in the stands suspect that when Jackie Robinson was robbed of a line-drive hit in the second inning, the stage was being set for a Perfect Game.

Robinson murdered the ball so hard that third baseman Andy Carey barely had time to fling his glove upward in a desperate attempt to get the ball. He could only deflect it. But, luckily, shortstop Gil McDougald was backing up, and able to grab the ball on one bounce. By a half-step, McDougald got Robinson at first base, and Larsen tonight can be grateful that it was not the younger, fleeter Robinson of a few years back but a heavy-legged, 40-year-old Jackie.

As the game wore on, Larsen lost the edge that gave him five strike-outs in the first four innings, and added only two in the last five. He had opened up by slipping called third strikes past both Gilliam and Reese in the first inning.

Came the sixth, and he got Furillo and Campanella on pops, fanned Maglie. Gilliam, Reese and Snider were easy in the seventh. Robinson tapped out, Hodges lined out and Amoros flied out in the eighth. And now it was the ninth, and the big

Scandinavian-American was going for the works with a calm that was exclusive with him.

Furillo gave him a bit of a battle, fouled off four pitches, then flied mildly to Bauer. He got two quick strikes on Campanella, got him on a slow roller to Martin.

Now it was left-handed Dale Mitchell, pinch hitting for Maglie.

Ball one came in high. Larsen got a called strike.

On the next pitch, Mitchell swung for strike two.

Then the last pitch of the game. Mitchell started to swing, but didn't go through with it.

But it made no difference because Umpire Pinelli was calling it Strike Number Three, and baseball history was being made.

Maglie himself was a magnificent figure out there all day, pitching hitless ball and leaving the Yankees a perplexed gang, until suddenly with two out in the fourth, Mickey Mantle, with two called strikes against him, lashed the next pitch on a line into the right-field seats to give the Yanks a 1-0 lead.

There was doubt about that Mantle homer because the ball was curving and would it stay fair? It did. In their own half of the inning, the Dodgers had no such luck. Duke Snider's drive into the same seats had curved foul by a few feet. The disgusted Snider eventually took a third strike.

The Dodgers were a luckless gang and Larsen a fortunate fellow in the fifth. Like Mantle, Sandy Amoros lined one into the seats in right, and that one was a near thing for the Yankees. By what seemed only inches, it curved foul, the umpires ruled.

Going into the sixth, Maglie was pitching a one-hitter — Mantle's homer — and being out-pitched. The old guy lost some of his stuff in the sixth, though, and the Yankees came up with their other run.

Carey led off with a single to center, and Larsen sacrificed him to second on a daring third-strike bunt. Hank Bauer got the run in with a single to left. There might have been a close play at the plate had Amoros come up with the ball cleanly, but he didn't and Carey scored unmolested.

Now there were Yanks still on first and third with only one out, but they could get no more. Hodges made a scintillating pickup of Mantle's smash, stepped on first and threw to home for a double play on Bauer, who was trying to score. Bauer was trapped in a rundown and caught despite a low throw by Campanella that caused Robinson to fall into the dirt.

But the Yankees weren't needing any more runs for Larsen today. They didn't even need their second one, because they were getting a pitching job for the books this memorable day in baseball.

Don Newcombe pitched for the Brooklyn Dodgers from 1949 to 1957 — with two seasons lost to military service — winning 123 games and losing 60 for a percentage of .672 during his tenure in Brooklyn. He was the only player ever to win the Rookie-of-the-Year, Cy Young, and Most Valuable Player awards. In 1956 he won 27 while losing just seven games for a .794 percentage, he hurled 268 innings and posted an ERA of 3.06. He has pitched in the final days of pennant races on one and two days' rest. It was said by some that he "couldn't win the big ones." They must have been looking at someone else!

THE LONGEST NIGHT

Michael Shapiro

[OCTOBER 1956:] Carl Erskine may have lost the fourth game but was in no mood to be pitied. He believed that his defeat was not in vain, that it was merely a stage in a greater plan. "There was a reason for it," he told a friend in the Dodger clubhouse that afternoon. He turned toward the locker where Newcombe sat. "There has to be another chance for him."

Don Newcombe did not sleep well the night before the deciding game. He woke four times, took a pill but still could not rest. His wife, Freddie, suggested that he move to another room, but he could not sleep there either. It was not the game that kept him awake, he told Milton Gross. "It was the other business I wanted to beat, but dammit I can't get away from it."

It was a brisk day but Newcombe was pleased with his warm-ups. Later, he would say that generally his troubles were early inning troubles, that if he got through the first and second and found his rhythm he would be fine. Just before Hank Bauer stepped in, Reese approached the mound. He had already spoken to Newcombe in the clubhouse but wanted to repeat what he said — "I told him how he'd gotten us this far and told him that this was the payoff but whatever happens don't worry. Just go out there and pitch."

Bauer led off with a single. But Newcombe threw three strikes in a row past Billy Martin and did the same to Mantle. Bauer was still on first when Berra came to bat. Reese came again to the mound, this time to remind Newcombe to keep the ball away from Berra. Newcombe got two quick strikes. Campanella signaled for a waste pitch, high and inside. "I was getting the ball where I wanted," he later said. "Except the first one Yogi hit. I tried to brush him back but I didn't get it inside enough."

Later, Campanella would say that Berra "hit it off his ear." The ball found the seats and Brooklyn came to bat in the first, down by two. Snider singled, but that was all.

In the top of the second, Newcombe fell behind two balls and no strikes to Kucks, the pitcher. Robinson approached from third and asked weather Newcombe was aiming his pitches. Newcombe replied he did not believe he was. An aimed pitch is a tentative pitch, a pitch directed at a spot but delivered without authority. Newcombe was a fastball pitcher who had the control that eluded so many men who threw hard. He did not need to aim the ball unless he did not trust himself just enough to throw. Still, the Yankees did not score. Neither did Brooklyn. The Yankees were batting in the third when once again, Newcombe looked in to face Berra, this time with Martin on first. Again Newcombe got two quick strikes. He seemed poised for a strikeout when Berra nicked his third pitch for a foul tip. Campanella wanted the next pitch wasted inside.

Newcombe threw and kept his back to the scoreboard when Berra's pitch sailed onto Bedford Avenue. He stared at the ground. In the pressbox men trained their binoculars on him. His lips appeared to be moving and someone was sure that when he brought his hand to his face it was to wipe away a tear.

The Yankees led 4 to 0 when Newcombe came to bat to modest applause in the bottom of the third. Berra, a notorious chatterbox behind the plate, offered Newcombe some backhanded consolation. "I hit a perfect pitch," he said. "It was perfect — low outside fastball and I hit the hell out of it." The Dodgers went hitless in the third.

ELSTON HOWARD'S HOME run in the fourth finished him. Alston came to fetch him and as Red Smith wrote later that afternoon, a boo was the last sound Newcombe heard as he stepped from the field into the dugout.

Irving Rudd found him in the shower. "Go away," Newcombe told him. "You'll get all wet."

"Look Don," said Rudd, "I know what you're going to do and you'll regret it afterward. Finish your shower and get dressed and then sit down and cool off. It won't be more than half an hour and the game will be over."

But Newcombe did not want to stay. He dressed and walked out to his car with Rudd chasing behind. James Newcombe was waiting by the car and Rudd asked, "Pop, can't you talk to him?"

A man standing in the parking lot called out, "It's tough, Newk. You can't win 'em all." Don Newcombe settled into the driver's seat of his station wagon. His father joined him. So did Milton Gross.

"I'm sorry, Pop," Newcombe murmured.

"What?" asked his father, who could barely hear him.

"I'm sorry."

"What do you have to be sorry for?" said his father.

They drove along Washington Avenue, then over to Flatbush. They left Brooklyn over the Manhattan Bridge and were driving through lower Manhattan when Newcombe switched on the radio. They heard Bob Wolf say, "After six innings it's Yanks 5, Dodgers 0. Roger Craig now takes over the mound." Gross was not sure whether Newcombe was listening. Twice he had to hit the brakes hard to avoid rear-ending other cars.

"You won 27," Gross told him. "You know there were some big ones."

"Remember that," said James Newcombe.

"I don't want to talk," Don Newcombe said. "I don't want to say anything."

He drove west toward the Holland Tunnel and New Jersey. He had his right hand on the wheel. In the left he clutched a handkerchief. He wiped his mouth and sometimes his eyes.

They lost the radio signal as they entered the tunnel. "Why didn't you change your shirt and go back to the dugout?" Gross asked.

"I don't know," Newcombe replied. "I don't know a lot of things."

Then, as they emerged into the light on the Jersey side of the tunnel, he said, "I felt good. I was throwing hard, real hard."

They were on the Pulaski Skyway when Bill Skowron came to bat with the bases loaded. The Dodgers had just walked Berra intentionally. Skowron's grand slam made it 9 to 0. Ebbets Field began emptying out.

"It can happen to somebody else, too," said James Newcombe. His son nodded.

"What about our hitters," said the father. "No hits the other day. Two hits yesterday and what have they got today." They had three.

Newcombe stopped at his father's house in Linden. He invited Gross in for a beer. In the kitchen his mother had the game on the television. "Get it over with," she said. "It's over and done."

"I'm sorry, Ma," Newcombe said.

"What's to be sorry?" said his mother.

Newcombe poured beer for himself, his father, and Milton Gross. "Drink up," he said. "I want to call my wife."

Newcombe and Gross soon left. They drove on and Gross asked what he had been thinking of as they drove from Ebbets Field.

"I was thinking about what I do wrong," Newcombe replied. "But I can't put my finger on why I do it." He paused, and then went on. "I was running in the outfield at the stadium the other day and a guy called me a yellow-bellied slob. How do you take things like that?"

He told Gross what Reese had said to him in the clubhouse, about how vital he was to the team. "And other people say I choke up. I think it's rubbed off in the clubhouse."

He dropped Gross at the commuter rail station. Five boys were standing on the corner, four black, one white.

"That Newk?" one boy asked. He wanted to know why Newcombe was there; the game had just ended.

"He left early," Gross said. The white boy, he noted, giggled.

"Don't laugh," said one of the others. "Just don't laugh."

NEWCOMBE STOPPED AT home and then went out and by dawn his wife could not find him. "He was in a state of mind I've never seen before in our eleven years of marriage," she told a reporter who called. "He isn't here and I don't know where he is. He was only here about ten minutes, then he left." She had called the liquor store, but he was not there. She called his relatives, who had not seen him. "He said he wouldn't be home last night. He left the car in case I need it."

In Brooklyn that night a funeral director in Ridgewood loaned a coffin to a bartender so that Warren DeMontreaux of Cooper Street could pay off his series bet by climbing in for a mock funeral. In Bedford-Stuyvesant, Dutch Pirozzi, who owned the Sportsman's Café, placed a casket by the front door. Matty Bosco made a mock casket that he placed in front of his flower shop on Atlantic Avenue. Inside he placed a doll dressed in a baseball uniform and announced that the memorial would stand for three days. And in a gas station out on Pennsylvania Avenue, Harold Whetstone was reading the sad news in the bulldog edition when three teenagers stirred him from his gloomy reverie to tell him they had come to rob him. They took $135 and vanished into the night.

The Dodgers had a small party. The team had planned nothing elaborate, certainly nothing like the gala of the year before, and nothing like the Yankee victory party in Manhattan at the Waldorf-Astoria. The Dodgers had a 12:30 flight the next day that would begin their voyage to Japan. Newcombe did not appear at the team party and by morning Buzzie Bavasi was warning that he had best make the flight: "If he doesn't show up it'll be a matter for the commissioner."

CARL FURILLO, WHO had fought in the Pacific, had refused to make the trip. So did Sal Maglie. Campanella announced that he would have surgery on his hand but would make the journey just the same. The Dodger wives were excited about visiting Japan, even if their husbands did not much want to go.

The players were milling around the gate at Idlewild Airport, drawing little attention, when Don Newcombe appeared. He wore a topcoat, a gray tweed suit, a red shirt, and a hat. He was chewing gum. He wore dark glasses over red-rimmed eyes. The reporters were on him quickly and he told them he had been home all night. "I told my wife not to tell anyone where I was," he said. "I felt terrible and didn't want to talk to anyone."

This was not true. Privately, he told Milton Gross that he had spent the night alone, walking. Gross had called the house. So had Jackie Robinson, Buzzie Bavasi, and the commissioner, Ford Frick. Newcombe admitted he had spent the night convinced he would break his contract and skip the Japan trip. He called his wife three times to let her know he was okay, but said nothing else. He wandered until dawn and then, at seven o'clock, called his lawyer. He was due in court to answer Michael Brown's charge that he had punched him in the stomach. A judge adjourned the case until November, after the team's return from Asia.

Newcombe left for the airport, bagless. When he arrived at Idlewild a crowd formed around the reporters who had gathered around Newcombe. Alston tried to buck him up. Campanella insisted his roommate did not choke. But Newcombe was on edge. "Where's my money for this trip," he said. "I'm not going until I get my check." A fellow from the front office took him by the arm and led him to the plane. His wife would take a later flight, and meet the team in Los Angeles.

He was loud on the plane. He sat near the front with Roy Campanella. Someone had brought a bottle on board and they were getting drunk. Walter O'Malley was on the plane with his wife. So were many of the other wives. Newcombe rose and on unsteady feet began noisily making his way to the bathroom. Walter Alston, who had seen and heard too much, got up. He was Newcombe's height and just as broad and now he stood in his path.

"Newk, I want you to go back to your seat and I want you to be quiet," Alston said. "You understand that?"

Clem Labine watched and listened as Newcombe replied. "Walter," he said, "get out of my way or I'm going to piss on you."

Alston stepped out of his way. But that, Labine later said, "was the beginning of the end for Newk. Newcombe was an alcoholic and none of us knew it."

The off season of 1956-1957 signaled the beginning of the end for the storied Brooklyn Dodgers. The first hints of the ballclub's deserting Brooklyn were beginning to surface; and Jackie Robinson retired.

JACKIE ROBINSON: MORE THAN A BALLPLAYER

J. Ronald Oakley

The offseason brought an end to the careers of two of baseball's greatest players, Bob Feller and Jackie Robinson.

Feller announced his retirement at a luncheon held at Cleveland Municipal Stadium on December 28. During a ceremony which saw his uniform number "19" retired, Feller said he planned to devote his time to his insurance business but would retain his job as president of the Major League Baseball Players Association until work on a new pension plan was completed.

Thus ended the career of one of baseball's greatest pitchers, certainly one of its fastest. Manager Bucky Harris of the Washington Senators once told his young hitters that the only advice he could give them when they were batting against Feller was to "go up and hit what you see. And if you don't see anything, come on back." Breaking into the majors at the age of 17 in 1936, the fireballer went into the record books with 266 wins and 162 losses. If he had not lost four years to the service during World War II he would certainly have made it into the 300-win circle. He was also credited with 3 no-hitters, 12 one-hitters, 6 seasons with 20 or more wins, 46 shutouts, and 2581 strikeouts. He once fanned 18 batters in one game and 27 in two consecutive contests. But the biggest prize always eluded him, a World Series victory. It was one of the major disappointments of his career.

The news of Feller's retirement was overshadowed by the controversial events surrounding the closing of Jackie Robinson's career. On December 13, Robinson had been traded to the New York Giants for $35,000 and left-handed pitcher Dick Littlefield. It quickly became the most sensational baseball story in New York since Leo Durocher crossed over from the Dodgers to the Giants in the middle of the 1948 season. The trade seemed to be a good deal for both clubs. The Dodgers needed to get

From *Baseball's Last Golden Age, 1946–1960: The National Pastime in a Time of Glory and Change* by J. Ronald Oakley. ©1994 J. Ronald Oakley. Used by permission of McFarland & Company, Inc., Publishers, Box 611, Jefferson NC 28640. *www.mcfarlandpub.com*

rid of some older players with high salaries, Junior Gilliam had already nudged Robinson out of his second base spot, and the team needed a left-handed pitcher. The Giants needed a first baseman, and Robinson would be a marvelous gate draw, especially when teamed with Willie Mays. Robinson was obviously nearing the end of his career, but in the past season there had been times when the old Robinson seemed to come to life with a clutch hit, a crucial stolen base, or a good defensive play.

Robinson was stunned at the news of his trade, which he learned about from a phone call from Buzzie Bavasi, the vice-president and general manager of the Dodgers. He felt betrayed, but he also faced a dilemma. At the time he received Bavasi's call he had already decided to retire from baseball and had concluded two important business deals. He had just agreed to take a $50,000-a-year job as the vice president of personnel with Chock Full O'Nuts, a restaurant chain, and had sold exclusive rights to his retirement story to *Look* magazine for $50,000, over $7,000 more than he ever made in one year as a player. For the article to be worth that much to the national magazine, news of his retirement would have to remain secret until the article appeared.

Caught in this awkward situation, Robinson was evasive. When contacted by reporters about the trade, he said that he was "disappointed in leaving Brooklyn" and that he hoped that "Brooklyn can win again unless the Giants can win it." He also told one reporter, "I'm going to play as long as I can. I'm going to give it all I've got."

The *Look* issue containing Robinson's article was received by most subscribers on Saturday, January 5, and the next morning the *New York Times* and other newspapers around the country carried the news. In the two-page article entitled simply, "Why I'm Quitting Baseball," Robinson said, "There shouldn't be any mystery about my reasons. I'm 38 years old, with a family to support. I've got to think of my future and our security. At my age, a man doesn't have much future in baseball — and very little security. It's as simple as that…. I'm through with baseball because I know that in a matter of time baseball will be through with me." Knowing that the secrecy surrounding his retirement would arouse considerable controversy, Robinson said, "I've always played fair with my newspaper friends, and I think they'll understand why this was the one time I couldn't give them the whole story as soon as I knew it."

The news of Robinson's retirement caused as much of an uproar as the news about his trade did back in December. "I still can't believe he won't play," Giants vice-president Chub Feeney said. "I can't believe he was just misleading the newspapermen he has spoken to and told he would play." Bavasi, who had often feuded with Robinson, left no doubt as to how he felt. "That's typical of Jackie," he told reporters. "Now he'll write a letter of apology to Chubby. He has been writing letters of apology all his life." Bavasi went on to say, "This is the way he repays the newspapermen for what they've done for him. He tells you one thing and then writes another for money. You fellows will find out you've been blowing the horn for the wrong guy." Bavasi's comments brought an angry retort from Robinson, who told reporters, "After what Bavasi said, I wouldn't play ball again for a million dollars."

Some members of the press felt that Robinson had deliberately deceived them and that it was unethical for him to sell his story to one publication. Many of them agreed with the *Washington Post's* Shirley Povich, who wrote that from 1947 on, Robinson "was a big leaguer all the way, until his final act of retirement. And then he went out bush." But other sportswriters wrote that Robinson had acted the best he could in a very difficult situation and that the press owed as much to Robinson, who had provided them with so much good copy over the years, as he did to them. Al Abrams of the *Pittsburgh Post-Gazette* wrote, "I just can't get ruffled over the charge that Robinson treated newspapers unfairly in concealing his retirement plans until the magazine broke the story. Let's just say that Jackie rode out of baseball on a controversial wave, just as he rode in some ten years ago."

Robinson's career had been a short one, for racism had kept him out of a major league uniform until he was 28 years old. In his decade on major league diamonds he had played 1,382 games and helped lead the Dodgers to six pennants and one world championship. He had a lifetime batting average of .311, hit over .300 six times, took the batting title in 1949 with a .342 average, hit 137 home runs, scored 947 runs, batted in 734 runs, and stole 197 bases, including 11 thefts of home (more than any post–World War II player). He led the league in stolen bases in 1947 and 1949, and his base-stealing totals would undoubtedly have been higher except for the Dodger style of play which emphasized power hitting. He was the Rookie of the Year in 1947, the National League's MVP in 1949, and drew millions of fans to tiny Ebbets Field and to parks all across the National League. In 1962 he would be elected to the Hall of Fame.

Statistics alone do not reveal Robinson's true worth to the Brooklyn Dodgers. He was a fiery competitor and leader who always played for keeps and was always regarded by opponents as the most dangerous player on the club. Leo Durocher, who supported bringing Robinson to the Dodgers and then feuded with him from 1948 on, said at the time of Robinson's retirement, "He can beat you in more ways than any player I know." Teammate Roy Campanella claimed, "Jackie could beat you every way there was to beat you.... I have never seen a ballplayer that could do all the things that Jackie Robinson did.... He could think so much faster than anybody I ever played with or against.... He was two steps and one thought ahead of anyone else." And Duke Snider later recalled, "He could beat you with his bat, his glove, his throwing arm, his legs, and his brain — and if he couldn't do it with any of those, he could beat you with his mouth."

Jackie Robinson was opinionated, argumentative, loud, aggressive, competitive, abrasive. He was often criticized for these traits, which were, incidentally, shared by Leo Durocher, Eddie Stanky, and many other white players. Roger Kahn would later write in *The Boys of Summer*, "Like a few, very few athletes, Babe Ruth, Jim Brown, Robinson did not merely play at center stage. He was center stage; and wherever he walked, center stage moved with him." When number "42" retired, baseball lost one of its greatest competitors and performers.

With his retirement, Robinson disappeared from center stage but not from the public eye. An active member of the NAACP and a friend and follower of Martin Luther King, Jr., he was outspoken on civil rights and politics. But he aged rapidly, his health and energy sapped by a heart condition, arthritis, and diabetes, which gradually robbed him of his sight. He also suffered a great tragedy when his son,

Jackie Jr., born during his historic year at Montreal in 1946, developed a drug problem, was rehabilitated, and then died in an automobile wreck in 1971.

In 1972 he threw out the first ball in the second World Series game at Riverfront Stadium in Cincinnati, and was honored with a plaque commemorating the 25th anniversary of his big league debut. As he accepted the plaque, he said, "I am extremely proud and pleased, but I will be more pleased the day I can look over at third base and see a black man as manager." Nine days later, at the age of 53, he was dead. Three years later, as part of the revolution Robinson had begun in 1947, Frank Robinson took the field as manager of the Cleveland Indians.

Jackie Robinson was always more than a ballplayer. He was an agent and symbol of integration and black progress, and he forced blacks and whites to talk about racism and integration long before *Brown v. Board of Education* and the civil rights activities of the fifties and sixties. His revolutionary integration of the national pastime had helped to publicize the problems of blacks, to promote black pride, to break down prejudices and racial barriers, and to pave the way for the acceptance of blacks in other areas of American life. The Reverend King once told Don Newcombe, "You'll never know what you and Jackie and Roy did to make it possible for me to do my job." More than anyone since Babe Ruth, Robinson had transformed the national pastime, and in the process had helped to transform America itself.

Pee Wee Reese spent 17 seasons in Brooklyn (minus three seasons in the military) and as captain of the Dodgers was most respected by players, fans and the press. He hit .269 with a career total of 2170 hits. He scored 1338 runs and led the Dodgers to seven World Series appearances. Reese was inducted into the Hall of Fame in 1984.

A Shortstop in Kentucky

Roger Kahn

So came the Captain...
And when the judgment thunders split the house,
Wrenching the rafters from the ancient rest, He held the ridgepole up....
— Edwin Markham

Pee Wee Reese was riding a ship back from Guam and World War II when he heard the wrenching news that Branch Rickey had hired a black. Reese had lost three seasons, half of an average major league career, to the United States Navy and he was impatient to get on with what was left when a petty officer said, "It's on shortwave. His name's Jackie Robinson. A colored guy to play on your team."

"Is that a fact?" Reese said, deadpan.

"Pee Wee," the petty officer said, in a needling, singsong way. "He's a shortstop."

"Oh shit," Pee Wee Reese said.

Across a brace of nights, Reese lay in a bunk, measuring his circumstances and himself. He'd won the job at short, in the double down caldron of two pennant races. Now the old man had gone and hired a black replacement. The old man didn't have to do that. But wait a minute (Reese thought). What the hell did black have to do with it? They'd signed a ball player. They'd signed others during the war. White or black, this guy was gonna learn, like Cowboy Bill Hart and Fiddler Ed Basinski, that the war was over now, and the *real* Dodger shortstop was still named Pee Wee Reese.

"Except—except suppose he beats me out. Suppose he does. I go back to Louisville. The people say, 'Reese you weren't man enough to protect your job from a nigger.'" In the bunk, only one response seemed right: "Fuck 'em." "I don't know this Robinson," Reese told himself, "but I can imagine how he feels. I mean if they said to me, 'Reese, you got to go over and play in the colored guys' league,' how would I feel? Scared. The only white. Lonely. But I'm a good shortstop. And that's how I've *got* to look at Robinson. If he's man enough to take my job, I'm not gonna like it, but dammit, black or white, he deserves it." Reese did not speculate on the reactions of other white ball players, but before the Navy transport docked in San Francisco he had made an abiding peace with his conscience.

Three themes sound through the years of Harold Henry Reese, son of a Southern railroad detective and catalyst of baseball integration. The first was his drive to win, no less fierce because it was cloaked in civility. A second theme was that civility itself. Reese sought endlessly to understand other points of view, as with Robinson or with Leo Durocher or with a news photographer bawling after a double-header, "Would ya hold it, Pee Wee, for a couple more?" the final theme echoed wonder. He played shortstop for three generations of Brooklyn themes, and came to sport droll cockiness. Yet near the end, sitting on a friend's front porch and watching a brown telephone truck scuttle by, he said with total seriousness, "I still can't figure why the guy driving that thing isn't me."

Reese played Dodger shortstop the year I entered high school. He played Dodger shortstop when I covered the team. The year I left the newspaper business, he batted .309. He was still able to play twenty-two games at short when he was forty and the Dodgers had moved to Los Angeles, in 1958. "He came from Kentucky a boy," Red Barber liked to say, his voice warmed by sparks of Southern chauvinism. "And he-ah, right he-ah in Brooklyn, we saw him grow into a man, and more than that, a captain among men."

By the time I met Reese he had been team captain for five years and had devised an unpretentious twinkly style of leadership.

"Good God A'mighty," he'd cry in the batting cage after cuffing a line drive to the right. "*Another* base hit." The big hitters relaxed and laughed and winked.

"How ya doin', Roscoe?" he greeted McGowen once after a long night game in Philadelphia.

"Not so good, Pee Wee," the gray-haired *Times* man said. He began a monologue on the bad hands he had lately drawn at cards.

Reese listened sympathetically. Then he said, "Roscoe. Did it ever occur to you that maybe it isn't the cards, that you just might be a horseshit poker player?" Even McGowen smiled.

It all seemed so casual that Reese stepped with apparent ease from pleasant trivia to more serious things. He was Jackie Robinson's friend. They played hit-and-run together and cards and horses. Anyone who resented Robinson for his color or — more common — for the combination of color and aggressiveness found himself contending not only with Jack, but with the captain. Aware, but unselfconscious, Reese and Robinson came to personify integration. If a man didn't like what they personified, why, he had better not play for the Dodgers.

Duplicity annoyed Reese. A younger Dodger pitcher sat drinking with a girl once when two newspapermen drifted into a hotel bar. "Christ," the ball player said. "Gotta get outa here, 'fore them guys see me and put it in the paper."

Splitting beers with Snider nearby, Reese called, "Hey. You have it wrong. The writers don't want to be treated like stool pigeons. You got caught with a dolly. Run and you make yourself look worse. Buy them a drink. Hell, writers get caught with dollies, too."

In the clubhouse Reese's drawl showed an edge, but between games of one important double-header Billy Cox angered him. "I can't play no more today," Cox said. "Bushed. I gotta save something." Gil Hodges gazed into a locker. Carl Furillo shrugged. But no one spoke. Finally Reese called, "What are you saving something for, Billy? An exhibition game in Altoona?" Cox played the second game.

Reese could have managed the Dodgers. After the overthrow of Dressen, he towered, the obvious successor. "It was not specifically offered," he says, "but they gave me the impression that if I wanted to run for office, ask real strong, I could have it. Thing was, I didn't want to run." Later he spent one season as a coach. From that point he might have succeeded Walter Alston and he certainly could have managed somewhere. But he quit after a single season. He was rejecting the eternal pressure, the abrasive life, the suffocating responsibility and, I suppose, the eventual firing that is part of a manager's condition of employment. His reason cut deeper than the outward calm. Before Pee Wee Reese retired as a shortstop, he had developed a case of stomach ulcers.

He took a job telecasting ball games once a week for NBC. "How do you like that?" he said, with cultivated mildness. "They're paying me to talk into a microphone and I still pronounce the damn word 'th'owed.'" But he was proud of this success, as he was proud of the others, and losing the NBC job to Mickey Mantle wounded him. When I telephoned Reese in Louisville, I said that I was sorry.

"That's show biz," Reese said. "Don't get lost coming here. Make it for brunch. The house is out in Bealesbranch Road."

He was comfortable, I knew. He owned a storm window business and a bowling alley and part of a bank in Brandenburg, Kentucky, and the Cincinnati Reds had hired him to broadcast for a season. "I liked the old NBC job," he said, "but face it. I was never a name like Mantle. I was hanging in and my time ran out. Now it's running out in Cincy, too."

The contentious present has whirled his name into controversy. According to newspaper accounts, a black group in Louisville accused Reese of renting bowling lanes only to whites. Driving out of Roe's Ozarks, through forests, into the Mississippi flats across west Kentucky hills, I wondered intermittently what could have happened. The man had worked ten years for integration, sharing a measure of Robinson's triumph, and ten years after that he stood as a segregationist.

"Come in," Reese said, at the door of a rambling, unpretentious house. Bealesbranch is a street of comfortable homes, with tidy lawns and landscaped plots, bespeaking means, if not wealth. Reese guided me through a large carpeted living room, to a veranda under a viny lattice. "Beulah will get coffee," he said. He wore slacks and a knitted shirt. His body looked trim. He eased onto a pale chaise lounge. His hair was sandy. You could still read Puck in his face. A choir of birds saluted the morning.

"Nice here," I said.

"We like it."

"What's this racial stuff about you?"

Reese sat up. "What racial stuff about me?"

"The papers said your bowling alley was lily-white."

He winced.

"Could Robinson bowl at your alley?"

"Look," Reese said. "What happened was that a black team wanted to use it on a night when all the alleys were taken by a league. Now maybe that *league* was all-white. I don't check on all the customers. In this climate, charges get wild. But hell"—disgust sounded—"I wouldn't run a segregated *anything*. A little while later, just by accident, I bumped into Robinson at an airport. He'd been speaking somewhere. He came over and asked if I was trying to make him look bad. I began to tell him what I told you, and he just started laughing."

Reese shook his head. "That Robinson. You remember the time he first got into the Chase Hotel in St. Louis. We're all on the bus and the black guys got in cabs to go to their hotels in the colored section. And Jackie gets on the bus.

"'Hey,' Campy shouts. 'Come with us, Jack.'

"Jack says, 'No, I'm going to the Chase.'

"Campy says, 'Oh man. Come *on*. We'll all get in the Chase eventually.'

"Jack says, 'I know. But I'm getting there *today*.'"

The housekeeper appeared with coffee. "I'm gonna make this man work," Reese told her. "He intends to write about me because he's forgotten how hard I am to write about. What I mean," Reese said, "is that Robinson or Durocher, stories about them write themselves, don't they?"

"Red Smith says he's waiting for a story that writes itself. He says he always has to push the keys himself."

"But there's nothing *colorful* about me."

"Well, why don't we start by talking about other people, say someone who's doing what you didn't want, managing—Gil Hodges."

"Okay, but I don't have a real good memory."

Reese raised his feet and sipped coffee. "When Gil first came up, a catcher, there were two other catchers around. Bruce Edwards, who was fine, until he put on weight. And Campy. We could play three catchers at once. Edwards at third, Hodges at first. And Campy where he belonged. Gil could play anywhere, but I didn't think he would *ever* manage. It's like me being a telecaster. If someone had told me I'd be doing national TV, I'd have said, '*No way*.' I wasn't that clever. I wasn't that much an extrovert. Rooming with Gil, and we roomed together on one of the trips the team made to Japan, I didn't think he'd be able to take over a club. He wasn't tough enough. Once Dressen put money in Gil's hand and said, 'If there's a play at first and you think the guy is out and they call him safe and you get th'own out of a ball game, I'll give you fifty.' Gil wouldn't do it. People like Maglie always knocked him down. I said, 'Gil. When one of those guys th'ows at you, why don't you just go up and grab him'—strong as Gil was—'and say, "If you ever come close to me again, I'll kill you."' Gil laughed. Nothing riled him. I didn't think he'd be tough enough. But he's become real tough, I hear. And I can't believe that's Gil."

"To your right," I said, "Billy Cox."

"Best glove I ever saw. He could be compared only to Brooks Robinson, but he had a better arm than Brooks and more speed. A lot of times he'd field the ball absolutely wrong." Reese sprang up and crouched to field a ball hit to his right. "Instead of backhandling, Cox would go for them like this." Reese reached right, but holding up his palm. "That's so awkward you know it's wrong. 'Cept Billy did it. They talk today about the six-finger glove. Billy wore a four-finger glove. So he picks up this terrific smash wrong, with a terrible glove, making it look easy, and then he'd hold the ball. I'd holler, 'Billy. Th'ow the damn ball.' Ol' Cox, he'd just set there, then he'd get the man by half a step."

"Campy was a man you enjoyed."

"Oh, I sure did," Reese said. His voice had been even and cheerful. Now sadness touched him. The voice changed from major to minor. "Damn terrible thing," Reese said. Then, picturing Campanella well again, "Campy was the best I ever saw at keeping the ball in front of him. Watching Johnny Bench, who will be one of the great catchers of all time, that's one thing he has to learn. On the breaking ball that bounces, don't try to catch it. Just keep it in front of you.

"Playing short, I was aware of signs. We might use the first sign after 'two.' A catcher goes 'one-three-two-one,' that's fast ball. The 'one' after the 'two.' But you have to change once in a while." Reese learned sign stealing on the 1940 Dodgers under Durocher and carried the lesson into the fifties. Whenever he reached second base, he tried to read the opposing catcher. If he detected a sign, he had ways of tipping the batter. Leading away in a crouch, hands on knees, might mean he had seen a curve sign. Leading away with hands on hips or standing straight might mean fast ball. "Robinson never wanted signs. Hodges always did."

"Of course," I said. "Hodges needed all the help he could get against good righthanders."

"Didn't we all?" Reese said. "But you see why I was so aware of signs. Once in a while Campy would just go down and pump 'two' for a curve, and I'd think, 'Hell, they're gonna pick that one off.' But what the hell, maybe I was giving the other teams too much credit."

Beulah brought more coffee. Reese was relaxing and moving easily from man to man. "Carl Furillo," he said, "had this great arm, but he threw a tough ball to handle. He was so close, especially in Ebbets Field. He played that wall better than anyone. If it hit the screen, the ball came straight down. If it hit somewhere else, it came straight back. If it hit another place, it went sort of up in the air. The guy, Furillo, would never miss. And here was a runner coming into second base and Furillo threw so damn hard the ball shot off the grass. You could get to dread that play. But you had to make it.

"Late in my career, I found out Carl was bitter against what he called a clique. Snider, Erskine, some of us out in Bay Ridge, our wives were close together, and we played bridge. Carl lived over in Queens. You didn't just drop by. I talked to Carl about it. I said, 'We have no clique. We have nothing against you. It's one of those things.' I don't remember what he did. I think he nodded. He feels he wasn't close to me, but, hell, I could never get close to Carl."

The telephone rang. Reese answered it and said softly that the figures seemed good. They seemed fine. But he wanted to think them over. He'd call back.

"Selling some shares in the bank," he said. "Where were we? To the Duke? I think he was an only child. They didn't call this guy 'Duke' for nothing. A big man in high school. Good basketball player. Could th'ow a football seventy yards. And he was hitting forty home runs. He could be tough to handle.

"Duke was the greatest going against the wall and catching the ball, but ground balls gave this guy a fit. With a man on first and a ball hit to center on the ground, Duke would not charge. The runners didn't even hesitate at second; they'd just go into third and all the time I'd say, 'Duke, goddamnit. Charge the ball. Sure you're going to make some errors, but you'll make the runners stop at second.' Duke would say, 'Pee Wee, I used to be an infielder. The reason I moved out here is that I hate those damn ground balls.'

"'All right,' I'd holler in a game. 'Move in.'

"He'd yell back, 'Ah, the hell with it.'

"'Goddamnit, Duke. Come in a couple steps.'

"'What kinda steps, Pee Wee? Giant steps or little steps?' In the middle of a damn major league game."

Reese laughed. "There was a day I heard him telling newspapermen, 'The fans right here in Ebbets Field are the worst fans in the world.' They'd been on him or attendance was off or something.

"Well, you know you can't win *that* one, and I said to one writer, Jack Lang, 'He's just hot. Don't use this.' Lang said he had to use it to protect himself. The way Duke shouted, ten writers heard and some of *them* were going to use it. So I hollered, 'Hey, Duke. You don't mean any of this.' He hollers right back, 'The hell I don't. The Brooklyn fans are the worst in the world and I want everyone to print it.'

"I said, 'Duke, you're gonna crucify yourself.'

"The Duke said, 'Fuck 'em.'

"The papers came out rough. Next game, we're playing Cincinnati and of all things a lefthander named Don Gross goes against us. Duke didn't care for lefthanders and he knew he was in for it from the fans. He didn't feel so mighty then. He wouldn't go out to warm up. Hell, they had signs: 'Snider, Go Back to California.' Finally I went out with him and started a catch. Man, they're booing like hell. Duke got mad and bore down hard and for as long as that lefthander was in there, he got base hits. And then they cheered him.

"I hated to be booed. I never read the papers when we lost or when I had a bad day. The guys may write tough things. You're better off not reading them. That helped with the writers, but you can't do anything about being booed. I didn't mind so much on the road or the Polo Grounds, but being booed on Brooklyn used to *kill* me. Maybe I'd booted a ground ball the night before. Then I'd tell my wife, 'Dottie stay home from the next one. I *have* to do this, but I don't want you there if I'm being booed.'

"Once she said, 'Look, honey, they never boo *you*.'

"I said, 'You must not listen sometimes then.'

"When I read a ball player saying he doesn't hear the boos, I think one thing: '*The hell you don't!*'"

"Preacher said after the first pitch he heard nothing."

"Pitchers are different," Reese said. "But did Preach try to tell you he didn't worry? In '49 we lost the first game of the World Series, 1 to 0, when Tommy Henrich hit one off Don Newcombe in the ninth. The next day we're ahead by 1 to 0, and it's a late inning and here comes Henrich and Preacher calls me in. You know how he used to take his cap off and play with his hair and mumble. It took him three hours to pitch a low-run game. I wanted to keep moving. I asked what the hell he wanted.

"'Man,' Preacher said. 'I see this Henrich up here and it sort of bothers me. I want you to talk to me awhile.'

"I said, 'What the hell we gonna talk about, Preach?'

"He says, 'Fishin' and huntin' are the only things I know enough to talk about.'

"I say, 'All right, Preach. How many hunting dogs you have?'

"I stood there talking for a bit. Then he says, 'Okay, I'm all right.' I go back to shortstop. He gets Henrich. We win, 1 to 0."

Reese remembered Erskine's reluctance to throw at batters, Labine's breaking stuff, Black's big year and how that season, 1952, he himself had lost his poise on a ball field. "I started slow," Reese said, "and one night Dressen sent George Shuba to hit for me. When Dressen whistled and here came Shuba, I couldn't believe it. They didn't hit for me much, not that I was such a great hitter. They just didn't. I saw George and I took my bat and heaved it against that little rack next to the dugout. Those damn bats in there ricocheted for five minutes. The people booed like hell. They were booing Dressen. To make things worse, George struck out.

"The next day in the clubhouse meeting, Dressen walked up and down kind of slow. In my own mind, I'm apologizing like crazy. Dressen said, 'I'm managing this club and if I feel I want someone out of the line-up, that's my decision and don't try to show me up. When you don't get a base hit, I don't raise hell with you. So I don't want you showing me up, but that's what you did to me last night, Reese. You showed me up.' And I said, 'Yeah, yeah. I did show you up and I showed George up and I'm sorry for it and I'll never do it again.'"

The remembrance troubled him. He sipped his coffee and thought and said, "It's funny. When you start talking about the team, I realize how great a ball club this was but how after we left the ball park we were not over all real close. Once you got in the clubhouse, you played bridge. Then boom. The game is over and, as Furillo says, 'We all went off in our little cliques.'

"And now the guys and I — what is it, ten years, fifteen? — we almost never see each other any more."

He was born July 23, 1918, during the last summer of World War I, on a farm, between Kentucky villages of Ekron and Brandenburg, forty miles downriver from Louisville. People were leaving farms, and three years later Carl Reese moved his family into the city and went to work for the Louisville and Nashville. As Pee Wee remembers him, his father had racial attitudes characteristic of his time and station. A railroad detective cleared bums out of the yards. Black bums were niggers.

Pee Wee grew, a slight, well-coordinated boy who won marbles tournaments but seemed a questionable baseball prospect. In his senior year at Du Pont Manual High School, he weighed slightly over 110. "I was strong," he says, "for a 110-pounder." He played second base for Manual that season and graduated and found a job with the Kentucky Telephone Company, splicing cables. The pay was $18 a week.

Baseball was for Saturday and Sunday. He had wanted to be a ball player, but his size kept him from taking his own prospects seriously. He spent two years with the phone company as cable splicer, and weekend shortstop, and ballooned to 140.

Then, to his surprise, the Louisville Colonels signed him out of a Presbyterian Church League. He had a good year for the Colonels, batting .277. He moved well. His hands were fast. He ran bases brilliantly. Then the Boston Red Sox bought the Louisville franchise for $195,000, and someone suggested that "five thousand was for the franchise. The rest went for the kid at short."

The next year, 1939, Reese blossomed. He led the American Association in triples and he led with thirty-five stolen bases. He stole the thirty-five in thirty-six attempts. But, in a move of minor, enduring mystery, the Red Sox sold him to the Dodgers for $150,000. Tom Yawkey, the president of the Red Sox, ran the franchise as a hobby. He hungered to have his team defeat the Yankees and spent millions in search of a winner. Why, then, would he countenance the sale of Reese?

At the time Larry McPhail bought Reese's contract, Joe Cronin, the manager of the Sox, was also the shortstop. Cronin was thirty-four. A suspicion persists that Cronin looked south and saw a rival of such talent as to drive him from the field. Cronin says no. Whatever, it is a matter of record that while Reese reigned in Brooklyn, seven men moved into and out of the shortstop's job at Fenway Park, Boston.

Leo Durocher became Reese's champion. He invited Reese to share his Brooklyn apartment and blanketed the rookie with advice and gifts. "Leo was a sharp dresser," Reese says. "I was a kid in polo shirts. If I liked one of his sweaters, he'd give it to me. Year or so ago, he was managing the Cubs and I saw him in Cincinnati. He wore a nice orange sweater and I said I liked it. Damn if the same thing didn't happen. I'm getting to be fifty years old and he's still giving me sweaters and I can't tell him no without hurting him."

Over two seasons, Reese acquired a toughness, somewhat like Durocher's without developing the older man's abrasiveness. Reese's first year went badly. He broke a bone sliding and later a pitcher named Jake Moody beaned him. The next season, 1941, his batting average sank to .229, and he made forty-seven errors, more than any other shortstop in the league. Durocher believes that Reese was asking out. "One day in August," Durocher says, "he kicked one in a spot and we got beat. I jumped him hard. He was down, and hoping that I'd take him out and play myself. But errors don't mean that much by themselves. The kid had everything, and the errors were just mistakes. I mean I couldn't field with him by then. So I said, 'Pee Wee. If you think I'm going in there to bail you out, you're nuts. You're playing even if you make twelve errors a day.'" Durocher pauses, milking the moment. "You know what happened then? Pee Wee didn't just play a good game. He played the game of the century. That's right. The kid played the fucking game of the century. And we won the pennant." The next season his batting recovered and he picked up more ground balls than any infielder in baseball. He married a sleek, black-haired Louisville girl named Dorothy Morton in 1942. He was maturing, everyone said, when he went off to war.

In the end his first concern about Jackie Robinson proved groundless. Robinson spent his prime at second base, complementing rather than challenging Reese at shortstop. Indeed, Reese found then that he had to fight for Robinson's job rather than his own.

In 1947, Rickey delayed promoting Robinson from the International League. The Dodgers and Montreal trained together in the Dominican Republic, and Rickey hoped that the Dodger veterans, seeing Robinson's skill, hungering for a pennant, would demand that Jackie join the team. Never was anyone more deaf to the tenor of his team.

On an exhibition series in Panama, Robinson batted .515. A half dozen Dodgers responded with a petition demanding that he not be allowed to play for Brooklyn. If Robinson was promoted, the petition read, the undersigned would refuse to play.

Reese, not captain then, was respected as a sensible young man. Dixie Walker of Villa Rica, Georgia, presented the petition and Reese shook his head. "I can't sign this thing. I don't know about you guys, but this is my living. I got a wife and a child. I *have* to play ball." Others, like Ralph Branca, a sensitive man from Mount Vernon, New York, and New York University, also declined to sign. But it was Reese's decision that shocked the petitioner's. He was a southerner and confidant of many. The petition was not presented to him again. It failed, and later Walker was traded and Robinson stayed.

After snacks, under the latticework, Reese began to talk about his old friend. His tones had warmth when he mentioned other teammates, but only Robinson moved him to intensity.

"Listen," he said. "This fella was a helluvan athlete. Tennis. Golf. Ping-pong. You name it. And making that double play, they didn't move him. He'd get over that damn bag. He didn't care how big you were, how hard you slid. He challenged you and he had those big legs and, playing alongside him seven, eight years, I don't remember seeing this guy knocked down. He didn't fear *anything.*

"Al Gionfriddo had a hearts game going in 1947 and Jackie was in it and they asked and I said, 'Yeah. I'll play.' Somebody said to me, 'Damn. How can you sit and play cards with *that* guy?' I said. 'What the hell's wrong with playing with a guy on your own team?'

"I don't know how he took it, to be frank. Mr. Rickey made me captain, maybe for the team but maybe to make me come out a little more, to come on stronger. I remember guys from other teams kidding Jackie. 'Hey, you have your watermelon today?' Or somebody trying to stick the baseball in his ear. Or yelling, 'You black bastard.' And the fans as we came north. Terrible. He didn't let on, but he musta heard.

"One time in Fort Worth, Texas, this guy was really on Jack. I said, 'Hey, Jackie. Don't pay attention to that son of a bitch. I'll take care of it.' I gave the guy a pretty good blast. He completely forgot Jackie and took after me. 'You ol' bastard, Reese. You shouldn't even be playin'. You're too damn old!' I laughed at him. He left Jackie alone.

"Jackie showed me letters he got. In Atlanta the Klan said they would shoot him if he played. During warm-up I said, 'Jack. Don't stand so close to me today. Move away, will ya?' It made him smile.

"There were times when I went over to talk to him on the field thinking that people would see this and figure we were friends and this might help Jack. And there were times when he was on his own. In Tampa, Florida, Ben Chapman had been cutting Jack strong. I wasn't aware how bad it was. Maybe Jack heard things I didn't; naturally I wasn't listening for them like he would be. Chapman was coaching third for the Reds in this exhibition game and we throw the ball around the infield and my throw goes to Jack pretty hard and he looks at me and makes a little motion shaking his hand. Ben Chapman hollered, 'Hey, Pee Wee. Don't throw it too hard to little Jackie now. You're liable to hurt his little hand.' Jack came across from second base, walked right in front of me, almost to third and said, 'Look, Chapman, you son of a bitch. You got on me for two years and I couldn't say a word. Now you open your mouth to me one more time during this game, I'm gonna catch you and I'm gonna kick the shit out of you.' Jack just turned around and walked back to second and Chapman did not say another word. Chapman was rugged, but you better believe Robinson would have been something in a fight. A guy that agile — and I've seen him kidding around with his fists. Well, you could see from the way he moved that he'd be something."

"The bean balls," I said. "Did Jack get the worst you saw?"

"I guess so," Reese said slowly. "Yes, sure, I would guess so. You know eventually they have had to have black people in baseball, but just thinking about the things that happened, I don't know *any* other ball player who could have done what he did.

"To be able to hit with everybody yelling at him. He had to block that all out, block out everything but this ball that is coming in at a hundred miles an hour and he's got a split second to make up his mind if it's in or out or up or down or coming at his head, a split second to swing. To do what he did has got to be the most tremendous thing I've ever seen in sports."

He rose and broke out a bottle of Scotch. "Okay?" he said. "Or am I still bad copy?"

"Excellent for a man with a poor memory."

He seemed settled now. The ulcers were healed. He looked contented. Mark Reese came home from school. Mark was twelve, very serious, very polite. "Could you and the gentleman throw some forward passes to me?" he asked.

"Soon as we finish the drink, Mark."

"Yes, sir. I'll meet you out front."

"How's your arm?" Reese said.

"Chicken."

"Don't worry about that," he said solemnly.

We walked to the front lawn. Mark began running what he called a post pattern, starting straight and curling toward a sycamore tree that symbolized a goal post.

Pee Wee threw flat hard passes to Mark's fingertips at the base of the sycamore. To throw that same distance, I had to loft the ball. The first throw brought down a few leaves. So did the second. After my third pass through the sycamore to Mark, Pee Wee looked at me and made a little grin.

"Hey," he said, "you got something against my tree?" I kept the next throws lower. Settled at fifty, the captain is the captain yet.

IV. Seventh Inning Stretch

When the Dodgers played the Giants, it was the most important game in your life. There will never be a rivalry like that again.

— Pee Wee Reese
Shortstop and captain, Brooklyn Dodgers
1940–1957

The great Dodger-Giant rivalry began to fester in the early years of the century, prodded in part by a riff between old friends John McGraw and Wilbert Robinson. In the spring of 1934, Giant manager Bill Terry was asked his opinion of Brooklyn's chances in the upcoming pennant race. His comment, "Brooklyn? Are they still in the league?" would come back to haunt him when the sixth-place Dodgers defeated the Giants on the last day of the season to finish them off and allow the St. Louis Cardinals to win the National League pennant.

IN THE COLD GRAY DAWN
OF THE MORNING AFTER

Tommy Holmes

[OCTOBER 1, 1934:] Bill Terry says: If the Dodgers had played all season as hard as they played against us in the last two games, it's a dead certainty that they'd have finished higher than sixth place."

Casey Stengel says: "If the Giants had played all season as they played against us in their last two games, they'd have finished in sixth-place themselves."

Groggy Giants Think It's All Over, but Wait Till They Reach Home

This morning's hangover was a terrible thing for New York's Giants. It seemed incredible to them; nevertheless, it is true. The Cardinals of old St. Louis won the National League pennant. The Giants set the pace for most of the year, moving into first place on a long-term lease on June 8. As late as Sept. 7 they led the pack by the majestic margin of seven games.

And then the New York machine that had won the flag and the World Series last Fall began to creak and groan and to fall apart and the Cardinals starting spurting forward through the marvelous pitching of the Dean brothers. On Friday the Cardinals tied the Giants. On Saturday the Cardinals took undisputed possession of first place. On Sunday — the very last day of the regular season — the Cardinals clinched the pennant, while the Giants fell before the Dodgers' tenth inning rally by the score of 8–5.

Col. Casey Stengel — yes, Casey is a colonel now, a Kentucky colonel like Mae

Originally published in the *Brooklyn Eagle*, October 1, 1934. Reprinted with permission of Historical Briefs, Inc.

West — is extremely pleased because the Brooklyn Dodgers played a most prominent part in the downfall of the Giants. But, in his enthusiasm, Mr. Stengel has not lost sight of the little, important things of life.

The Worst Is Yet to Come

Said he today, "The Giants thought we gave 'em a beating Saturday and yesterday. Well, they were right. But I'm still sorry for them when I think of the beating they still have to take. Wait until those wives realize that they're not going to get those new fur coats this year. I've been through it and I know."

The story of the September drive down the National League homestretch is that the Giants abruptly passed their peak as a winning ball club and literally fell over a precipice while the dazzling Deans of old St. Louis drew on their reserve for the most astonishing exhibition of high pressure pitching ever delivered in the major leagues. The further it went, the more terrific was the tempo set by the country boys from Oklahoma. On Friday, Dizzy shut out the Reds; on Saturday, Paul beat the Reds; on Sunday, Dizzy came back with one day of rest and shut out the Reds again.

Whom will the Deans beat on Monday? Nobody, I guess, and I don't know how they'll be able to stand the inactivity. They are strange critters. In August, they were tearing up uniforms and declaring that they were quitting to go fishing in Florida. Suspended by the club, they howled to high heavens and Judge Landis because they weren't allowed to play. And here as September came to a close they had pitched the Cards to a flag and were shuffling in their corners, ready to go to work on Schoolboy Rowe and the rest of the Detroit Tigers in the World Series.

Some Little Consolation

The Giants must be glad it is all over, even happy that the regular race didn't result in a tie. In that event they'd have had to face the Deans in a play-off. For the New York players, no future experience can ever bring about the dark despair of Saturday and Sunday when Brooklyn's Dodgers twice knocked them off to lay their once bright pennant hopes among the sweet peas.

I don't know whether Brooklyn fans predominated in the mob of more than 45,000 up in the Harlem horseshoe yesterday, but the band from Brooklyn was certainly noisier than the followers of the Giants.

Brooklyn scored one in the second and one in the fourth and Fred Fitzsimmons hit a home run in the last of the fourth to make the score 5–2 in New York's favor. In the eighth, the Dodgers blasted Fitzsimmons out of the box and tied the score. Three Brooklyn fans raced madly through the lower stands. The first carried an automobile claxon, the one in the rear violently shook his cowbell, the one in the center held aloft a 3 by 2 placard bearing an answer to Bill Terry's famous February query. It read —"Yep, Brooklyn is still in the league."

And so as the Dodgers opened fire on Hal Schumacher and the tired Carl Hubbell for three in the tenth, making the score 8–5, it was an anti-climax except to the jubilant Brooklyn fans. Johnny Babich, the newest of the Dodger regular pitchers, mopped up the Giants in the last half.

The Giants raced across the field as though they wanted to get away from it all as quickly as possible. The Dodgers had to squirm and shove their way through the fans who almost tore off Stengel's uniform. Three or four rooters grabbed Al Lopez and carried him on their shoulders to the clubhouse. His gray uniform, bobbing above the heads of the whirling mob in the deep twilight was the last visible evidence of the most hectic of National League finishes.

The rivalry between the Brooklyn Dodgers and the New York Giants was the greatest in all of sports. It was never more intense than in the sizzling pennant race of 1951.

1951 AND THE MIRACLE PENNANT RACE

James D. Szalontai

Douglas MacArthur was among the 32,445 fans who witnessed a serious bean-ball war at the Giants' home ballpark the following afternoon. Once again, the Dodgers won by a 7–3 score. The game almost turned into a backroom brawl. Under Burt Shotton, the Dodgers were less willing to retaliate for the beanballs. Dressen on the other hand had a two for one rule. If they hit one of our batters we hit two of theirs. Coincidentally, Durocher had the same rule. Larry Jansen was a gentle man playing a hostile game who for years had given up far more homers than he should have allowed. Hitters took a firm toehold in the box with the knowledge that Jansen was unlikely to brush them back. Like Sheldon Jones, he had resisted Durocher's orders to throw the beanball, but like Jones, he would submit and heed Leo's order of "stick it in his ear."

In the fifth inning Durocher gave Jansen a direct order. It was time for Campanella to go down. He ignored Leo's orders and threw the first two pitches for strikes. Campy was bailing on the second pitch, concerned that the ball was coming at his head. Durocher implored his pitcher to brush the batter back and this time he threatened him with a fine: "It'll be a C-note if you don't!" Campy was confused; he stepped out of the box, bent down to rub some dirt on his hands and asked Westrum if Jansen was going to throw at him. Westrum replied,

"Who, Larry? He wouldn't throw at Adolf Hitler."

With Jansen under the threat of a fine, he unleashed a pitch at Campy's head but took a little off so the hitter could get out of the way. Campanella was livid, arguing with umpire Donatelli that the ball hit his shirt sleeve and therefore he should be awarded first base as a result. He told Westrum, "You gonna pay for that." Westrum was in a bind because he had just told Campanella that Jansen would not throw at him. Durocher had been grinning at the Dodger catcher the whole time and Campanella finally looked at a third strike on the outer edge of the plate.

From *Close Shave: The Life and Times of Baseball's Sal Maglie,* ©2002 James D. Szalontai, by permission of McFarland & Company, Inc., Publishers, Box 611, Jefferson NC 28640. *www.mcfarlandpub.com.*

In the sixth, Chris Van Cuyk threw at Westrum. Westrum went sprawling into the dirt and came after Campanella but a fight was averted as the umpire stepped in. In the eighth inning, Jansen pitched close to the Dodgers catcher once again. Campanella went after Westrum, shoving him back into the umpire. Westrum retaliated and shoved Campy towards the pitcher's mound. Westrum began shedding his catching equipment, the "tools of ignorance" as they say, and preparing for an all out fight with Campy. Both benches emptied before the hostilities finally settled down. When Ralph Branca came into the game he nailed Bobby Thomson. Branca was not shy about throwing inside and would protect his players.

The other events of the day included Stanky knocking the ball out of Reese's hands when he stole second. Rocky Bridges throwing a shoulder block at Bobby Thomson during a pickoff play. Van Cuyk knocked Hank Thompson down. Thompson took offense and had some words with the Dodger hurler.

The season was not even a week long, but the Giant/Dodger war was already in mid-season form. When the teams exited the premises after the game, Dressen taunted Durocher. Leo responded by giving him the finger.

The Giants and Dodgers were set to play the Labor Day weekend with two games at the Polo Grounds to begin September. If Durocher's club wanted to keep a flicker of hope alive they had to win both games. Maglie enjoyed a 3–1 record against the Dodgers on the season and he toed the slab in the opener. The Dodgers countered with Ralph Branca. Charlie Dressen was home in bed with the flu; therefore coach Cookie Lavagetto ran the team in his stead. Despite the manager's absence the game was a typical Dodger/Giant war, filled with beanballs, bench jockeying, and arguments. The Dodgers looked helpless in the contest as New York won easily by an 8–1 score behind the exploits of Maglie, Mueller, and Stanky. The Barber finally won his eighteenth game as he limited the Dodgers to seven singles. He did not walk a batter and struck out seven. Mueller hit three home runs and drove in five. Thomson hit his twenty-fourth homer. In the fifth inning, Reese lined into a triple play as Dark speared it, flipped to Stanky for the second out and "The Brat" tagged Furillo for the third out.

The day started out hot and muggy but by the time the 40,794 persons began to take their seats below Coogan's Bluff, it was overcast, windy, cold, and dreary with the threat of rain. When the Brooklyn batting order was announced the crowd booed powerfully to make sure the enemy knew they were not welcome guests. New York took the early lead as Mueller hit a solo shot in the first and Thomson hit a two run homer in the second to put them up by a 3–0 score. Tensions were high right from the start. In the first inning the moody but reserved Duke Snider exploded when Lee Ballanfant, the home plate umpire, punched him out on a 3–2 pitch. Robinson and Lavagetto ran towards Snider and tried to calm him down. In the second inning, Sinister Sal sharpened his razor and threw close to Campanella a couple of times. Jackie Robinson faced Maglie with the bases loaded and two outs in the third inning. Maglie broke off an inside curve that didn't break as he had expected. Jackie hung in and then ducked away at the last moment, raising his hand to protect his face, but the ball glanced off his left wrist. It forced home a run. Maglie was hot and trotted towards the umpire insisting that the ball hit his bat not his wrist. Westrum was also arguing, as was Durocher. The argument raged for several minutes, at which time the four umpires huddled to discuss the situation.

There were *four umpires* instead of three because of the combative nature of Giant/Dodger games. Ballanfant told Durocher and Lavagetto to make their pitchers cease throwing at each other. Pee Wee Reese later stated that nobody was throwing at anybody. Robinson and Lockman had no complaints. This was baseball, a rough and tumble sport that employed the beanball, the brushback, and the knockdown as a part of baseball strategy. Durocher suggested that the umpires should stick to umpiring instead of mind reading.

One of the reasons for the Giants' late surge attributed to the fact that they were stealing other teams' signs. They had a powerful naval telescope pointing out of one of the windows of the clubhouse in dead center field. A spotter watched the game from behind the telescope and relayed the type of pitch through a buzzer system that had been hooked up and connected to the Giants' first base dugout and the right field bullpen. Sal Yvars usually watched for the signal and relayed the sign to the batter. If there wasn't a buzz it meant a fastball was coming, one buzz indicated that a breaking ball was on the way. Yvars told the batters to watch the baseball in his hand as they batted. If he tossed the spheroid into the air it meant a breaking ball was coming; if he held it, a fastball. Some players took advantage of the intricate system while others preferred not to. The two days in which Mueller feasted on Dodger pitching and hit five homers, it was suggested that he knew what pitch was coming. Bill Rigney stated that the Giants stole signs from second base. The first runner to advance to the midway would find out the sequence from the catcher and give it to Rigney. The runner at second would also flash the signs to the hitter. Former Giant Willard Marshall recalled, "There was a lot of sign stealing going on back then. When I was with the Giants we had Bill Rigney in the clubhouse with a spyglass." Wes Westrum, who later became a coach and a big league manager after his playing career finished, stated: "I must have helped Willie Mays to at least another twenty-five homers in his career by letting him know what pitch was coming."

The Giant-Dodger rivalry became even more personalized when Leo Durocher left Brooklyn to manage the Giants. The antagonism was greatest between Leo and Jackie Robinson and Carl Furillo. This incident occurred in 1953.

THE RIVALRY

Roger Kahn

As the Dodgers worked their way North, I had a beer with Carl Furillo. "It's gotta stop," he said.

"What's gotta stop."

"Maglie throwing at my head. I know why he's doing it. Durocher orders him to do it. Next time Maglie throws at me, I go for him."

"Who?"

"Durocher. I'm gonna get him."

The Dodgers reached their mountaintop in century 1953. As a team, Brooklyn batted .285. No club has matched that for more than a quarter century. The '53 Dodgers led all baseball with 208 home runs. They scored 955 runs, about 200 more than any other club in the league, and they were the best defensive team as well. The Dodgers made eleven fewer errors than any other team in the league.

The Brooklyn weakness—and this was relative—was the pitching staff. The Dodgers had a good strikeout staff, but the team earned run average was unimposing: 4.10. By contrast, the Yankee pitching staff, with Reynolds, Raschi, and Ford, posted an ERA of 3.20. The difference, a run a game, would be significant.

The Dodgers ran off from everyone else in the second and on September 6, eleven games out front, they played their last game of the season against the Giants. The Dodgers had beaten the Giants nine times in a row.

The Giants went ahead in the first inning when Al Dark hit a home run, but the Dodgers took the lead in the second on Roy Campanella's two-run homer.

Gil Hodges bounced out. Ruben Gomez threw an inside fastball that hit Furillo on the left wrist. Furillo walked toward the mound. He pushed aside two umpires who tried to stop him. He pushed into Charlie Dressen, who threw both arms around him. Gomez, a willowy six-footer, stood his ground. To reach him, Furillo would have to trample his own manager. Gomez now circled back toward second base. Dressen talked urgently, "Come on. Come on. Get hold of yourself." At length Dressen led Furillo to first base.

Order returned. Gomez threw two strikes and two balls to Billy Cox. Furillo stared into the Giant dugout. He saw Durocher glaring at him, lips moving. He could not hear what he was saying. Durocher made a beckoning gesture with one finger. Furillo bolted from first base toward the Giant dugout.

Durocher, flanked by ten players, rose to meet Furillo. They grappled and fell to the ground. Furillo clamped a headlock on Durocher, who lost his cap. Durocher's bald pate went pink, then red, then purple. Two powerful Giants, Monte Irvin and Jim Hearn, moved to rescue their manager. Clawing and stomping they worked Durocher's bald head free. Someone stamped on Furillo's left hand. The umpires threw both Furillo and Durocher out of the game. (The Dodgers defeated the Giants 6–3.)

Furillo's hand puffed. In the clubhouse, he seemed oblivious to pain but his breath came in snorts. "I told you I'd get him," he said. "He made them throw at me one time too many."

I said that taking on Durocher at the Giant dugout stacked the odds.

"I wasn't worried about the other players ganging up on me," Furillo said. "A lot of the Giants hate him too."

Furillo played no more that season. He suffered broken bones in his left hand. He was batting .344 and his average froze. While on the bench, Furillo won the batting championship, beating out Red Schoendienst of the Cardinals (.342) and Stan Musial, who hit his customary .337.

More than one baseball writer fell to temptation and wrote that Furillo's fractures were a lucky break.

And then it happened. Branca threw, Thomson swung, and Pafko looked up — and "Wait till next year" was once again on the lips of the Flatbush Faithful ... only with a little less enthusiasm.

LAST CHAPTER

Red Smith

[OCTOBER 4, 1951:] NOW IT IS done. Now the story ends. And there is no way to tell it. The art of fiction is dead. Reality has strangled invention. Only the utterly impossible, the inexpressibly fantastic, can ever be plausible again.

Down on the green and white and earth-brown geometry of the playing field, a drunk tries to break through the ranks of ushers marshaled along the foul lines to keep profane feet off the diamond. The ushers thrust him back and he lunges at them, struggling in the clutch of two or three men. He breaks free and four or five tackle him. He shakes them off, bursts through the line, runs head on into a special park cop who brings him down with a flying tackle.

Here comes a whole platoon of ushers. They lift the man and haul him, twisting and kicking, back across the first-base line. Again he breaks loose and crashes the line. He is through. He is away, weaving out toward center field where cheering thousands are jammed beneath the windows of the Giants' clubhouse.

At heart, our man is a Giant, too. He never gave up. From center field comes burst upon burst of cheering. Pennants are waving, uplifted fists are brandished, hats are flying. Again and again, the dark clubhouse windows blaze with the light of photographers' flash bulbs. Here comes that same drunk out of the mob, back across the green turf to the infield. Coat tails flying, he runs the bases, slides into third. Nobody bothers him now.

And the story remains to be told, the story of how the Giants won the 1951 pennant in the National League ... The tale of their barreling run through August and September and into October ... Of the final day of the season when they won the championship and started home with it from Boston, to hear on the train how the dead, defeated Dodgers had risen from the ashes in the Philadelphia twilight ... Of the three-game play-off in which they won, and lost, and were losing again with one out in the ninth inning yesterday when — Oh, why bother?

Maybe this is the way to tell it: Bobby Thomson, a young Scot from Staten

From *Red Smith on Baseball.* ©2000 by Phyllis W. Smith. Reprinted with permission of Karen Weiss for Phyllis W. Smith.

Island, delivered a timely hit yesterday in the ninth inning of an enjoyable game of baseball before 34,320 witnesses in the Polo Grounds.... Or perhaps this is better:

"Well," said Whitey Lockman, standing on second base in the second inning of yesterday's play-off game between the Giants and the Dodgers.

"Ah, there," said Bobby Thomson, pulling into the same station after hitting a ball to left field. "How've you been?"

"Fancy," Lockman said, "meeting you here!"

"Ooops!" Thomson said. "Sorry."

And the Giants' first chance for a big inning against Don Newcombe disappeared as they tagged him out. Up in the press section, the voice of Willie Goodrich came over the amplifiers announcing a macabre statistic: "Thomson has now hit safely in fifteen consecutive games." Just then the floodlights were turned on, enabling the Giants to see and count their runners on each base.

It wasn't funny, though, because it seemed for so long that the Giants weren't going to get another chance like the one Thomson had squandered by trying to take second base with a playmate already there. They couldn't hit Newcombe and the Dodgers couldn't do anything wrong. Sal Maglie's most splendorous pitching would avail nothing unless New York could match the run Brooklyn had scored in the first inning.

The story was winding up, and it wasn't the happy ending which such a tale demands. Poetic justice was a phrase without a meaning.

Now it was the seventh inning and Thomson was up with runners on first and third base, none out. Pitching a shutout in Philadelphia last Saturday night, pitching again in Philadelphia on Sunday, holding the Giants scoreless this far, Newcombe had now gone twenty-one innings without allowing a run.

He threw four strikes to Thomson. Two were fouled out of play. Then he threw a fifth. Thomson's fly scored Monte Irvin. The score was tied. It was a new ball game.

Wait a moment, though. Here's Pee Wee Reese hitting safely in the eighth. Here's Duke Snider singling Reese to third. Here's Maglie, wild—pitching a run home. Here's Andy Pafko slashing a hit through Thomson for another score. Here's Billy Cox batting still another home. Where does his hit go? Where else? Through Thomson at third.

So it was the Dodgers' ball game 4-1, and the Dodgers' pennant. So all right. Better get started and beat the crowd home. That stuff in the ninth inning? That didn't mean anything.

A single by Al Dark. A single by Don Mueller. Irvin's pop-up. Lockman's one-run double. Now the corniest possible sort of Hollywood schmaltz—stretcher bearers plodding away with an injured Mueller between them, symbolic of the Giants themselves.

Then went Newcombe and here came Ralph Branca. Who's at bat? Thomson again? He beat Branca with a home run the other day. Would Charlie Dressen order him walked, putting the winning run on base, to pitch to the dead-end kids at the bottom of the order? No, Branca's first pitch was a called strike.

The second pitch—well, when Thomson reached first base he turned and looked toward the left-field stands. Then he started jumping straight up in the air, again and again. Then he trotted around the bases, taking his time.

Ralph Branca turned and started for the clubhouse. The number on his uniform looked huge. Thirteen.

V. Late Innings

During Hahn's (Kenneth Hahn, Los Angeles County Supervisor) stay in New York, he received a note from Walter O'Malley indicating he would like to discuss a move to Los Angeles. Hahn reported that he shook hands with O'Malley on the transfer of the Dodgers..., although O'Malley cautioned the supervisor not to mention the decision publicly lest the outrage in Brooklyn be overwhelming.

— Neil J. Sullivan
The Dodgers Move West

During the winter of 1956-1957, the tale of two cities began to unfold in earnest.

OVERTURE FROM THE COAST

Neil J. Sullivan

Grist for conspiracy theories surrounding the timing of Walter O'Malley's decision to move the Dodgers to Los Angeles can be found in O'Malley's first meeting with Los Angeles officials in October 1956. Having completed their final subway series with the Yankees, the team stopped in Los Angeles on the way to visiting Japan. During the layover, O'Malley met with Kenneth Hahn, the County Supervisor, to discuss the possibility of the Dodgers' moving to Los Angeles. Hahn recalls that he had been in New York during the 1956 World Series to see if the Washington Senators could be induced to move West. This venture had been authorized by the County Board of Supervisors, which operated independently of city officials. The county anticipated a municipal stadium constructed with revenues drawn from county employees' pension funds. During Hahn's stay in New York, he received a note from Walter O'Malley indicating he would like to discuss a move to Los Angeles. Hahn reported that he shook hands with O'Malley on the transfer of the Dodgers during subsequent meetings in Los Angeles, although O'Malley cautioned the supervisor not to mention the decision publicly lest the outrage in Brooklyn be overwhelming. As subsequent events would prove, the agreement between O'Malley and Hahn could have been nothing more than an understanding in principle. Hahn himself says that once the Dodgers decided to move to Los Angeles, he withdrew from the picture, leaving the contract negotiations to the city.

In November 1956, as the Brooklyn Sports Center Authority continued to flounder, Poulson [Mayor of Los Angeles Norris Poulson] commissioned a study of Chavez Ravine by a group of civil engineers, who reported that the land might be used for the construction of a baseball stadium and recommended that $2 million be appropriated to that end in the mayor's 1957 budget.

There were two major obstacles to this proposal. First, the unanswered question of whether a baseball stadium would conform to the requirement, still pertinent, that Chavez Ravine be put to an appropriate public purpose. Second, $2 million was only a fraction of the sum needed for a new stadium. For the city to finance the

From *The Dodgers Move West* by Neil Sullivan, ©1989 by Neil Sullivan. Used by permission of Oxford University Press, Inc.

structure, additional revenues would have to be secured through bonds requiring two-thirds approval by the electorate.

Although Poulson played a pivotal role in bringing the Dodgers to Los Angeles, he was not blindly committed to bringing just any major league team to the city. Shortly after assuming office, he declined to make an offer to entice the Browns because, as he wrote, "They did not have a good team or baseball organization." Several years later he also declined to pursue the Washington Senators, who were also looking for new quarters. Poulson's reluctance stemmed from his days as a congressman, when "I had seen them play too many times in Washington, D.C., and they were also 'tail-enders.'" Poulson remained determined to secure only a top-caliber team.

Poulson was remarkably naive or else remarkably Machiavellian. He either simply assumed that a successful firm would willingly relocate to an untried market, or he foresaw the difficulties facing the Dodgers in New York and positioned Los Angeles to take advantage of them. Judging from future negotiations between Poulson and O'Malley, naivete is the more plausible explanation. But there was a rational basis for Poulson's optimism. He was aware that the first modern transfer shift in professional sports had occurred in 1946 when the Cleveland Rams of the National Football League relocated in Los Angeles. Within five years they won a championship, and Poulson concluded that as far as baseball was concerned, "Los Angeles rated the best because we had championship teams in football and track and other athletic activities." Poulson later recalled sitting in the bleachers and rooting for the Dodgers during the 1955 World Series, but he dismissed any speculation that he had designs on the team at that time.

The recommendation to construct a baseball stadium in Chavez Ravine was made at a time when major league baseball had recently spread to Baltimore, Milwaukee, and Kansas City. In a short time, Los Angeles would become the focus of national attention as a prospective major league site. The attention, of course, would center on whether the Dodgers would transfer to the West Coast, and in the heat of the controversy many would forget the rich history of baseball in Los Angeles and of the intriguing earlier opportunities for bringing major league baseball to the West....

In February 1957 Walter O'Malley purchased from the Cubs their minor league franchise, the Los Angeles Angels, and the Angels' home park, Wrigley Field, near downtown Los Angeles. Just as he had forced the action in New York with his announcement in August 1955 that the Dodgers would schedule games in Jersey City, now O'Malley inspired city officials in Los Angeles to formulate a plan that would lure him across the country to a market fifteen hundred miles from the nearest major league franchise....

At the same time O'Malley acquired the Los Angeles Angels, he began to negotiate with city and county officials in Los Angeles. He met with Mayor Poulson and other officials at Vero Beach during spring training. Poulson described the session as "a sparring match," although from the outset the participants overestimated each other's strength. The Dodgers had already sold Ebbets Field and their lease was due to expire in 1959. Because they had been rebuffed by the New York Board of Estimate, their only sure option for the immediate future was scheduling home games in Jersey City. Somehow, despite that predicament, Los Angeles officials concluded that O'Malley was holding all the cards....

In a common version of the story, when Robert Moses and Mayor Wagner refused to cave in to Walter O'Malley's exorbitant demands, the Dodger president suckered the gullible Californians who, in their eagerness to attract the team, gave away the store. The rendition has the symmetry and passion of a morality play but, the record is considerably more complicated.

By February 1956, New York had two eminent prospects for securing the Dodgers' future in Brooklyn. The first was Robert Moses's option as chairman of the mayor's Slum Clearance Committee to invoke his powers under the Federal Housing Act to assemble at Atlantic and Flatbush the parcel of land that O'Malley could have then purchased for the construction of a stadium. The second opportunity was to erect a public stadium under the auspices of the Brooklyn Sports Center Authority. Since this course required the cooperation of the mayor, the city council, and the Board of Estimate, as well as the governor and the state legislature, it was necessarily a far more torturous path. O'Malley's interests were blocked completely on the first prospect, and were slowly expiring on the second. For the Dodger president to retain control of the club's future, new options needed to be created; accordingly, O'Malley opened a tie to Los Angeles through the purchase of the Angels.

In California, meanwhile, long-standing interest in acquiring a major league franchise had combined with a keen desire to do something about the white elephant of Chavez Ravine. City engineers had concluded even before O'Malley purchased the Angels that the area could serve as a site for a baseball stadium. The evidence further shows that Chavez Ravine had not been acquired for Walter O'Malley's benefit; rather, federal law required the city to reserve the acreage for an appropriate public purpose after the original public housing project had lost support. A number of observers wrote during the winter of 1956 that the Dodgers might eventually relocate in California, but these were mere conjectures that associated a team in search of a new playing field with a market which had been seriously interested in major league baseball since before World War II.

The interpretation which argues that Walter O'Malley orchestrated events in Los Angeles by manipulating the officials of that city ignores the highly pertinent histories both of baseball and the public housing controversy in Southern California. The overemphasis on O'Malley's role misses the vital contribution of major political actors in Los Angeles to the transfer of the Dodgers. The city council vote of October 7, 1957, culminated a concerted effort by the city leaders to overcome formidable opposition to the final contract. Poulson, Wyman, McClellan, and others faced legal, political, and economic restraints similar or identical to those confronting New York officials. In Los Angeles those obstacles were overcome not because they were less imposing, nor even because the city's officials were uniquely skilled; rather, Poulson and the other advocates were committed to attracting the Dodgers, while their counterparts in New York were indifferent or hostile to the measures necessary for keeping the team.

When New York realized that the threat from Los Angeles was real, officials renewed efforts to keep the Dodgers in Brooklyn, or at least in a nearby community. Until those efforts were fully spent, Los Angeles could not be sure that its arduously constructed proposal to Walter O'Malley would finally succeed.

Phil Foster, the Brooklyn comedian, recorded this comedy song in 1957. It aptly expressed the feelings of the Brooklyn Faithful.

LET'S KEEP THE DODGERS IN BROOKLYN

Samuel Denoff, William Persky, and Roy Ross

Say, did you hear the news
About what's happening in Brooklyn
We really got the blues
About what's happening in Brooklyn
It ain't official yet
We hope official it don't get
But beware my friends and let me warn ya
They're thinkin' a takin' the Bums to California
Chorus:
Let's keep the Dodgers in Brooklyn
A house is not a home without some love
Don't let 'em leave our premises
LA would be their nemesis
Cause Brooklyn fits the Dodgers like a glove.
Mister Walter O'Malley, we always called you pally
We stuck with you thru thick or thin
But if you take away the Dodgers
Guys like Campy, Newk and Hodges
We ain't your pal no more the way we been.
Chorus: Repeat
We offer you our bridges
You can take 'em whitcha
We have a couple we could spare
But we all feel so glum
Without the Duke and Gilliam
We need one left to jump off in despair.

Really, what would Brooklyn be without the Dodgers?
Well — Brooklyn would be…
Like a pair of socks that's holey
Without Jackson and Cimoli
Like a bed without a pilla
Without Oiskine and Furilla
Like a ship without a harbor
Without Podres and the Barber
Like the sun without its shine
Without Zimmer and Labine
Like the birds without a bee
Without Alston and Pee Wee
And here I am a poet
And I didn't even know it
So send the Phils to Trenton
The Giants to St. Paul
But keep the Bums in Brooklyn
The greatest borough of all.
So let's keep the Dodgers in Brooklyn
You heard our plea, at last we had our say
Your mind is in a bog
If you take them to that smog
Keep the Dodgers in Brooklyn, USA
We really love 'em
Keep the Dodgers in Brooklyn, USA
O'Malley, do me a favor
Mind your own business
And stay home and don't leave town.

Jimmy Cannon of the New York Post *takes on Walter O'Malley in this 1957 column. The antagonism toward the Dodger president was heating up.*

Walt, You Can Go, but Own Up as to Why

Jimmy Cannon

[JULY 7, 1957:] The sport of baseball once had a beautiful innocence, a marvelous tournament running across the spring into autumn, grace and strength measured by the arithmetic of the scores. There was about it a wonderful purity, an exercise performed by the young, a glad festival of skill and excitement, played on the grass of big cities and never on rainy days.

The athletes belong in the sun as if the night were a hostile time, a shift for watchmen and burglars and the trash of café society. But now that the night has claimed it, baseball has been soiled by darkness and the greed of café proprietors and those who embrace the blackness to shield their clandestine schemes.

The truth of the athletes hasn't been impaired and they work at their assignments as if they were inhabitants of glorious afternoons. But the darkness, illuminated by electric apparatus, appears to have influenced the stockholders, the general managers and the franchise owners. They act with the secrecy of those who run businesses after the dusk has protected sneaky enterprises. Only P.K. Wrigley, who controls the Chicago Cubs, refuses to succumb to the nighttime and his ball games are played in daylight.

It is a game that belongs in the afternoon, a sort of festival depending on heat and glitter. It is as if the darkness contaminated those who dominate it, has turned them into night people, furtive and cautious with the special trickery of those who flourish by moonglow.

Now they have stolen the attitudes and the mugger's commandments that govern their behavior. Always have they been ruthless and cruel, but now they are brazenly contemptuous and appear to be proud of their falsehoods which are told with a smug glibness. Always they have operated with a gay liar's audacity. Now the truth seems to be their foe. It is as if facts were worthless comments and only the lie was dignified.

It was natural that the Braves traveled from Boston to Milwaukee and the A's quit Philly for Kansas City, the Browns sought refuge in Baltimore. The apathy of the buffs caused this and there is no rancor in me because they made the shift. It has always been a business disguised as a sport, but the illusion was perpetuated because people have faith in those migratory workers who represented their home towns. But Crying Walter O'Malley, the president of the Dodgers, behaves as if the people of that borough were running him out of town. There is no malice in me because Crying Walter intends to open the store in Los Angeles. It is his privilege to travel to any settlement where his team can take down the bigger profit.

But his grieving became nastily comical when what he made in Ebbets Field proves he has benefited financially from his stay there. It also exposes the peculiar weakness of Ford Frick, commissioner of baseball, and Warren Giles and Will Harridge, the presidents of the big leagues. Never before, including the term of Happy Chandler, has baseball been handled by such subservient men.

The congress that granted O'Malley and Horace Stoneham the privilege to lam to Los Angeles and San Francisco was a parliament that employed the tactics of the night rider.

It was explained to ball journalists that the gathering was a favor to Gussy Busch, who owns the St. Louis Cardinals. At the All-Star game in St. Louis, it was contended, the owners intended to revel at fetes and they didn't intend to muss up pleasure with business. Normally, such meetings are held during the All-Star festival. Inconsequential matters would be taken up at the conclave at the Cincinnati gathering. At least one reporter telephoned Giles, who assured him the matters were trivial and not worth a stick of tape. But as permission was granted to the Giants and Brooklyn to make the journey, the announcement was made. It fractured the theory that Judge Kenesaw Mountain Landis had maintained during his time as the only baseball commissioner with a feeling that the sport was also the property of the people.

I'm sick of O'Malley's jovial slyness, his hearty evasion, his absurd claims that a ball club is a municipal necessity. So embarrassed was Stoneham at Mayor Wagner's press conference that he left before it was over. He couldn't handle Crying Walter's double talk either.

The great Brooklyn Dodgers are in their declining years. As an era ends, a clown is hired and strong hints are dropped about leaving Ebbets Field. The faithful may be about to give their last hurrah.

TWILIGHT OF THE BUMS

Robert Creamer

[APRIL 1, 1957:] Pee Wee Reese stood at home plate, waiting. The Detroit pitcher on the mound was a large young man named Jim Bunning. He was very fast this sunny March afternoon and very wild.

Pee Wee waited with a quiet confidence that became a 37-year-old man who still felt 19, who was the proud father of a practically brand-new six-weeks-old son and who in the four times he had appeared at bat in this young exhibition season had had a walk, a single and two lovely home runs.

Bunning threw. The fast ball went directly at Pee Wee's head, and Reese fell in a lump at the plate, hit by the pitch. There wasn't a man in the press box or in the dugout or in the stands who knew Reese who didn't feel a little sick to his stomach.

Pee Wee rolled over and held himself tautly, in an odd position, stretching his body in pain as he supported himself on his toes and his left forearm. People gathered around him, and after a while Reese stood up and allowed himself to be led from the field. Dr. Harold Wendler, the Dodgers' trainer, carried Pee Wee's right arm.

"Thank God, it wasn't his head," was the first reaction among those who knew Reese. But, from the way the trainer held the arm, it looked broken, and if it *was* broken that could be the end of the road as a ballplayer for Pee Wee Reese and the end, too, for this year's Dodgers.

"Bunning just settled the National League pennant race," said Jack Lang of the *Long Island Press.* However, an inning or so later word came up from Dr. Wendler that it was only a bruise, a bad bruise but no more than that, on the fleshy inner part of the forearm where Pee Wee had raised it protectively in front of his face. Jack Lang was wrong then. The race was still wide open.

But, even so, Lang's comment and Reese's injury suddenly brought the status of the 1957 Brooklyn Dodgers clearly into focus. They were, indeed, as everyone has charged, an old team, a collection of marvelous baseball players but old ones, past

243

their prime, prone to injury, prone to ailments, losing slowly but surely to age. Carl Furillo's cranky elbow still bothered him; Carl is 35. Roy Campanella's hand, which crippled him so badly last season, was still a question; Roy is 35, too, and some say older. Sal Maglie is fine, but Sal eases past 40 on April 26 and Sal has a history of back trouble; most men of 40 with back trouble feel it strike after a half hour of cutting grass. How can a 40-year-old man with a trick back pitch 200 innings of baseball?

And Don Newcombe's arm was hurting, and Carl Erskine's probably was, too, though with Carl a sore arm is as much a part of his baseball life as his glove and he tends to ignore it. Don and Carl are both past 30. Duke Snider, hit by a pitched ball, had picked up a bad bruise on his leg, and he's 30, too.

Clearly, then, this was a team of old and ailing players. And it was a team that depended on those old and ailing players for its strength. Lose a Reese or a Campanella or a Furillo, and where would they be?

The exhibition game went on. Bunning continued to be wild but the Dodgers had not scored against him when, with two men on base, Don Zimmer came to bat in the second inning.

Zimmer is a young man on this team, 26, and a fascinating study in courage. In 1953, when he was with St. Paul, Zimmer was batting .300 and leading the American Association in home runs and runs batted in, when he was hit in the head with a pitched ball. His skull was fractured, and he nearly died. It took him months to regain full control of his speech and his reflexes. But he did, and he returned to baseball. He moved up from the minors to the Dodgers and for three seasons has been a valued utility player for Brooklyn, though Zimmer resents the role of substitute and burns with an angry ambition to play regularly, every day. Last year, early in the season, he was struck full in the face by another pitched ball. This time he nearly lost his sight: the retina of his left eye had become detached. He was forced to lie completely immobile for several weeks while the eye slowly healed, and it was said that almost certainly his career as a baseball player was over.

Zimmers Don't Flinch

But here he was, back again, playing for the Dodgers again, and batting now against the wild, fast right-hander. Bunning's pitch came wailing in, high, inside, right at Zimmer's head. People who knew Zimmer's history flinched. Zimmer didn't. He fell to the ground like a cat, under the pitch, safe. He popped up to his feet and moved back into the batter's box at once, his bat cocked.

"He's been beaned twice, hasn't he?" A Detroit man said in the press box. He was thinking, along with everyone else, of Reese's arm and Zimmer's head and wondering how the player could possibly generate enough nerve to face the pitcher again.

"Watch him," a Brooklyn writer said. "He won't give an inch. The crazy bastard." He said these last words proudly, affectionately.

Bunning threw. Zimmer stepped into the pitch, swung and hit a three-run home run over the left field fence.

"Guts," the Detroit man said, almost to himself.

The Tigers rallied later on to bring the score to 3–2, and they loaded the bases with no one out in the eighth. In to pitch for Brooklyn came a tall, lanky Cuban named Rene Gutierrez y Valdes, who won 22 games in the Pacific Coast League last year. Valdes' nickname, he will tell you, is *Latigo*, The Whip, and he exudes confidence. "I want to pitch only against Yankees," he announced, when he finally reported to camp after brashly holding out for a higher salary. Why the Yankees? He was asked. "If I beat Yankees I make team," he argued logically.

But The Whip made his debut against the Tigers instead, and the bases were loaded and no one was out. The tying run was on third base. *Latigo* pitched. The first batter fouled to the first baseman. One out. The second popped up to the infield. Two out. The third also popped to the infield. Three out. The Whip retired three more Tigers in succession in the ninth, and the Dodgers had the ball game 3–2, thanks principally to Don Zimmer and Rene Valdes.

It was only a spring training game, but suddenly the status of the Brooklyn Dodgers was out of focus again. Their great players were old, true enough, but now it appeared that it wasn't just that simple. There were some young players in the background, and their skills and energy could have a significant bearing on the success or failure this year of what almost everyone has come to think of as the old, old Dodgers.

A good part of this blanket thinking about the Dodgers as an old team stems from the sheer greatness of the key Brooklyn players, greatness that keeps young players from breaking into the lineup. No other group of stars in the long history of baseball has played together so many years so successfully as the eight-man nucleus of the modern Dodgers: Reese, Furillo, Gil Hodges, Snider, Campanella, Newcombe, Erskine and the departed Jack Robinson. Reese came to the Dodgers in 1940; Furillo in 1946; Robinson, Snider, and Hodges (except for two times at bat in 1943) in 1947; Campanella and Erskine in 1948; Newcombe in 1949. A couple of them made one or two return trips to the high minors, but 1949 can be designated as the year this collection of extraordinary players became a team. In the eight seasons from 1949 through 1956, they won five pennants and tied for a sixth, lost another on the last day of the season and finished second the one other time they failed to win. And the same group was chiefly responsible, year after year. Aside from pitching (where first Preacher Roe, then Joe Black, then Clem Labine and Sal Maglie made significant contributions to success), only one other player, the resourceful Junior Gilliam, has become an integral part of the Dodger lineup. Compare the Brooklyn starting nine in the memorable first game of the 1949 World Series against the New York Yankees (when Tommy Henrich beat Don Newcombe 1–0 on a ninth inning home run) with that which started the memorable last game of the 1956 Series (when Yogi Berra destroyed Newcombe with two two-run home runs). Newcombe was the pitcher in 1949, Campanella the catcher. Hodges was at first base, Robinson at second, Reese at short, Snider in center, Furillo in right. In 1956 Robinson had moved to third base, but the others were all in precisely the same positions. The Yankees, who won seven pennants in the same eight years, had an almost complete overhaul in that time: of the nine who started against Brooklyn in 1949, only Yogi Berra was in the lineup for that final game of the 1956 Series.

The point being so laboriously made is simply this: the greatness of the Dodger nucleus makes it hard to believe that the Dodgers can continue to win without them, and the rapid turnover of personnel common in baseball makes it hard to believe that the Dodger nucleus can keep going much longer. The retirement of Jackie Robinson, the greatest of all Dodger ballplayers lends strength to this argument. The nagging feeling persists that perhaps this at long last will be the year that the fabulous one-hoss shay falls apart, all at once.

But talk to Walter Alston about this. He's the fourth man to manage this extraordinary collection of players and the most successful, when you consider the declining ability of his stars and the rising ability of his opponents. Admirers of Leo Durocher, Burt Shotton and Charlie Dressen may possibly object indignantly to that statement and it is admitted that Alston may well be the weakest tactician of the lot. But as a strategist he is by far the best. Someone once explained the difference between tactics and strategy in describing Leo Durocher as a manager: "If you were in a building and it started to collapse, Leo would get you out. I don't know what he'd do, but he'd think of something, and you'd get out. That's tactics, and that's Leo. But someone else would have seen to it beforehand that the damn building was safe."

And that's strategy, and that's Alston. Durocher seldom thought past today's game. Alston is almost irritating in his consideration of the future. One of the standard joke lines of Brooklyn baseball writers is, "We'll have to wait and see about that," which is Alston's stock reply to most questions seeking his opinion. Alston doesn't pop off. Ask him, for instance, if he thinks the Dodgers will miss Robinson this year. It's a ticklish question in the first place because the fiery, outspoken Robinson was a constant bur in Alston's hide.

"I can't say yet," Alston replies. "Have to wait and see how the player who takes his place will do."

Press him a little further. "Hell," he says, "any team would miss a competitor like Robinson. He was a great player. But Charley Neal (a young infielder) had a better batting average than Robinson last year. Randy Jackson (Robinson's alternate at third base) hit about the same, and he batted in more runs." Talk to Alston about the other old players, about the possibility of one or two or several of them breaking down this year. "There's always that chance, but I don't see any sign of it yet. And I don't think the whole bunch is going to break down at once."

But the possibility *is* there, and Alston knows it, and so he is constantly working his young players in and out of the lineup: Don Demeter, a 21-year-old string bean of a center fielder who hit 41 home runs for Fort Worth last year; Jim Gentile, a 22-year-old first baseman, who hit 40 homers as Demeter's teammate; John Roseboro, a left-handed hitting catcher who is not yet on the Dodger roster but who hits sharply, throws well, runs fast and, all in all, looks like a fine baseball player. Alston has been using Neal and Chico Fernandez at second and short. And Zimmer, of course, and others.

All this is an attempt to reinforce the dike, to add insurance. The Dodgers have had, for the past decade, brilliant fielding and powerful hitting. Lately, both have become just a little frayed.

Pitchers and Hitters

Last year Alston insisted he wasn't worried about his hitting. "We'll get enough runs," he said at that time. "I'm not worried about that. I'm worried about my pitching." A year ago Johnny Podres had just been drafted, Billy Loes had a sore arm and so did Karl Spooner, and Don Bessent had been operated on for abdominal obstruction. "That's four pretty good pitchers we didn't have," Alston said the other day. "But it turned out our pitching came through better than we ever expected. Newcombe won 27, and we got Sal Maglie. Roger Craig was very good the first part, and Erkine was good. The bullpen was strong: Labine was very valuable in relief, and so was Bessent when he came back. Drysdale did pretty good. The pitching won for us. But the hitting didn't get us enough runs, except the last 10 days of the season. That was the only time all year we had a sustained attack. It carried through the first two games of the Series, then it stopped cold."

He made a wry face, remembering that the Dodgers scored a total of six runs in the last five games of the Series after scoring 19 the first two.

"This year now we're not worried about our pitching. I don't know if Newcombe and Maglie will win 40 games between them again, but you have to expect them to do pretty well, and we have Podres back. We have Erskine and Craig, and they're reliable pitchers. We have a very good bullpen, with Labine and Bessent. And Ed Roebuck. Young fellows like Sandy Koufax and Spooner and Fred Kipp can help us. They're all lefties, like Podres. Did you know we didn't throw a left-handed pitch against the Yankees in the Series last year? We can use lefties. Koufax and Spooner have been throwing hard. Koufax has very good stuff; all he ever needed was control, and now he seems to have it. Everyone knows how hard Spooner can throw when he's right (Spooner struck out 27 men in pitching two consecutive shutouts when he made his major league debut in 1954, and then pitched well in the latter part of 1955 before hurting his arm). Now and then he looks all right again. Kipp looked awfully good in Japan on that trip we took after the Series. And I'm very high on young Drysdale; he could be one of our big pitchers. You can't be sure, of course, but it could turn out we might have a hell of a pitching staff. We better have, because I'm worried about that hitting."

The pendulum has swung, then, over the years. Where once the Dodgers were accepted as a team of power hitters and great fielders who made up for a mediocre pitching staff, now the once-great team is carried by its pitchers.

Baseball people have an almost reverent respect for good pitchers, and the Dodgers' chief rivals for the pennant—the Milwaukee Braves and the Cincinnati Redlegs—always praise Brooklyn's pitching staff. But pitching is a delicate thing. The odds that say there's a chance that Kipp and Spooner and Koufax and Drysdale will blossom into full-fledged major leaguers are no better than those that say Newcombe's arm will stay sore or that Maglie's age will trip him up or that Podres and Erskine and Craig will fail.

The Dodgers are a fragile team in their twilight years, and if they manage to hang on to win the pennant one more time it will be a signal tribute to their lingering greatness and to the skill of their unpraised manager in utilizing his Zimmers and Kipps and *Latigos*. And it may well be their last hurrah.

Be sure to see them play this year if you can, because the fabulous Bums of Brooklyn won't be the same much longer. For one thing, they may be moving cross-country to Los Angeles. For another, Jackie's gone and the rest of the old gang can't be too far behind.

This was the finale at Ebbets Field. Danny McDevitt pitched and Gladys Gooding played the organ, and only 6702 fans showed up.

Take Them Away, L.A.!

Chris Kieran

Flock Cops Finale, 2–0

[September 25, 1957:] A lot of strange things have happened at Ebbets Field since it was built in 1913, but the strangest occurred last night. They played the last game there. Of course that's not official and won't be until the announcement is made — probably next Sunday. But from the repertoire of songs played by organist Gladys Gooding which included, "After You've Gone," "Thanks for the Memories," "What Can I Say Dear, After I Say I'm Sorry," "Say It Isn't So," "If I Had My Way," "Whatever Will Be, Will Be," this was it.

And to make the situation more bizarre, only 6,702 members of the Faithful showed up to kiss the boys goodbye. They had a pleasant evening as they watched their heroes ring up their 18th shutout of the campaign with a 2–0 whipping of the Pirates. It wasn't as exciting a game as the score might indicate. Just another night affair played in a chilly September breeze, something the Dodgers shouldn't expect to feel in Los Angeles.

The Faithful few seemed reluctant to leave when the festivities were over. A crowd hung around the Dodger dugout for more than 15 minutes — probably the first time most of them had ever watched the batboy file away all the lumber. As Miss Gooding was playing, "Auld Lang Syne," there were some cries of "Don't go, don't go."

There were no instances of three men sliding into one base at the same time, no crucial third strikes were dropped, no homers were hit and nobody passed nobody on the basepaths. It was strictly a routine affair, hardly befitting the antics that the customers had come to expect. If they give the Los Angelenos more of the same, they won't like it.

Even Tex Rickart, the public address announcer, didn't put on a show. He came through with his usual blurb of "Please don't go on the field at the conclusion of the game, use the nearest exit."

It had been suggested that he close out with "Use the nearest leading to Chavez Ravine." No guts — or maybe he knows something.

As for the game itself, it was over in the first inning the way Danny McDevitt was pitching. He limited the Bucs to five hits and fanned nine to move the Brooks to within 21 of the major league strikeout record of 896. Junior Gilliam led with a walk, went to second when rookie Ben Daniels threw wild in attempting to pick him off first, and came home on Elmer Valo's double off the right field wall. Then, just to make sure, they added another in the third on Gino Cimoli's single and Gil Hodges' slicer to right.

Every one of the Bucs hits was of the infield variety. They didn't get one good belt off the young lefty, and he wasn't in trouble at any stage. They'll love him in Los Angeles.

It's over! It's done! The song has ended. The fat lady has sung. King Kong has fallen from the Empire State Building. It is the winter of our discontent. The Dodgers have left Brooklyn!

IT'S OFFICIAL—DODGERS GO TO LOS ANGELES

Tommy Holmes

New York Loses 2d N.L. Club

Wagner Hopes to Attract One

[October 9, 1957:] The Dodgers yesterday took the irrevocable step from Ebbets Field to Los Angeles. Less than twenty-four hours after the City Council of the sprawling California metropolis had approved a controversial offer for the Brooklyn baseball franchise, stockholders and directors of the ball club unanimously voted to move.

Together with the formal announcement just a week ago that the Giants quit the Polo Grounds for San Francisco, the Dodger action constitutes the abandonment of New York by the 81-year-old National League.

Although long expected, the definite Dodger decision to go west triggered flurries of official statements.

Wagner Has a Plan

At City Hall, Mayor Wagner again declared his intention to appoint a group of citizens within the next few days "to help us get another National League club."

The Mayor refused to discuss a question whether the city would seriously consider a municipal stadium in Flushing Meadows, Queens, as an inducement to attract another team, but added, "Naturally, they must have some place to play."

At Borough Hall, Brooklyn, Borough President John Cashmore said, "I have personally done everything I could to keep the Dodgers in Brooklyn, but I couldn't do it alone."

He said he would "leave nothing undone to have National League baseball continued in Brooklyn. It is important to the economic life of the borough."

Originally published in the *New York Herald-Tribune,* October 9, 1957. Reprinted by permission of Historical Briefs, Inc.

But baseball men regarded the prospect of a National League return to this city in the foreseeable future as bleak, indeed.

O'Malley's Statement

The announcement came from Walter O'Malley, president of the Dodgers and was followed by a statement from Warren Giles, president of the National League. Neither was present at the World Series press headquarters at the Waldorf-Astoria to preside over the liquidation of National League baseball here.

VI. The Last Out

This put into the Big Oom's (Walter O'Malley) head the idea for the biggest snatch ever pulled off in baseball: the kidnapping of the Dodgers away from their loved ones in Brooklyn.

— *The Lords of Baseball*
by Harold Parrott

It is still there 30 years later. The seething anger, the sadness, and most of all, the memory.

30 Years of Perfidy

New York Daily News

[SEPTEMBER 24, 1987:] Sept. 24, 1957. A chill was in the air. An autumn wind was sweeping across Brooklyn. And all across Brooklyn, there was weeping and gnashing of teeth. For as this summer season ended, so did the seasons of joy. Walter O'Malley was taking his cold, cold heart to warmer climes, and breaking other hearts in the process. The Borough of Kings was being brought to its knees by a knave.

This day, Sept. 24, is the 30th anniversary of the last Brooklyn Dodger game at Ebbets Field. Lower the flags to half-staff, please, to mark the demise of Dem Bums. The entity that plays in California has as much to do with the real Dodgers as quiche has to Crackerjack.

Dem Bums. No team was ever as beloved; no fans as faithful. And then The O'Malley betrayed them. For 30 pieces of California gold. As early as 1948, he had been whining for a new stadium; in '55 he began mewling about a move. The official announcement came in October '57. But those at Ebbets that chilly night of Sept. 24 had already accepted the worst.

They numbered a scant 6702. Those who were absent should not be berated; perhaps they couldn't stand to say goodbye in public.

THOSE WHO WERE PRESENT SAW the Dodgers beat the Pirates 2–0. They heard organist Gladys Gooding play a suitable repertoire: "After You've Gone," "Thanks for the Memory," "Say It Isn't So," "Auld Lang Syne." And they sang the Dodger theme song, "Oh, Follow the Dodgers/Follow the Dodgers around/The infield, the outfield/the catcher and that fellow on the mound..." But now, they couldn't follow. Unless they wanted to trek 3,000 miles.

The O'Malley moved the franchise as if it were a hamburger stand, sans tradition, sans heritage. Caring not a whit for either — and even less for the loyal following. When the Dodgers left Brooklyn, they left it bereft.

Thirty years. An entire generation has grown up deprived of Dodgerdom. There are children who will never hear the Dodger Sym-Phony play, "The Worms Crawl In, The Worms Crawl Out" as the opposing team changes pitchers. Children who confuse Pee Wee Reese with Pee Wee Herman. Who think Preacher Roe is a TV evangelist. Who believe "The Shot Heard 'Round the World" has something to do with the American Revolution and ergo, celebrate it.

This is the legacy of the late, unlamented O'Malley, wherever he may be.

But, as any Brooklyn Dodger fan knows, where he is, it is never ever chilly.

In 1972 Roger Kahn wrote what is arguably the best baseball book ever written. It is more than a book about baseball and baseball players. It is a book about men and about life.

HOW *THE* BOYS OF SUMMER GOT STARTED

Roger Kahn

You'd like to know how *The Boys of Summer* got started? Well, sometime in the 1950s I went from the *New York Herald Tribune* to *Newsweek,* which was memorable only because I got to know John Lardner, Ring Lardner's son. Later the *Saturday Evening Post* asked me to become an editor-at-large, which meant that I'd write a certain number of stories a year. Some were sports stories but not many. Around 1967 Al Silverman, who has become chairman of the board of the Book-of-the-Month Club, had *Sport* magazine and said, "It's our 20th anniversary. Would you do a retrospective on 20 years of baseball?"

Well, I'd gotten away from baseball a little bit, and I told Silverman that I really wasn't the person to write the piece. Silverman kept after me anyway.

Now, Billy Cox had always fascinated me because he, rather than Brooks Robinson, was the best glove at third I've ever seen. And he'd been in the first wave at Guadalcanal or Anzio which had done terrible things to him ... being under mortar fire for five days, hearing all those screams of death. Cox never spoke about that, but we'd have little talks about things that interested me, and he had a kind of wit. He drank and would disappear from the team for a few days and then come back. And there was, of course, still in my head after I had switched my allegiance as a kid from playing first base to third base the idea that if Cookie Lavagetto, my childhood Dodger hero, was a good third baseman, then Cox was a matchless third baseman. I also remember this little black glove Cox had used that Vin Scully used to say he got at Whalen's Drugstore for $3.95. Billy simply fascinated me. He was very hard to write though; I only wrote once or twice about him because he didn't say much. So finally I told Silverman — lord knows why — "Look, I'll do a 20-year baseball retrospective for you if you let me find out where Billy Cox is so I can just go and say hello to him."

I don't know where that came from, but it was something I wanted to do passionately. And Silverman said, "Sure." I then found out where Billy was and phoned him down in Newport, Pennsylvania.

From *Baseball: The Writer's Game* by Mike Shannon. ©2002. Reprinted by permission of Brassey's, Inc.

I said, "What are you doing?"

He said, "I'm the substitute bartender at the American Legion hall." Substitute bartender? Billy Cox?!

He said, "The hall's not hard to find. You come to Newport, make a left at the Gulf station, and go up the hill."

Who the hell knew where Newport, Pennsylvania, was let alone the Gulf station. But I made my way, found the American Legion hall on top of one of those severe hills you find in western Pennsylvania. And there was Billy, now with Falstaff's belly, but the face was the same.

Newport was an old railroad town through which the railroad had stopped going. Three or four old and hostile-looking people, hostile to an outsider, were sitting at barstools, wearing the striped caps that railroad engineers wore.

I was excited to see Billy, and Billy was excited to see me. He ran out from behind the bar, and then he said, "You seen me. Could I play ball?"

I said, "Billy, you were the best damn glove I ever saw."

He turned to these guys drinking beer, guys who'd been drinking beer since the trains stopped running, and he said, "You hear that?

"A New York writer said that."

And I got a stab. I felt the same way Pete Rose felt about being cut from the Western Hills High School football team. "When I got cut from the team," he said to me, "it was a pitchfork in my heart."

It was a pitchfork in my heart when Billy said, "A New York writer said that." Why do I have to tell these solemn bastards that Billy Cox was a great player? Why don't they know that? Why don't they know what the glove was?

I wrote the piece for *Sport*, but the meeting with Billy stayed with me as I was finishing a book about the Columbia University student uprisings called *The Battle for Morningside Heights*. I wanted to do more with Cox, but I was practical enough to know that I had to finish the book I was supposed to finish before I could go to work on another one. So I finished *The Battle for Morningside Heights*, and I began to find out where the Dodgers were.

I knew that Roy Campanella was in a wheelchair in Tarrytown, New York. I knew Clem Labine's son had lost his leg in Vietnam. And Jackie Robinson I always saw. I knew Robinson was a great man, and I wasn't going to let that get away. If there was any kind of excuse, I'd say to Jack, "Let's have lunch." And he'd say, "Why?"

"Well, we can talk about Goldwater and Nixon and Rockefeller." Robinson was very interested in Republican politics.

And I knew that Jack had gone through an ordeal with his child. Jack and his wife, Rachel, didn't know what to do with Jackie Robinson Jr. He was a good athlete and a fine student, but he was always in trouble. The Robinsons sent him to a private school for kids with problems, but that didn't help much. Finally, they suggested to young Jack that he join the army, a European way of dealing with a difficult child. "The army will make a man out of you," you know.

And Jack Jr. joined the army. He had some of his father's hand-eye coordination, so he became a great rifle shot. He starred in Vietnam, was a terrific rifleman in Vietnam. But he also learned about heroin there and came back and dealt, didn't just use, but dealt heroin in the Stamford, Connecticut, railroad station.

In a hotel near there he was picked up, and he actually drew a gun on a detective. Somehow he wasn't shot. He was disarmed.

After that terribly painful scene, a young journalist who'd never seen Jackie Robinson play baseball said, trying to get him to talk, "Mr. Robinson, it must comfort you to know that you have helped so many children with your career."

And Jackie said fighting back tears, "I couldn't have helped many children. I haven't helped my own son." The boy had just been arrested.

I just had this powerful feeling that "I want to get this down. I don't care how broke I am when its over, or if I have to go to work for *Time* magazine writing dreary stories for dreary editors, I am going to get this book finished. This is the book I am going to write."

I got a relatively small advance, $25,000, small because I would have to travel the whole country and at least half the advance would go for traveling expenses; but I was doing this as a book of moral purpose. I thought it was a book that should be done, and I wanted to do it.

In order to survive, I had to agree to do a medical book, the story of "the training of ten surgeons in a hospital." Once in a while I went to work in this hospital, but finally the chief surgeon wrote a letter saying, "I don't think we are going to continue to cooperate with you. You're more interested in these boys from Brooklyn. You admire Jackie Robinson more than you admire me." That was true.

I took some money on the medical book because at that time I had three children, an ex-wife, and a current wife who didn't work. I felt I was supporting a large part of the United States of America. I was making no progress on the medical book, and now this surgeon pulled out, for some good reasons and some crazy doctor-type reasons. I remember wondering what would happen if Harper & Row found out. I wasn't going to lie, but I didn't have to volunteer anything either.

As I began talking to these extraordinary ballplayers, they became less Olympian, less god-like, and more human, and I started gathering these wonderful human stories. Doing the book was encountering the people; it wasn't interviewing. As I saw them as older, they saw me as older. All of them were too polite to say that. But it was emotional for all of us. *The Boys of Summer* was a very emotional book to write.

When I finished, I had no thought of a number one bestseller. But I thought I had done good work. And I also thought that the children continuing to eat meant that I had to do something fairly lucrative, but I didn't know what. I figured that this was probably the last book I would ever write and that, as I said, I'd probably be doing dreary stories for a news magazine.

The lady I was married to then was Alice Russell. One of Alice's comments during the course of the book, about a year and a half into it was, "I'm becoming the world's outstanding expert on Pee Wee Reese under the age of 35." At the end I had $380 left in the bank. I probably owed back alimony and probably owed back taxes. So I said to Alice, "This is something pretty good. Work that I'm proud of. Maybe the children will be proud of it and you will be too. We have $380; we might as well have nothing. Let's throw a party and invite everybody in New York we care about."

Alice went to a gourmet food store, Zabar's, and bought a Norwegian salmon which she poached. And everybody that we cared about in New York City who was free came.

Jackie Robinson had never visited my home. I don't know if it was some subtle black-white thing or not, but he'd never come over. I said, "I've finished the book." Jack was not the kind of guy who'd say, "Congratulations!" He'd say, "Well, that's what you get paid to do, right?" That was Jack, hardnosed conversationally. So I said, "I'm having a party, and I'd like you to come. And I'd like to thank you for helping me."

He said okay and asked what time, how many people and all that. He came without Rachel. I had a sense he was checking out the party, to see if this was some kind of red-neck party transposed to New York. Jack didn't know my friends. We were close, but maybe I was a secret racist. There were no racists at the party.

Two things happened that night which I remember very clearly. One of my guests was Howard Fast, who was either a communist or a fellow traveler. In either case, Fast, who wrote *Spartacus* and *Citizen Tom Paine* among other books, was far left. And it was then public that Jack had diabetes. There was a couple at the party who had a diabetic child, and Jack was talking to them about living with diabetes and how you could live a rich and full life with the disease. Jackie was in no way aggressive. He was actually quite shy. He just found this couple with trouble where he could help them.

And suddenly Howard Fast said, "Why did you testify against Paul Robeson?" Right here is Arthur Ashe's book, *Hard Road to Glory*, about black sports in America, and in it Ashe talks about Paul Robeson's leftist, "siren song in bass," which is from Jack's testimony. Robeson said, "If the United States went to war with the Soviet Union, no black person would fight for America because he has nothing for which to fight." That was public statement. Congress asked Robinson to come, and Robinson said, "I'm not an expert on Communism, Fascism, or any other 'ism.' I'm only an expert on being a Negro in the United States because I've had thirty years of experience at it." Great forgotten speech. And somewhere in that speech he says, "We must not listen to this siren song in bass." Well, this offended the extreme left and Fast said to Jackie, "How could you possibly testify against Paul Robeson."

Jack was startled and not ready for that because he was comforting these people about their daughter. And he said, "If Branch Rickey had asked me to jump off the Brooklyn Bridge I would have done that." Fast began to lecture Robinson on politics. At that point I stepped between them, and I can laugh today when I say that if Fast had said one more word I was going to hit him.

If Robinson had hit him, he would have knocked him 10 blocks! But I was not going to have anybody be that rude to Jack. And Jack was upset. Who wants to have his politics challenged at a party? I don't think there's anything in Robinson's statement to Congress that he ever has to apologize for.

So the evening went on, and more drinks were served, and Zero Mostel was there. Suddenly, Zero shouted in the booming voice of Tevya, the "Fiddler on the Roof": "MISTER JACKIE ROBINSON!" Robinson, who had his back to Zero, cringed. His shoulders went up, and his head went into his shoulders. He turned as if to say, "What now?"

Then Zero said, "You … are … my … hero!" And he walked up and hugged him.

So the party winds down, it's Monday morning, and now we have $80. We've blown the $300 on the salmon and the booze. And I just had no thought of where I would go; I didn't want to go work for *Time*. Well, the phone rang, and it was somebody from Harper & Row saying, "Have you heard? Have you heard?"

My editor was cruising the Aegean Islands, so this was the editor's assistant. And she said, "*The Boys of Summer* is the main selection of the Book-of-the-Month Club." That was about $100,000. I went from $80 to $100,000 that quickly, and I thought, "If there is a God, I wish he'd stop playing these games with me."

The book did well, though it was sharply attacked in the beginning by numbers of people. It got a terrible review in *Life* by Wilfrid Sheed. He said, "This is about eight ballplayers"… it's about 13; he said my parents were "immigrant culture-vultures" … my great-grandmother was born in New York, and both my parents were born in New York. And he said that I "romanticized" the players; "they're really oafs." A cocktail waitress told Sheed that the players were poor tippers, and that was the basis for the *Life* magazine comment on the book. Some years later Wilfrid Sheed wrote a novel that didn't do anything called *The Boys of Winter*. So I'd like to give him not a CASEY Award (for best baseball book of the year) but a chutzpah award. He couldn't stand *The Boys of Summer* and then he wrote a book he called *The Boys of Winter*!

The *New York Times* gave it to a woman to review, in what was a parody of women's liberation. She said that any sports book that begins with a line of poetry can't be all good. That's from W.C. Fields: "Anybody who hates dogs and small children can't be all bad." Then she said that the book had much too much about the *Herald Tribune* and much too much about growing up in Brooklyn. Finally, she said I was all wrong. The 1952 Dodgers were not so great. The 1955 Dodgers were great. Well, she was full of it. Because the 1955 Dodgers were the 1952 Dodgers older and slower. Robinson didn't get better from 1952 to 1955; Pee Wee Reese didn't get better. Cox was gone, Gil Hodges didn't get better, Campanella didn't get better. They got older. And now, instead of being 30-ish, they were 33-ish, 34-ish. The Yankees also got older. The Dodgers finally won the World Series in 1955 because Johnny Podres pitched a good game and Sandy Amoros made a fine catch in the seventh game.

So I was thinking, "Geez, what do I have to do?" They were pummeling me. And there was another slap in the face. Roger Angell had a collection of *New Yorker* pieces called *The Summer Game* come out in the same spring. The *Times* carried a front-page review which said I was Vinegar Bend Mizell and Roger Angel was Warren Spahn. How terribly cute. The reviewer called *The Boys of Summer* a pastiche of New Journalism and obscenity. The word "fuck" appears once in 550 pages.

Ed Fitzgerald was running the Book-of-the-Month Club, and as *The Boys of Summer* got to be number one, he took me to lunch at a place I had never been before, the Banker's Club. After a few martinis he asked, "I bet you think you beat the bad reviews in the Sunday *Times*."

And I said, "I think I did. Mostly because I'm number one."

He said, "Think of how many more books you would have sold if you had gotten the reviews you deserve."

Newsweek's review was great. Most reviews were great, but you remember the ridiculous shots people take at you. Jonathan Yardley said, "It's two books. It's a book about growing up, and it's a book about these players." Well, no, it's not two books; it's one book. I was pleased after the documentary of The Boys of Summer came out, and the Times movie critic said it left out the sense of what growing up in Brooklyn was like. Good call. I believe you need an Aristotelian sense of place. The Boys of Summer begins with my father and me in Brooklyn. It begins with Sam Leslie and Pete Coscarart and Lonnie Frey, who made 55 errors in a good year—they're not Boys of Summer. It ends at the tomb of Ebbets Field. It's all one; it has the Aristotelian unity of place. And I get somebody saying, "It's two different books."

Later there was a love feast between many people and the book, and as it went on and on, one day the editor at Harper & Row called me and said, "I have a bottle of Chivas Regal. Come over, and you'll be pleased when you see why I have the bottle of Chivas Regal." He had the Sunday Times book review which showed that the book was number one, and he asked, "How does that make you feel?"

Well, I didn't feel anything. I just felt dazed. I'd written the book I'd wanted to write. It was certainly nice to get a little money and pay off the medical book I didn't have to write anymore. But I felt dazed, and after a while I said, "Gosh, I hope it doesn't fall to number two next week." It stayed up there an honest eight weeks. Some writers will say, "My book was number one for 41 weeks," and people don't look it up and they get away with it. But there's no reason for me to do that. The Boys of Summer was on the list for 25 weeks, number one for eight.

Two weeks after the book came out Gil Hodges died. I was in Philadelphia then, and the Philadelphia Inquirer ran a headline, "It's Winter for the Boys of Summer." I was doing a TV show, Live at Five or whatever the hell it was, and the interviewer asked me, "Do you think Gil Hodges' death is helping the sale of your book?" That remains the worst question I have ever been asked.

Dick Cavett brought in some of the players, and we did his show. Everybody was excellent; Reese, Clem Labine, Joe Black, and Carl Erskine. I told a few Bums stories. For instance, Frenchy Bordagaray seems to be out at the plate but may have a chance if he slides. He doesn't slide, and he's tagged out standing up. Casey Stengel says, "For Chrissakes, why didn't you slide?" Bordagaray says, "I was gonna, Case, but I was afraid I'd crush my cigars." That was 50 ... 50 Depression dollars.

In another one, Bordagaray was standing on second base tapping the bag with his foot, and ZIP, "Yer out!" They picked him off. "Case, he musta caught me between taps."

Erskine talked with great beauty about raising a Downs Syndrome child. Black talked about growing up black, also with great beauty. Labine talked about visiting his son in a hospital where there were 32 people like Clem Labine Jr., who had lost a leg in Vietnam, and in the ward there were two wheelchairs. He said, "This war is costing this country more than a million dollars a day. I think for a million dollars a day we ought to be able to afford a wheelchair for every kid who's lost a leg in Vietnam." The audience stood up and cheered. So the book goes into, I think, the America of the time and is not just about curveballs and sliders.

Reese talked about Robinson, and I guess we all talked about Robinson. And there was no Robinson on the show. After a while, Joe Black or Pee Wee or somebody called me and said, "Gee, why wasn't Jack on the show?"

I said, "I don't know. I don't produce the Dick Cavett show."

But I called the producer about it, and he said, "Oh, god! We just forgot."

So then they had a special segment for Jack. And, in truth, Jack wasn't very good. He was embarrassed by all the praise that we had given him. Right after that Jack called me and said, "You son of a bitch, the fan mail has started again."

There was some talk that because he was a Republican and an executive in capitalist industries that Jack was an Uncle Tom. The book showed some of the fire in Jack. Long after that sad October day when Jack died, I was pleased that my book had made him current again in the last summer that he would know.

The Boys of Summer was quite a long book, more than 700 pages on my typewriter. Some of the stories were quite searing. There was a New York City B'nai B'rith dinner giving Gil Hodges the Baseball Sportsman of the Year Award. I went there and Erskine had come in. I congratulated Gil and went off to Toots Shor's restaurant with Erskine.

I said, "I can't finish this. It never ends. These stories are so searing to my soul. I can't get this finished."

Erskine gave me a Knute Rockne pep talk. He said, "Roger, the story should be written, and everybody is counting on you. Pee Wee is and Jackie is and I am, and you're the only person who can do this. If you don't do this, we'll all be forgotten."

The next day I shook the cobwebs out of my head, and I started to finish the book. That was Carl Erskine's gift to me.

You saw that poem at the house, hanging on my living room wall, called, "My Masterpiece" by Robert W. Service. It ends:

> A somber way I go tonight,
> With all my thoughts and dreams remote,
> Too late a better man must write
> The little book I never wrote.

Carl Erskine transcribed that poem in his own hand for me in 1987, saying that this was for me from my friend Carl Erskine for "having the courage to finish this book that no better man had to write."

I framed that on paper which will last for a long time, and I wrote Carl how moved I was by it. And then I wrote, "P.S. You owe me $40.00 for a frame." We can joke around like that.

When Furillo died, Erskine did a eulogy — how hard that must have been to do. He said, "The man was velvet and steel." The little part of the eulogy printed in the *New York Times* read to me like Carl Sandburg. Erskine told me, "Isn't it amazing? You always wanted to be a major league ballplayer. And I have always wanted to know literature and music, and we're so close."

So when he did the Furillo eulogy, I didn't make any joke at all. I just said that describing Furillo as velvet and steel sounded like Carl Sandburg. I told Carl, "You are a poet." I thought that was the nicest thing I could tell him. So you joke, and you don't joke.

Shoot, the three strongest guys on the team are dead: Robinson, Hodges, and Furillo. What do you make of that? I don't know what to make of it. We're getting to an age where we're all going to go.

Four different newspapers, including the *Los Angeles Times,* asked me to do a Carl Furillo obituary. I decided the piece should go in a New York paper because Furillo played in New York; he wasn't a Los Angeles Dodger. He had a couple of burnt-out years there. It was 10 o'clock at night, and I had some of the piece done. I was upset because Furillo was such a good fellow, and life was so cruel to him, even giving him leukemia while he was working four nights a week as a watchman because he had no money. He'd say, "Everybody's got to work, even writers, ha, ha." And as I was lying here in bed, resting, I found tears on my face. I thought, "What are you crying for?" Then I thought, "Carl Furillo is worth tears."

The Boys of Summer brought us closer together. After my son died, I was touched that Pee Wee called to comfort me. I know how hard it was for Reese to have made that call ... because when Jackie Robinson's son died, I called. When Jack answered the phone, I wanted to say something, but I choked up for a second. I finally said, "Jack, I'm trying to tell you you have my love."

Jack said, "You don't have to tell me that. By making this phone call you already have."

So when Reese called me, he said, "You remember, I was the captain. I just wanted to say for all the fellas ... we are very, very sorry."

As Erskine said, "A family is more than blood."

Yes, I suppose I'll always be known as the author of *The Boys of Summer,* no matter what else I write.

It was painful. A one-ton iron ball painted like a baseball came crashing down on the dugout.

Wreck-Ball Caps Ebbets Field

Dana Mozley

[February 24, 1960:] They had a funeral, with all the trimmings, in Brooklyn yesterday. Dead, and now put to rest, was Ebbets Field, which would have been 47 on April 9. Home of the Robins, Superbas, and Dodgers for 45 memorable seasons, Ebbets Field is being razed and will be replaced by a $22,300,000 middle-income housing development. It was bought for that purpose for $3,000,000 by Marvin Kratter … after the Dodgers moved to Los Angeles.

Several Dodgers of the past and city officials paid their respects as about 200 sentimental fans mourned. Then, as the 69th Regiment Band played "Auld Lang Syne," they began to demolish the ancient edifice.

There were odd things at Ebbets Field, right to the last. Gladys Gooding, who played the organ and sang the National Anthem for many years, wasn't there. The Star Spangled Banner was sung yesterday by Lucy Monroe, a familiar voice at Yankee Stadium.

Then there was loveable Tex Rickart, the Dodgers' long-time public announcer, taking the mike for the last time. "Ladies and Gentlemen," he intoned, "coming in to pitch for the Dodgers is Ralph Branca, No. 14." In all his days in Brooklyn, Branca wore no uniform but No. 13.

Al Helfer, once one of the voices of Brooklyn, announced the players, each of whom said a few words. There were Branca and Carl Erskine and Tommy Holmes. And there were the catchers who crouched behind the plate in the first and last games at Ebbets Field—Otto Miller and Roy Campanella.

Miller could remember that on opening day, April 9, 1913, the Phils edged out the Dodgers, 1–0. In the very last game there, and the last one ever played by Campanella, the Dodgers shut out the Pirates, 2–0, on Sept. 24, 1957.

Before making a few presentations to Campanella and the Hall of Fame in Cooperstown, Kratter promised "that Ebbets Field will be reborn within 24 months." He said the housing development will include a Little League baseball field to be called Ebbets Field. The home team will be the Brooklyn Dodgers.

Campy, three times the NL's Most Valuable Player, was given his old No. 39 uniform, his clubhouse locker and an urn of sod from behind home plate.

TO LEE ALLEN, historian of the Hall of Fame, was presented the key — mounted on red velvet — which Charles Ebbets used to open the doors to Ebbets Field on April 9, 1913. Walter O'Malley used the same key to close the doors after the finale on Sept. 24, 1957.

Home plate was also turned over to Allen for baseball's shrine.

It was 11:55 A.M. when a huge crane moved over near the third base stands. From it hung a one-ton cast-iron ball, painted white with stitches to resemble a baseball.

UP WENT THE ball and down it crashed, beginning the demolition by crumbling the roof of the visiting team's dugout.

That crash ended the last rites for a stadium in which Babe Herman stumbled under many fly balls, Mickey Owen missed the third strike to open the gates for the Yankees to win the '41 World Series, Cookie Lavagetto's two-out double in the ninth inning that broke up Bill Beven's World Series no-hitter and Johnny Vander Meer made history in 1938 by pitching his second consecutive no-hitter.

Joe Raposo wrote this lament, so poignant that when you listen to Sinatra sing it you can smell the fresh bread baking at the Bond Bread Company across the street from Ebbets Field.

THERE USED TO BE A BALLPARK

Joe Raposo

And there used to be a ballpark
Where the field was warm and green
And the people played their crazy game
With a joy I've never seen
And the air was filled with wonder
From the hotdogs and the beer
Yes, there used to be a ballpark right here.

And there used to be rock candy
And a great big fourth of July
With the fireworks exploding
All across the summer sky
And the people watched in wonder
How they'd laugh and how they'd cheer
And there used to be a ballpark right here.

Now the children try to find it
And they can't believe their eyes
Cause the old team just isn't playing
And the new team hardly tries
And the sky has got so cloudy
When it used to be so clear
And the summer went so quickly this year.

Yes, there used to be a ballpark right here.

In his 15 years in Brooklyn Red Barber used euphemisms, phrases and expressions in his mellow southern vernacular that led one Brooklyn fan to exclaim, "How come he don't talk no English?" But they understood every word.

I'M SORRY THEY LEFT

Red Barber and Robert Creamer

The fifteen years I had in Brooklyn were wonderful. The Ebbets Field we've been talking about was a part of America that's gone, and there never will be anything to equal it. I don't criticize O'Malley for moving the Dodgers (and, because of that, the Giants, too); that was a most complex situation, and certainly the introduction of major league baseball to California was a boon to baseball. But, personally, I was very sorry when the Dodgers left and moved to Los Angeles. I regretted seeing a unique institution die. There was never another ball park like Ebbets Field. A little small, outmoded, old-fashioned — well, MacPhail stuck a lot of paint on it and spruced it up, but it was still a dirty, stinking, old ball park. But when you went in there as a fan, it was *your* ball park. You were practically playing second base, the stands were so close to the field. Everybody was in touch with everybody else at Ebbets Field. There have been other small old parks in the major leagues, but none quite like this one — with its double-decked stands across left field into center and that big wall in right. And the people. And the rivalry with the Giants. When you add that in, it clinches the argument. There never was before or since, and probably never will be again, two teams in the same town in the same league. Those great rivals met *twenty-two times a year* in the same city. Whenever the Dodgers and Giants played — whether it was at Ebbets Field or the Polo Grounds — you had both factions in the stands. In other words, it wasn't a rivalry just on the ball field, with a home crowd rooting for their team and booing the visitors. At the Dodger-Giant games in Ebbets Field and the Polo Grounds, you had a constant back-and-forth roaring from the first pitch to the last, *for* both teams and *against* both teams. I think there was a reluctant affection down underneath for the rival team; that is, there was no team a Brooklyn fan would rather see play the Dodgers than the Giants, and the same thing went for Giant fans as far as the Dodgers were concerned. It was an invigorating, emotional rivalry, and I think that emotion explains a good part of the success of the New York Mets. When the Dodgers and Giants pulled out of New York and went to California and left the

Reprinted from *Rhubarb in the Catbird Seat* by Red Barber and Robert Creamer, by permission of the University of Nebraska Press. ©1968 by Walter L. Barber and Robert Creamer.

Yankees as the only team in New York, the Yankee attendance did not go up. It stayed at about the same level where it had always been. The National League fans—the Giant fans, the Dodger fans—did not care about the Yankees and the American League. Their ball clubs had left them, and they were bereft. But when the National League came back into New York with the Mets, and put this clownlike ball team — so like the old, old Dodgers of the Babe Herman–Uncle Robby era — in the Polo Grounds, the old home of the Giants, those bereft fans were back in business. Or at least enough of them were to form a strong nucleus for the so-called new breed of Met fans.

Those were great days, those days of the Dodger-Giant rivalries, and I miss them. I miss the Polo Grounds, which was torn down after the Mets moved into Shea Stadium, and I miss Ebbets Field, which was torn down before that. I pride myself on being an objective, professional sports reporter, but down inside I'm an emotional human being, too. Ebbets Field meant so much to me, even after I had left to go to Yankee Stadium, that I never went back to look at the place after it became a ghost park. I never have gone back because I can still see Ebbets Field. As far as I am concerned, it is still standing.

APPENDIX: BROOKLYN DODGERS IN THE BASEBALL HALL OF FAME

Managers

Wilbert Robinson
Leo Durocher
Walter Alston

Players

Zack Wheat
Burleigh Grimes
Dazzy Vance
Roy Campanella
Billy Herman
Jackie Robinson
Arky Vaughn
Pee Wee Reese
Duke Snider
Wee Willie Keeler
*Sandy Koufax
*Don Drysdale

Broadcasters

Red Barber
Vin Scully

Executives

Larry MacPhail
Branch Rickey

Special Mention

Gil Hodges, who belongs

*Achieved stardom in Los Angeles

INDEX